Recovering the Piedmont Past

RECOVERING THE PIEDMONT PAST

Unexplored Moments in Nineteenth-Century Upcountry South Carolina History

Edited by Timothy P. Grady and Melissa Walker

Foreword by Orville Vernon Burton

THE UNIVERSITY OF SOUTH CAROLINA PRESS

© 2013 University of South Carolina

Published by the University of South Carolina Press
Columbia, South Carolina 29208

www.sc.edu/uscpress

Manufactured in the United States of America

22 21 20 19 18 17 16 15 14 13   10 9 8 7 6 5 4 3 2 1

Library of Congress Cataloging-in-Publication Data

Recovering the Piedmont past : unexplored moments in nineteenth-century
Upcountry South Carolina history / edited by Timothy P. Grady and Melissa Walker ;
foreword by Orville Vernon Burton.
    pages cm
    Includes bibliographical references and index.
    ISBN 978-1-61117-253-9 (hardbound : alk. paper) — ISBN 978-1-61117-336-9
(ebook) 1. South Carolina—History, Local—19th century. 2. South Carolina—
Social conditions—19th century. 3. Education—South Carolina—History—19th
century. 4. African Americans—South Carolina—History—19th century. 5. South
Carolina—Church history—19th century. I. Grady, Timothy Paul, author, editor of
compilation. II. Walker, Melissa, 1962– author, editor of compilation.
    F273.R32 2013
    975.7′03—dc23

                                                              2013010907

Contents

Foreword

The essays in this collection attest to the value of local history. Although many in the profession are moving to global and transnational studies, some fail to realize that these "higher" or "broader" levels are in fact intellectual constructs rather than concrete realities. It is also true that no history, properly understood, is merely local. On the local level, where the complexities of human endeavors transpire, is where we find the substantiation of national and international experience. Local historical study has the potential to illuminate behavior in a given community and to provide perspective for understanding behavior in other communities. Whether as a reflection or as a stark contrast, a study of a particular place illuminates U.S. history, and even world history. As Eudora Welty has suggested in *The Eye of the Story*, "One place comprehended can make us understand other places better. Sense of place gives equilibrium; extended, it is sense of direction."

This collection of essays also corrects an imbalance. Too much of our nation's history has been written from the northeastern urban historical perspective. In addition studies of Charleston, the earlier European-settled black-belt regions of the coast, and in the midlands state capital of Columbia, with its political maneuverings, have dominated the history of South Carolina. We need these histories of the South Carolina upcountry to get an evenhanded story of South Carolina and American history. These articles highlight the advantages of studying history in a particular place. Places have history and tradition. Local history deals with all the people in the community, with all their ambiguities and contradictions, all their negotiations across lines of race, class, gender, and power. Local history offers a way to explore Jon Gjerde's idea of community (which he expressed in *The Minds of the West*) with its "curious amalgam of cultural retention and cultural change, tradition and modernity, authority and freedom." Local history includes practicalities and metaphysics. It brings to the profession the capacity to challenge a historiography and methodology that now tends toward the study of ideas and ideologies, discourses and cultural stances. Moreover, local studies provide the evidence for historical generalization, sometimes verifying and sometimes challenging popular interpretation. It can examine a larger subject, such as the civil rights movement, viewing it in microcosm to see how it really worked at the ground level. The civil rights movement from a national perspective, as explained by Taylor Branch (see *Parting the Waters* and *Pillar of Fire*), can look one way, but examining it in three Alabama cities as J. Mills Thornton in *Dividing Lines* did at the grassroots level makes community studies more than simple local history and gives the context that macrohistory misses.

Many of my generation and I were part of a revolution in history, the so-called new social history, which fundamentally altered historians' understanding of the nature of their discipline and opened the door to local studies. To revert briefly to nostalgia and talk a little bit about what we tried to do in the 1970s, in those heady, early days, new social history employed systems and comparisons to explain human behavior and analyze patterns of change over time. Guidelines as presented decades ago included a quantitative emphasis in the use of records and in statistical presentation; the explicit use or refinement of social theory; and a spotlight on the lower social strata. One could add a fourth characteristic: a focus on community studies as an important tool to investigate social change.

The social and cultural history of the South has grown steadily in recent decades, but it remains dominated by models illustrating a few themes—honor, paternalism, kinship ties, industrialization, race relations—through analyses that tend to sweep aside the complexities of life in local communities. A small group of scholars has focused closely on the retrieval of the dynamics of local life or the careful reconstruction of particular incidents, sometimes with the aid of anthropological insights: for example, Charles Joyner's *Down by the Riverside,* Melton McLaurin's *Celia, A Slave,* or my book on the South Carolina piedmont, *In My Father's House Are Many Mansions.* These studies, more than a quarter century old now, tended to approach the past with the certainty of a social scientist. The best of these drew inspiration from European and Chinese social historians such as Emmanuel LeRoi Ladurie, Nathalie Zemon Davis, and Jonathan Spence, whose brilliant books, including *The Return of Martin Guerre* and *The Death of Woman Wang,* cleverly and vividly built up social context before introducing elements of human contingency that were central to the plot. Here painstaking archival research was harnessed to the task of propelling readers from the solid ground of fact across a speculative void toward the conclusion that this must have been the way things worked out. Following this, Alain Corbin has taken this approach about as far as it might go, "rediscovering" in *The Life of an Unknown* a French clog maker—who apparently never did anything much of moment—entirely by reference to what he must have experienced, given the social coordinates of age, class, sex, and location that the author plots. Here the question of human agency drops out entirely.

Working from a different set of assumptions, another group of culturally inspired historians, including Carlo Ginzburg in *The Cheese and the Worms* and

Edoardo Grendi in "Storia sociale e storia interpretativa," have drawn strength from Italian proponents of *microstorie*. They revel in documentary research and in the new adductive methods of analysis they have brought forward. Although scholars such as Simon Schama (*Dead Certainties*) or Robert Darnton (*The Great Cat Massacre*) stopped short of invoking insight as method, they showed a greater willingness to treat seemingly irrelevant documents as potentially crucial clues, to follow their lead even down interesting trails which finally went cold. Books such as Laurel Ulrich's *The Age of Homespun* or Asa Briggs's *Victorian Things* turned social historians' assumptions upside-down to great effect, treating material objects as clues from which layered strands of gendered cultural significance, political meaning, and social relations could be teased and interwoven. Other works, such as Spence's brilliantly playful *The Question of Hu* or Greg Dening's *Mr. Bligh's Bad Language,* combined a willingness to let readers draw their own conclusions about complex, confusing, and deliberately ambiguous arguments with a powerful desire to retrieve the narrative form and the simple pleasure of reading history. These social scientific and culturalist tendencies have produced many estimable works, such as Edward Muir and Guido Ruggiero, eds., *History from Crime;* R. Po-Chia Hsia, *Trent 1475;* Patricia C. Cohen, *The Murder of Helen Jewet;* Carlo Ginzburg, *The Judge and the Historian;* Angela Bourke, *The Burning of Bridget Cleary;* and Richard D. Brown and Irene Q. Brown, *The Hanging of Ephraim Wheeler.*

In southern history the only examples that offer much assistance are Winthrop Jordan's pathbreaking examination of a forgotten slave conspiracy—if such it was—*Tumult and Silence at Second Creek,* and Scott Nelson's published journey in search of the legend of John Henry, *Steel Driving Man.* So far scholars of the South have been slow in developing the questions advanced by either the so-called New Social Historians or the culturalists inspired by the "linguistic turn." They have also wavered between narrative and analysis. While there are abundant partial examples of scholarship, writing microhistories of what occurred in the South Carolina upcountry breaks new ground methodologically in southern history. The last twenty-five years of scholarship has pointed the way to microhistories that allow historians to investigate communities and local areas in different ways—politically, militarily, socially, culturally, intellectually, and, best of all, as total history. The essays in *Recovering the Piedmont Past* heighten and bridge the social/cultural/political divide by exploring compelling incidents, stories, and places through the patient examination of the clues engendered, drawing together the need for both storytelling and explication of the upcountry of South Carolina.

The various essays offer comprehensive analyses of change in the South Carolina upcountry. I believe they also answer the criticism that a focus on communities had caused an intellectual fragmentation that has been ongoing for some time. In fact a concentration on a broader locale, such as the upcountry of South Carolina, answers the challenge of how to reunite the elements of the overall story.

One of the reasons to study the South Carolina upcountry is to gain new knowledge of behavior—to learn how people lived, how they reacted to and treated others, and what their lives meant to them. These essays deal with particular people in particular communities, with all their ambiguities and contradictions. They reveal the complexity of people without reducing them to simplicity. A historian brings order out of chaos and, in doing so, constructs an artificial presentation that makes sense out of the chaotic past. By admitting this, we find a study of communities allows us to approximate the total truth of the complexity and confusion of the human experience. One of the greatest values of local studies as a genre is a holistic view, an insight into real life experience writ large. A comprehensive portrait of U.S. society must include the culture and daily existence of the elite and ordinary people. One needs to know about daily routines of household, work, play, church, and school. Thus the historian can look at society in the microcosm of the community. As Maurice Stein has emphasized in *The Eclipse of Community,* "every community study is to be viewed as a case study. . . . They should all be studies of the effects of basic processes and historical events on changing social patterns. . . . Every good community study is a study of transitional processes."

The study of any particular locale enables scholars to understand larger human concerns. Local studies can include more than geography and more than family, community, mobility, or assimilation; they can probe religion, capitalism, racism, politics, and other processes which intricately involve the people of every community. In this collection the topics for study include resort areas and the role of tourism on economic development and also education as it developed among the people and in the actual classrooms. They include the men in cavalry units, the people who "gave flesh and blood to government policies," as Andrew Myers has put it in his essay in this volume. They include a story of religious motivation in freedmen's churches and schools and give depth to the larger narrative of African Americans moving from slavery to freedom. Even if attention has been given to a particular controversy, the processes of local study give a unique focus to national debates. And in gender issues and questions of justice, the processes in a local study show how newspaper coverage and use of symbols can effect mob behavior in a particular instance.

Several years ago I was sitting with the historian C. Vann Woodward at a Southern Historical Association meeting. Near the end of the conference Woodward mentioned that he had heard a lot about race and gender, but there was another important lens for viewing southern history that no one had discussed.

I thought that this disciple of Charles Beard and author of *Origins of the New South* would certainly say class. Instead he said . . . region.

As this collection illustrates, Woodward was onto something quite important and something that we as historians have too often neglected, not just studying the South as a region, but those regions within the South that helps us as historians to put together the whole. Regions such as the upcountry provide the stories necessary for any sweeping synthesis, for any comprehensive and accurate portrait. This collection highlights regionalism at its best.

Introduction

Timothy P. Grady and Melissa Walker

In the nineteenth century South Carolinians referred to the far western counties of the state as the "upcountry." Bordered on the north by North Carolina and on the west and south by Georgia, the region today is made up of fifteen counties, including Oconee, Pickens, Greenville, Spartanburg, Cherokee, York, Anderson, Laurens, Union, Chester, Abbeville, McCormick, Greenwood, Edgefield, and Newberry. Geography distinguishes the upcountry counties from others in the state. The northern portions of Oconee, Pickens, Greenville, and Spartanburg Counties are home to the foothills of the southernmost chain of the Blue Ridge Mountains with peaks rising to just over three thousand feet. A series of monadnocks, single rocky crests that project from relatively level terrain, line the North Carolina border, their colorful names less forbidding than their daunting terrain: Table Rock, Glassy Mountain, and Hogback Mountain. To the southeast, mountains give way to piedmont—rolling countryside punctuated by valleys and well drained by streams born on mountain peaks. The elevation in the piedmont ranges from three hundred to twelve hundred feet above sea level, and the soil is mostly sandy loam or thick clay. Once upon a time the upcountry boasted rich topsoil, but poor farming practices in the late nineteenth and early twentieth centuries led to severe erosion. In many places the piedmont's ubiquitous red hills are all that is left. The major rivers of the region—the Reedy, Enoree, Broad, Saluda, Tyger, Pacolet, Savannah, and Catawba—provided transportation and power to early settlers.[1]

More than geography distinguishes the upcountry from the rest of the state. From colonial times until the present, upcountry residents often found themselves at cultural and political odds with powerful lowcountry planters and merchants. For example, at the time of independence, each lowcountry vote carried as much weight as six votes in the upcountry. Upcountry residents complained that the government was unresponsive to their needs.[2] The upcountry developed a reputation as the home of political mavericks, as demonstrated by the region's legacy of independent-minded political leaders. Many events and individuals from the region's history are recognized nationally for their importance. Patriot victories at the Battles of Kings Mountain and Cowpens, made possible in large part by the commitment of upcountry militiamen, marked key turning points in the American Revolution. John C. Calhoun, whose political career helped shape the politics of the nation in the early nineteenth century, called the upcountry his home, as did Joel Poinsett, a member of the U.S. House of Representatives, ambassador to Mexico, and a noted horticulturalist who introduced the poinsettia to the United States. Representative Preston Brooks, who infamously assaulted Massachusetts senator Charles Sumner on the floor of the U.S. Senate during the sectional crisis of the 1850s, hailed from the upcountry.

After the Civil War, the upcountry continued to produce local, state, and national leaders. The region gave birth to such benevolent figures as Ann Pamela Cunningham, one of the founders of the American historic preservation movement, and to less benevolent figures such as the firebrand white supremacist politician Ben Tillman, who led the effort to write a new constitution in 1895—a constitution that enshrined disfranchisement. The region continued to contribute prominent figures in both state and national politics throughout the twentieth century. Some examples include the long-lived senator Strom Thurmond; Elizabeth Johnston Patterson, the first and only woman from South Carolina elected to the United States Congress; and the civil rights leader Jesse Jackson. From prominent figures of literary history such as W. J. Cash to famous names from the world of sports such as Shoeless Joe Jackson, South Carolinians from the upcountry played an important part in the history of the state and the nation.

In spite of the upcountry's pivotal role in South Carolina's history, historians have given far less attention to the history of the region than that of the lowcountry, and much of that attention has focused on either the eighteenth century or the twentieth century. Fine local histories, such as Archie Vernon Huff's *Greenville: The History of the City and County in the South Carolina Piedmont,* explore the past of several upcountry communities across the sweep of three centuries. Most of the existing scholarship on the nineteenth-century upcountry focuses on the region's political and economic history, while large swaths of upcountry social history remain unexamined. Important studies of the nineteenth-century upcountry, such as that by Lacy K. Ford, have focused on economic and political history. Other works, such as that of Orville Vernon Burton, have pointed the way toward a more extensive study of the social history of the upcountry, but that promising beginning has been largely unfulfilled.[3] Scholars have also paid considerable attention to the history of textile mills, particularly in the postbellum period, and more recently the historian

Bruce Eelman has explored broader commercial development in the upcountry.[4] In addition historians have turned their attention to the history of race relations and racial violence in the nineteenth-century upcountry.[5] Yet much work remains before people fully understand the social landscape of the South Carolina upcountry.

It is the relative scarcity of scholarship regarding the social and cultural life of the upcountry during the nineteenth century that provides the rich opportunity for this anthology. Outside of political and economic histories of the upcountry, academic historians have largely left entire segments of this region's history untapped, thus missing opportunities to find there an array of unexplored moments. These are not moments in the sense of a minute or an hour of chronological time, nor are they unexplored in the sense that the topics or themes considered here are completely unknown. The idea of these unexplored moments is simply to uncover in even the most localized of topics the themes interwoven throughout the historical tapestry that exists between the people and communities of the upcountry, the state, the region, and the country. The concept behind this anthology, then, is to bring to light a variety of different social and cultural narratives from the nineteenth-century South Carolina upcountry. Each narrative in its own way deals with something relatively unknown and unexplored when considered in the larger historiography of a particular account. But collectively the narratives provide unique and valuable insights into the diversity of experiences of the people who have called the upcountry their home. Together they allow all people, in the upcountry and beyond, a better appreciation of the beauty and vibrancy of this place and time.

The essays in this collection provide a window to the social and cultural life of the upstate during the nineteenth century, illustrating larger trends of social transformation occurring in the region at this time. Some of the essays add depth and complexity to our understanding of nineteenth-century southern history, while others challenge accepted narratives about a homogeneous South. All were produced by historians from colleges and universities around the upstate and allow the scholars the opportunity to use their skills to promote a better understanding of the region. This anthology is also unique in that collectively the authors bring a variety of backgrounds to their topics. They not only are historians but also bring interdisciplinary expertise from American studies, library science, and women's studies to their historical interpretations.

The goals of this anthology are twofold. First, the authors in this work seek to demonstrate the wealth of potential topics that exist in the social and cultural history of the nineteenth-century South Carolina upcountry. It is hoped that this volume will serve as the impetus for veteran and new scholars alike to take a closer look at this area when seeking fodder for fresh and innovative local, regional, and national research. The authors share a strong consensus of opinion that a multitude of unexplored moments remain from this area, and it is the hope of all that new scholarship will result from our collective efforts.

The second goal is for this work to provide local residents of the upcountry fuller knowledge and a greater appreciation of their region. The original inspiration for this collection came when one of the editors endured a wait in a long line of voters during a recent election. In that two-hour wait, an elderly gentleman, who proudly boasted of his multigenerational roots to that community, regaled voters with tales of that particular precinct's history. After a brief investigation revealed the potential underlying those intriguing stories, the idea for this book began to develop. Other regional scholars responded enthusiastically with additional tales of local interest from around the upcountry. As a result this volume might serve as the inspiration for all residents of the upcountry to understand better and appreciate the unique and revealing history of this influential region.

A note about terminology is in order. In many cases descriptive terms in use during the nineteenth century are no longer current. For example, the terms "district" and "county" both referred to the primary judicial and administrative subdivisions in the state. These subdivisions were historically tied to the courts. In 1799 the South Carolina General Assembly designated the principal subdivisions "districts." The state constitution of 1868 subdivided some of the districts into smaller entities, and the resulting judicial and administrative units were called "counties." For consistency we have used the names that were current for those times being discussed. For example, when writing about the 1820s, authors refer to the Spartan District; when writing about 1890, they refer to the area as Spartanburg County.[6] Another source of potential confusion is in the names of counties or districts; at various points during the nineteenth century, the legislature divided districts/counties into two or created new districts or counties from parts of other counties. We use the geographic designation appropriate to the area we are discussing at that moment in time. Similarly the area we call the upcountry was referred to as the "backcountry" in the eighteenth century. Today it is called the "upstate." The authors in this work call the region the "upcountry," the term most commonly used in the nineteenth century.

The editors would personally like to thank the contributing authors for the enormous effort that is so readily apparent in the follow chapters. We are certain that the authors' skill and dedication to their craft have produced a volume that will benefit historians of the upcountry for many years.

Notes

1. Archie Vernon Huff Jr., *Greenville: The History of the City and County in the South Carolina Piedmont* (Columbia: University of South Carolina Press, 1995), 1–2; Walter Edgar, *South Carolina: A History* (Columbia: University of South Carolina Press, 1998), 7–8; Paul R. Surratt Jr., ed., "South Carolina Rivers and Creeks Map," South Carolina Department of Archives and History, available online at http://www .usgwarchives.org/sc/sca_maps.html (accessed September 20, 2011).

2. Edgar, *South Carolina,* 251.

3. Huff, *Greenville.* On antebellum political and economic history, see Lacy K. Ford, *The Origins of Southern Radicalism: The South Carolina Upcountry, 1800–1860* (New York: Oxford University Press, 1988); and Orville Vernon Burton, *In My Father's House Are Many Mansions: Family and Community in Edgefield, South Carolina* (Chapel Hill: University of North Carolina Press, 1985). In 2007 Furman and Clemson Universities cosponsored an interdisciplinary scholarly conference with the theme "Our Past before Us—The Search for the South Carolina Upcountry." While a great deal of fine research was featured at the conference, little of it has made its way into print.

4. Jacquelyn Dowd Hall et al., *Like a Family: The Making of a Southern Cotton Mill World* (Chapel Hill: University of North Carolina Press, 1987); David L. Carlton, *Mill and Town in South Carolina, 1880–1920* (Baton Rouge: Louisiana State University Press, 1982); Allen Tullos, *Habits of Industry: White Culture and the Transformation of the Carolina Piedmont* (Chapel Hill: University of North Carolina Press, 1989); Bruce W. Eelman, *Entrepreneurs in the Southern Upcountry: Commercial Culture in Spartanburg, 1845–1880* (Athens: University of Georgia Press, 2008).

5. W. J. Megginson, *African American Life in South Carolina's Upper Piedmont* (Columbia: University of South Carolina Press, 2006); Bruce E. Baker, *This Mob Will Surely Take My Life: Lynchings in the Carolinas, 1871–1947* (London: Continuum, 2008).

6. For more information on districts and counties, see South Carolina Department of Archives and History, "The Formation of Counties in South Carolina," available online at http://archives.sc.gov/formation/ (accessed September 20, 2011).

Mineral Water, Dancing, and Amusements

The Development of Tourism in the Nineteenth-Century Upcountry

Melissa Walker

In October 1886 a *Spartanburg Herald* reporter journeyed to the mineral springs resort at Glenn Springs, twelve miles south of town. He traveled through the "life-giving air" of a pleasant autumn morning, passing underneath luxuriant fall foliage and between "fields of cotton, clad in fleecy white robes." The reporter visited the fifty-year-old spa "believing he might find something interesting . . . concerning the . . . justly famed resort." He was not disappointed. Even late in the season he found twenty guests at the hotel, all of them enthusiastic about the health benefits derived from partaking of the waters at Glenn Springs. Many of the guests, the reporter learned, were from the state's lowcountry, and they had come seeking "health, rest, [and] recreation." The altitude, the "pure air, the social and health giving features of the spot" all attracted guests to enjoy the "balls and billiards; . . . [the] bowling allies [*sic*] and beautiful promenades." Impressed with the comfortable facilities and with guests' testimonies about the healing properties of the mineral water, the reporter gave the resort a glowing review.[1]

The *Spartanburg Herald* reporter was one of many nineteenth-century travelers who extolled the beauty, comfort, entertainment, and healing available at one of upcountry South Carolina's resorts. Tourism was an important engine in the economic and social development of South Carolina's upcountry districts, particularly in the modern-day counties of Greenville, Spartanburg, Cherokee, Oconee, Anderson, and Pickens. Historians of the twentieth-century South have only recently begun to consider the role of tourism in the region's economic development, and less attention still has been given to tourism in the antebellum South.[2] As in other parts of the South and the nation, resort tourism was an important factor in the development of the economy, culture, and infrastructure of upcountry South Carolina during the nineteenth century.

In the 1760s white settlers began to arrive in the upcountry of South Carolina. The early settlers, most of them Scots-Irish immigrants, came to the upcountry from the Pennsylvania and Virginia backcountry by way of the Great Philadelphia Wagon Road. They established small farms on former Cherokee lands near the region's rivers and creeks. They built grist mills, sawmills, and ironworks to serve the local populations. By the last quarter of the eighteenth century, small communities of yeomen farmers dotted the upcountry, and here and there villages grew up around newly established courthouses, most notably in Spartanburg in 1785, Greenville in 1786, and Pendleton in 1790. These villages became the centers of commercial and court life in upcountry districts. Economic development in the upcountry proceeded slowly at first, largely because the region's connections to the rest of the state and to other parts of the South were hindered by poor transportation links.[3]

The upcountry districts boasted a cooler summer climate than in many other parts of the South. Nestled in the foothills of the Blue Ridge Mountains, the far western districts also possessed scenic vistas and several mineral springs that attracted visitors from other areas. By the early decades of the nineteenth century, a number of upcountry businessmen had realized that they could exploit the attractive landscape and climate to lure out-of-town visitors—visitors who came with full wallets. This essay explores the development of resort hotels in upcountry South Carolina with a particular focus on Glenn Springs Hotel in Spartanburg, the best-documented of the nineteenth-century tourist attractions.

Over the course of the nineteenth century, entrepreneurs developed several resorts in the upcountry districts. The earliest visitors were elite planters from the lowland regions of the South, but by the postbellum period the South's growing middle class had become the core of the tourist trade. Visitors brought cash to the small towns and rural communities of the upcountry. They also took an active role in developing the transportation infrastructure, the churches, and the schools of upcountry districts. Tourism became an important vehicle through which upcountry business leaders built the local economy. For the tourists, a visit to one of the upcountry's resorts was a social statement, a means of marking oneself as part of the social elite. In the critical antebellum and postbellum years, upcountry resorts provided places where lowcountry and upcountry political leaders shared ideas and reinforced their ideological and economic ties.[4]

The districts in South Carolina's northwestern corner began attracting the attention of visitors in the opening decade of the nineteenth century. Elite white residents of the South Carolina lowcountry had long sought refuge from the summer's heat, humidity, and disease by fleeing to cooler, drier locations. As Dr. S. H. Dickson explained at a meeting of the State Agricultural Society, "In the Lowcountry, there are few plantations which admit of permanent residence; the whole region being pervaded by a pestilential infection . . . during the Summer and Autumn." Cases of epidemic and endemic diseases such as cholera, malaria, yellow fever, and typhoid peaked in the warm-weather months. Fearing the onset of these warm-weather diseases that they believed were caused by "miasmas" lingering in the humid air of the marshy land, lowcountry planters routinely fled their plantations from May to the first killing frost in late October or early November. Some went to town houses in Charleston, Beaufort, or Georgetown. Others decamped to the Sea Islands or to the pine barrens around Summerville, where a summer resort grew up in the early 1800s. A handful traveled to salubrious destinations in the northern United States.[5]

By the beginning of the nineteenth century, many lowcountry residents began to venture to the higher elevations of the state's interior. For example, the town of Pendleton, incorporated in 1790 and now in modern Pickens County, attracted a number of Charlestonians looking to establish homes or farms in the interior. Charles Cotesworth Pinckney, a Revolutionary War veteran and South Carolina delegate to the Constitutional Convention, built Woodlawn Plantation near Pendleton in 1810. Pinckney's brother Thomas and Charles Gaillard, another Charleston planter, built homes nearby. The nearby Greenville District also attracted planters seeking locations for summer homes, including the Charlestonians Henry Middleton and Joel R. Poinsett and Joseph Alston, a Georgetown District planter.[6]

Visiting Charlestonians hosted family and friends at their upcountry summer houses, but those who could not afford second homes sought other lodgings. Soon the lowcountry traffic was heavy enough to entice upcountry entrepreneurs to open hotels catering to visitors from the coastal regions. Squire Edmund Waddell opened an elegant eponymous resort hotel in Greenville in 1815. Col. William Toney followed suit by opening the Mansion House nearby in 1824. Known for its excellent fare, the Mansion House boasted heart-pine floors, a tin roof, a circular staircase, and a parlor with two fireplaces.[7]

East of Greenville lay Spartanburg, a village that had grown up after the establishment of a courthouse there in 1785. Though its road connections were less regular than those of Greenville and Pendleton, Spartanburg too attracted lowcountry folks. By midcentury the family of the revered South Carolina writer William Gilmore Simms summered at the town's elegant Walker House Hotel. The nearby Palmetto House also attracted visitors. Home to parties, dinners, business meetings, and political gatherings, the Palmetto House was praised by many nineteenth-century residents of Spartanburg as one of the finest hotels in the state. Lowcountry tourists who were headed for the mountains of western North Carolina often spent an evening or two in Spartanburg, and the city's Merchants' Hotel was advertised as "a pleasant stop-over place for tourists en route to the mountains."[8] By the 1840s tourism was becoming a significant segment of the upcountry economy.

The development of a tourism industry in upcountry South Carolina was part of a larger national trend. Although the earliest American tourism was the province of the wealthy, by the early nineteenth century growing numbers of Americans enjoyed enough disposable income and leisure to travel. At the same time, transportation became safer and more comfortable throughout the nation because of the rapid construction of canals, turnpikes, and eventually railroads. Entrepreneurs responded by building comfortable lodging places at scenic or historic destinations. Travel writing emerged as an important genre in journalism during the early national period, and travel writers' reports fueled popular interest in new destinations. The historian John F. Sears noted that many of the most popular tourist destinations in the early national period were scenic landscapes. "Tourism," he contended, "played a powerful role in America's invention of itself as a culture."[9]

Tourism aided upcountry economic and cultural development in a number of ways. The establishments catering to tourists employed local people, bringing dollars into local economies. Lowcountry visitors helped develop the infrastructure of upcountry communities by using their influence in the state legislature to obtain funding for road improvements. For example, lowcountry tourists lobbied the North Carolina legislature for funding for the Buncombe County Turnpike, which opened in 1827. The turnpike connected upcountry South Carolina to western North Carolina, where lowcountry planters owned summer homes in Flat Rock and Fletcher. In 1848 the South Carolina legislature chartered the Keowee Turnpike to connect the Pendleton District to North Carolina. Because lowcountry lawmakers wielded most of the power in South Carolina's legislature, their support played a critical role in gaining approval for the Keowee Turnpike project. In addition summer visitors generated the demand for reliable stagecoach lines, enhancing the links between the western districts and the rest of the state. Because the lowcountry visitors usually brought along entire families, they sought good churches and schools. One Pendleton proprietor advertised that his establishment was convenient to "two excellent Academies, male and female." In Greenville summer residents helped to found St. James's Episcopal Mission in 1821, ten years before the town was incorporated. (St. James's would eventually become Christ Episcopal Church.) A village grew up around the Glenn Springs resort in Spartanburg, including a store, a post office, a male academy, and an Episcopal church. Churches were developed near many of the upcountry's most popular resorts. Eventually the resorts also became cultural centers for the region, hosting musicians and other entertainers from all over the nation.[10]

Upcountry citizens undoubtedly welcomed the dollars generated by the visitors from coastal regions, but tensions sometimes arose. In 1836 the Greenville lawyer Benjamin F. Perry, a good friend of several summer residents, complained, "We have had a good deal of company here this summer but not much company as would interest a man of sense and reading—They all seem disposed to gratify their animal propensities without cultivating their interests at all, if they have any to cultivate—drinking, eating, gambling, and whoreing [*sic*] is the summit of their ambition." It is not clear whether the visitors were gambling and whoring among themselves or with the locals.[11]

In spite of occasional tensions, the number of upcountry resorts grew throughout the antebellum period. By the 1820s entrepreneurs were developing resort hotels near natural mineral springs that punctuated scenic rural areas of the upcountry. Resort hotels had begun to appear in the United States in the 1790s. Like the European spa towns that these lodgings mimicked, American resort hotels sought to capitalize on the tradition of visiting thermal and mineral springs in pursuit of improved health. The first major American hotel designed on the European model was the Sans Souci Hotel, a grand one-hundred-room facility that opened at Ballston Spa, New York, in 1806. In the 1820s similar establishments opened at Stafford Springs, Connecticut; Saratoga Springs, New York; and Virginia Springs, Virginia.[12] Scenic landscapes also inspired the construction of resort hotels before the Civil War. One of the first in the nation was the Catskill Mountain House, which opened in upstate New York in 1824.[13] The fashionable Keith-Sutherland Hotel, an upcountry example of an inn built to feature a scenic landscape, opened in 1848 near Table Rock Mountain in the Blue Ridge foothills north of Greenville.

Entrepreneurs launched mineral springs hotels all over the eastern United States in the antebellum years, spurred in part by a new interest in natural remedies, improved diets, and healthy atmospheres among health reformers. Even doctors who practiced the traditional "heroic" treatments of bleeding and purging frequently recommended a change of climate for their ill patients. In the 1840s the mineral springs craze was boosted as hydropathy became a distinctive branch of American medicine. Hydropathic practitioners believed in the benefits of various water treatments, especially the consumption of mineral water. One such man was the Philadelphia physician John Bell, who published his *Treatise on Baths and Mineral Waters* in 1831. Bell wrote that "mineral waters . . . produce the therapeutical effects . . . with more ease and with less perturbation and even in a painless manner" than many drugs. Newspaper ads promised that the nation's mineral springs could cure everything from kidney stones and hemorrhoids to dyspepsia and consumption, from female complaints and syphilis to rheumatism and "melancholia."[14]

In addition to attracting invalids, mineral springs resorts catered to a healthy clientele. The historian A. K. Sandoval-Strausz has pointed out that nineteenth-century resort hotels were true destinations rather than places people passed through on their way to other places. Resorts became a vehicle used by the affluent to escape the "urban hoi-polloi" for a time. As Sandoval-Strausz observed, the new scenic and mineral springs resort hotels "represented a new economy of travel, one based not on moving goods, workers, or information, but rather on transporting people to safe pleasurable surroundings where they could occupy and consume the land in new ways."[15]

The hotels found at mineral springs resorts proved fairly uniform as to architecture. They were often frame buildings, which were inexpensive to build and provided adequate weather protection for the seasonal operation of hotels. Usually large and sprawling, most hotels featured long, low facades that capitalized on bucolic views. Most boasted a rustic exterior style and interior furnishings. Nineteenth-century resorts were frequently nestled in scenic or pastoral surroundings. Mineral springs resorts with their focus on natural surroundings were part of a larger trend in nineteenth-century America—that of creating genteel landscapes where the dangers of wilderness were removed and guests could commune with the natural world.[16]

Several mineral springs resorts opened in the upcountry in the decades before the Civil War. One local historian called Pacolet Spring the first mineral spring in the Spartan District to gain attention, though it was some time before a hotel opened there. Apparently this mineral spring south of Spartanburg was a regular stagecoach stop as early as the 1790s, though it is not clear whether any overnight accommodations were available there. It was renamed Poole Springs by 1825, and by 1855 records indicated that R. C. Poole was operating a hotel for sixty or so guests in "plain decent country style." Poole advertised that his springs had been "resorted to for the last century or more by those afflicted with most kinds of diseases."[17]

In the 1830s a joint stock company made up of Charleston and Columbia businessmen purchased land around popular springs known as Limekiln or Limestone Springs, near the village of Gaffney, then in northern Spartanburg County. In 1835 these stockholders invested somewhere between sixty thousand and seventy-five thousand dollars, a substantial sum, in the construction of a four-story hotel and some guest cottages at Limestone Springs. Featuring more than one hundred guest rooms, a large dining hall, drawing rooms, family parlors, a racetrack, and well-landscaped grounds, the hotel attracted many lowcountry residents, who arrived by carriage with entourages of relatives and slaves. Contemporary newspaper accounts indicate that the guests enjoyed horse racing by day and dancing and card playing by night. Unfortunately the depression of 1837 dealt the new venture a severe blow. After several years of financial struggle, the hotel at Limestone Springs closed in 1844. The bank that held the mortgage sold the large hotel building for use as the Limestone Springs Female High School, a forerunner to modern-day Limestone College.[18]

In the Greenville District, the Charlestonian Dr. Burrell Chick built a hotel at Lick Springs (soon renamed Chick Springs), about five miles northeast of the village of Greenville. Chick discovered Lick Springs on a deer-hunting trip in 1838 when his Indian guides showed it to him, claiming that the water from the springs would heal sores. When it opened for business in 1842, Dr. Chick's hotel soon attracted influential visitors from around the state. When Chick died in 1847, two of his sons purchased the property and expanded the operation, adding billiards and a tenpin alley on the lawn. Gala balls were held for the patrons at Chick Springs, including an 1853 celebration honoring South Carolina governor John L. Manning. The Chick brothers sold the property to investors from the lowcountry in 1857. The hotel continued to operate successfully until the Civil War halted the tourist trade, and the building burned in 1862.[19]

As the descriptions of Limestone Springs and Chick Springs Hotel suggest, the provision of amusing activities was at least as important as the presence of healing waters at upcountry resort hotels. Hotels offered numerous entertainments for guests, including nature walks, billiards, lawn games, lectures, concerts, balls, and dances. Some activities, such as billiards and gambling, were intended only for male patrons, but most activities were enjoyed by male and female guests. The provision of these activities encouraged patrons to stay for weeks or even months. Many families returned during the same time period year after year. Regular visitors soon formed something of a community. Mineral springs resorts provided spaces where male and female guests socialized freely, belying a popular notion of antebellum southern society as a world segregated by sex. Chaperoned by family members or older friends, unmarried young women often traveled to the resorts in search of eligible young men, giving hotels a reputation as marriage marts. For example, extant copies of the Glenn Springs Hotel register are filled with the names of single men and women, suggesting that the hotel was popular with the courting set.[20]

In the antebellum years, visits to mineral springs often served as markers of class status. The historian Thomas A. Chambers said, "A trip to the springs was a social statement, an expression of one's class identity."[21] A visitor signified him- or herself as part of a social elite—or an aspiring member of that group—by vacationing at a resort location. By developing a network of friends among elites from other parts of the South or the nation, seeking marriage partners among them, and engaging in conspicuous leisure, elites distinguished themselves as social leaders in the developing nation.

*Exterior of the Glenn Springs Hotel, 1926. Courtesy of the Herald-Journal
Willis Collection Spartanburg County (S.C.) Public Libraries.*

The best-documented and longest-lived of the upcountry's resorts was Glenn
Springs, southeast of the village of Spartanburg. According to various historical
accounts, the healing powers of the mineral springs at this location were first
discovered as a result of a fortuitous accident. A farmer, just returned from
service in the Revolutionary War, was plagued with scabies contracted in the
army. Soon he had passed the "irritating disease" to his entire family. One day
after the soldier's homecoming, his cows did not come back to the barn at milk-
ing time. He sent his son to look for them. The boy found the livestock in a
quagmire known locally as "Sulphur Springs," and he tumbled into the muddy
water in his attempt to drive the cattle home. Soon thereafter the son found that
his scabies had cleared up. As the local historian Mrs. T. Sumter Means wrote,
"The father must have been a man who thought, for he took the cue, marched
the whole family up to the swamp for a mud bath, and the result was they were
all healed. True, some of them, had to dip more than once, but finally all were
cured." Of course, word spread of this cure for the dreaded skin disease commonly called "the itch."[22]

Soon the value of drinking the water with the "queer taste" was established in
local lore. A man who suffered from dropsy (or edema) visited the family, and
he was convinced to try drinking the water. Believing that the water was helping
his condition, he continued to drink it until he was restored to health. As word
of the springs' healing power spread, they became popular with local residents
suffering from various afflictions.[23]

Sometime around 1815 James P. Means, the springs' owner (and perhaps an ancestor of Mrs. T. Sumter Means), built a two-story frame house, where he occasionally lodged visitors to the springs. Means sold the property to Mr. John B. Glenn in 1826, and the property became known as Glenn's Springs (later shortened to Glenn Springs). Glenn enlarged the house and opened a regular inn for summer visitors, and the resort's fame began to spread. In 1837 a joint stock company called the Glenn Spring Company purchased the land and the inn from Glenn. The main partner in the joint stock company was a physician, Maurice E. Moore, who hoped to add scientific legitimacy to the springs' reputation with his expert testimony about the therapeutic properties of the sulphurous waters. The Glenn Springs Company constructed a large wood-frame establishment with finely landscaped grounds and cottages. Opening in 1838, the main body of the hotel was reported to be sixty feet square, three and one-half stories high, with twelve-foot ceilings. The dining room, drawing room, and ballroom were reported to be fifty feet in length each. The owners purchased "handsome furniture" from New York, secured "a fine meat and pastry cook," and employed a "string band" to entertain the guests. Mrs. T. Sumter Means reported that "the public showed its appreciation by giving a liberal patronage." Liberal patronage was no guarantee of success, however. Like the Limestone Springs venture, the Glenn Springs Hotel seems to have been a victim of the economic downturn of 1837. In spite of a steady stream of summer visitors, the joint stock company was unable to recoup its huge investments. As Mrs. Means put it, "The season . . . was too short, and the expenditures had been too lavish for pecuniary success, and after about five brilliant social seasons at the Spa, the company found themselves nigh insolvent." The inn was sold at a sheriff's sale in February 1842.[24]

The new owners of Glenn Springs included a Mr. Murphy (his first name was not recorded) and his nephew John C. Zimmerman. Zimmerman, the child of German immigrants, had managed to become one of Spartanburg's largest landowners after moving to the area from St. Matthews, South Carolina, in 1830. Zimmerman became the sole proprietor of the hotel in 1845. He managed the property until 1853, turning it into a very successful venture. The local historian J. B. O. Landrum described Zimmerman as "frank, genial, and generous, ever ready to lend a helping hand to the poor" and "a gentleman of unbounded hospitality." Zimmerman was not only a good host but also a good businessman, and he saw the potential to generate year-round income by bottling the springwater and shipping it to customers throughout the Southeast. A number of local merchants sold Glenn Springs Water, including H. A. Ligon, a Spartanburg druggist whose store was known as "The Immense Drug and Paint Establishment." Ligon and his family were frequent guests at the hotel. Other testimonies as to the healing power of the mineral water from Glenn Springs came from further afield. The New York City physician and medical professor

John Darbly claimed to order Glenn Springs water for his own patients, noting that "in certain disorders, it is invaluable."[25]

Not only did Zimmerman sell bottled mineral water, but he also expanded the offerings of the hotel. In the late 1840s Zimmerman added "cold, warm, and shower baths" as an attraction for guests. The establishment proved popular with many of the state's most influential leaders, including one governor who moved his office to Glenn Springs for several weeks each summer and was accompanied by his family and many state officials. Judges and state legislators frequented Glenn Springs Hotel, and after the Mexican War a number of veterans of the much-revered Palmetto Regiment retired to the resort to recoup from war wounds and illnesses. The infamous South Carolina congressman Preston C. Brooks had a home nearby and frequently dined at the Glenn Springs Hotel. Brooks gained fame after he beat the abolitionist senator Charles Sumner of Massachusetts on the floor of Congress in 1856. Other notable visitors were Mrs. John C. Calhoun and Edmund C. Ruffin, a secessionist firebrand from Virginia.[26]

Less well-known fixtures at Glenn Springs during the antebellum years were the widows Mrs. Fernandes (sometimes spelled Fernandis) and Mrs. Bacon. According to Mrs. Means, in 1840 Mrs. Bacon was brought "on a bed to Glenn Springs. Her stomach was intolerant of all food, to such a degree that . . . she was fearfully weak and emaciated." By the end of the season of treatment with Glenn Springs mineral water, "she could walk up and down the steep hill to the Spring, and eat what she chose." She came for a month each year for thirty years thereafter. Her friend Mrs. Fernandes was known to one and all as "Aunt Sally." She came to Glenn Springs for treatment of injuries she had received in a bad fall as a young woman. Though the waters did not cure her, they did improve her symptoms, and she returned each summer until the Civil War. Of Aunt Sally, Mrs. Means commented, "untiring in kindness, cheerful in affliction, she was for years a central figure at the watering place."[27]

In 1853 Zimmerman sold the hotel, and the trail of ownership is unclear between that year and 1876. Mrs. Means reported that the hotel continued to operate until the outbreak of the Civil War. In fact, she claimed that the 1860 season "was the most brilliant that Glenn's [sic] Springs ever knew," with more than a thousand visitors. "Driving, games, and dancing gave pastime to pleasure seekers, as freely as the spring ran water for the invalids." One visitor that summer was Samuel Burges, a traveling fee collector for a Charleston newspaper. In August 1860, on a journey through the upcountry districts to conduct a round of collections, Burges spent three days relaxing at Glenn Springs. In his travel journal, Burges reported that he found seventy or eighty guests at the hotel when he checked in on August 29. The next day he "loafed about store, billiard room, spring, &c. At night the tableaux very good."[28]

The Civil War sparked changes to upcountry tourism. While the upcountry saw little in the way of actual hostilities during the war, the economic and
social disruptions seem to have taken their toll on tourist traffic to the region.
Some attractions never regained their former glory. The Chick Springs Hotel
in Greenville burned during the war. The hotel was not rebuilt until 1885, and
efforts to revive it were not successful; the property was sold in 1903.[29] Although
it is not clear whether the Glenn Springs Hotel remained open during the war,
it operated after hostilities ceased. Mrs. Means reported, "Since the war, in spite
of the fact that Glenn's [sic] Springs is not on a railroad, and has only a country
market to rely upon; the old resort still has a good patronage."[30]

The makeup of the upcountry's tourist population changed markedly after
the war, reflecting trends taking hold around the country. Many lowcountry
elites had suffered financial reverses, while others traveled elsewhere for their
summer retreats. Western North Carolina's resorts became increasingly popular
with lowcountry residents after the war. However, a growing middle class was
seeking places to spend its leisure time, and this group found its way to the
upcountry resorts. While some middling folks, such as the newspaper collector
Simon Burges, had visited the upcountry's tourist attractions for short periods,
hotel records suggest that after the Civil War the middle class made up the majority of tourists in the upcountry. The historian Cindy Aron points out that vacationing became a common middle-class practice in the 1870s and 1880s. Many
labor relations experts and physicians began to recommend a respite from the
pressures of the workaday world as beneficial to workers' physical and mental
health as well as their productivity.[31]

Several factors fueled the middle class's embrace of tourism. First, the rapid
expansion of clerical and managerial occupations gave more families the leisure time and the financial resources for vacation travel. The construction of
railroads helped make travel more comfortable. Second, in the South the Civil
War had devastated the fortunes of many in the planter class, forcing hoteliers
to seek out new audiences for their services. Third, promotion of tourism was
an element of New South boosterism. The phrase "New South" was coined by
the *Atlanta Constitution* editor Henry W. Grady in a speech to New England
businessmen. Soon the phrase became shorthand for the idea that a new and
improved South, a South committed to a progressive economy, had replaced the
old slaveholding plantation society. New South boosters sought to modernize
the southern economy and to bring the region into the national mainstream by
attracting outside investors as well as cultivating local entrepreneurship. Much
of the rhetoric of New South boosterism pervaded the language of promoters of
post–Civil War upcountry tourism.[32]

Evidence of this New South boosterism is found in a number of publications
publicizing the county's assets. In 1888 a group of city businessmen published a

pamphlet titled *Spartanburg City and County, South Carolina: Their Wonderful Attractions and Marvellous Advantage as a Place of Settlement and for the Profitable Investment of Capital.* The brochure featured the county's vibrant manufacturing economy, its modern agriculture, its arts and culture, and its tourist attractions. The copy proclaimed, "Spartanburg is in the line of and is the object of a heavy summer travel, and from the first of May to the first of October the city is at her very best with life and bustle." The boosters noted that downtown hotels housed visitors in comfort and style. The annual Farmer's Summer Encampment, an agricultural fair launched in 1887, drew twenty thousand visitors to hear "addresses on every conceivable subject of practical importance." In addition, the brochure explained, each year two thousand "health and pleasure seekers" from several states visited Glenn Springs, a mineral springs and spa located in a scenic rural community southeast of town. Fifteen years later the Chamber of Commerce produced *Spartanburg City and Spartanburg County, South Carolina, 1903,* an update of the 1888 publication. In addition to the attractions listed in 1888, the brochure described the South Atlantic States Music Festival, an event organized by the Converse College Choral Society, which drew world-class musicians to town to mount performances of *Aida, The Messiah, Faust,* and other works. Clearly city leaders saw tourism as intrinsic to both the economic and cultural life of the county.[33]

Several upcountry resorts, including Glenn Springs, managed to thrive in the postwar period thanks in part to improved railroad access. For example, in 1859 a railroad connector from Union to Spartanburg was completed. The Glenn Springs Hotel provided a hack service (buggy transportation for hire) from the Spartanburg station to the resort, considerably simplifying the process of traveling to the springs. Postwar entrepreneurs capitalized on the improved access. Around 1876 the Glenn Springs Hotel was purchased by Dr. John W. Simpson and his son J. Wister Simpson. The Simpsons operated the hotel throughout the rest of the century. They also expanded the bottling operation, building a large bottling house from which water was shipped throughout the country and to some parts of Europe. Unfortunately no information on the scale of the bottling business survives.[34]

Mrs. Means's book, published in 1888, reprinted newspaper accounts of visits to the springs from several southeastern publications. These accounts provide a glimpse of the guest experience. As in the prewar period, guests seem to have been attracted as much by the activities and the fare offered at Glenn Springs as by its healing waters. On July 10, 1883, a correspondent from the *Charleston News and Courier* provided this account:

> Of course on rising in the morning the first thing in order is a visit to
> the spring, where an unlimited amount of water is drunk, and an hour

Glenn Springs Hotel Dining Room. Courtesy of the Herald-Journal Willis Collection Spartanburg County (S.C.) Public Libraries.

or more is passed in pleasant conversation. Then all await breakfast with a comforting sense of duty done, and all even including the confirmed dyspeptics, are ready to respond to the call of the bell, take their places at the table, and indulge their newly acquired appetites. A tempting bill of fare is offered and none are able to resist.

The day is spent in strolling, reading, conversation, and playing ten-pins, cards, billiards, bagatelle, chess, croquet, &c. Pistol and rifle shooting, fancy work and swinging are also indulged in, and everyone does just what he or she may feel like doing. In the evening dancing is in order, and quadrilles, waltzes, &c. follow each other in quick succession. There is also much instrumental and vocal music which is greatly enjoyed.[35]

Music for the gala evenings was sometimes provided by visiting performers such as Vito Reale's Orchestra from Washington, D.C. Elite citizens of local communities joined the visitors for these weekend extravaganzas. Several times a year the hotel re-created the days of Camelot by organizing a jousting match; locals and guests competed for cash prizes and the right to choose a "queen" as escort to the evening's banquet.[36]

The resort's popularity seems to have grown in the closing decades of the nineteenth century. In 1894 the Simpsons renovated the Glenn Springs Hotel, expanding it to provide accommodations for five hundred. They probably made this investment in response to the opening of a railroad spur linking Glenn Springs directly to the railroad line at Roebuck, south of Spartanburg. Passengers generally traveled by train from Spartanburg to Roebuck, where they transferred to a special two-car train bound for Glenn Springs.[37]

Evidence of the increasingly middle-class clientele at Glenn Springs can be found in an extant hotel register for the years 1891–93. A comparison of guest names with census and city directory records clarifies the socioeconomic status of some of the guests. A few landowning planters appeared on the guest list, but so did family members of the state's growing professional and business classes. For example, Mrs. T. S. Farrow, her daughters Jennie and Julia, and her sons Stryder and Farrow checked into the hotel on May 20, 1891. Mrs. Farrow was the wife or perhaps the widow of T. Stobo Farrow, a Spartanburg editor and lawyer. Another 1891 guest was A. Judson Watkins, a Richmond, Virginia, merchant. In July 1891 Thomas John Moore and John Crawford Anderson checked into room 83. The two were Civil War veterans, longtime friends, brothers-in-law, and prosperous landowners. Both had also served in the South Carolina House of Representatives. Landowning farmers, merchants, and physicians were also well represented in the register.[38]

The hometowns of guests in the extant register suggest that few postwar Glenn Springs guests came from outside the Southeast and that indeed most came from the upcountry. A handful of visitors listed hometowns as far afield as New York state, and others came from distant southern towns such as New Orleans or St. Augustine, Macon or Richmond, Charlotte or Atlanta, Charleston or Georgetown. The vast majority, however, came from within a one-hundred-mile radius of the hotel—from Edgefield, Allendale, Newberry, Greenville, Union, Columbia, or Spartanburg.[39]

Of course the postwar resorts of the upcountry, like other tourist facilities throughout the South, catered to white guests only. Any African Americans who visited the hotel were undoubtedly servants, as was the case of the "servant" whom L. G. Waring listed in the hotel register. In 1891 Waring listed his servant as a companion and hotel guest. In some cases these servants might have slept on pallets in the rooms of their employers; in other cases they may have stayed in rooms that the hotel provided especially for servants. There are simply no records to tell us what accommodations the hotel made for servants.[40]

Little is known about the staffs at Glenn Springs Hotel or at any of the other upcountry resorts. In the antebellum period, presumably, some of the staff members were enslaved. The 1850 slave census shows that John C. Zimmerman owned ninety-seven slaves; some undoubtedly worked his land, but others probably worked in the hotel. After emancipation both black and white people probably were hired to serve hotel guests, but there is no information on staffs in the available records. The hotels provided seasonal wage-earning opportunities in small rural communities. Locals could have found employment ferrying hotel guests and supplies to and from the train stations, providing maid service and meals, and maintaining hotel property. Jobs in bottling plants probably provided year-round employment. Local farmers would have found a ready market for fresh fruits and vegetable as well as milk, eggs, meat, and butter. General storekeepers such as a Mr. Cates in the Glenn Springs community would have welcomed the increased trade from the hotel and from individual guests. In short, resort hotels gave small but important boosts to the prosperity of the rural communities where they were located.[41]

The hotel at Glenn Springs continued to operate after the turn of the century, when it was joined by another Spartanburg County mineral springs resort, White Stone Lithia Springs. White Stone was located about eight miles from the city in the southeastern part of the county. Visitors apparently summered in cabins at the spring site as far back as the 1850s, but not until 1902 was a hotel constructed there. The amenities offered at White Stone Springs Hotel indicate that travelers were demanding an increasing number of modern conveniences at resorts. James T. Harris, a Laurens native and Wofford College graduate who also developed the Harris Lithia Springs in Laurens County, built the hotel, a grand building lit by electricity and with a steam heat system. An electric car line connected the hotel to a railroad station two miles away. According to a promotional brochure, the "White Stone has become celebrated in all parts of the United States" under Harris's management. Not only did he run the hotel, which could accommodate 350 guests, but he also began a bottling operation to bottle and ship White Stone Springs water. Harris claimed to be shipping a railroad car load of bottled water a day to points as far away as the Philippines and Alaska. White Springs Lithia Water was awarded a first prize medal at the Louisiana Purchase Exposition in St. Louis in 1904.[42]

In the postwar period, other resort hotels that capitalized on mountain settings or scenic vistas opened in the upcountry. In 1873 Robert and Mary Anderson opened a hotel in Travelers Rest, north of Greenville on the Buncombe Road (which went to Asheville, North Carolina). A Charleston newspaper reported that the Andersons' hotel was often full and that "Col. Anderson and his wife are untiring in their attention to the guests and everyone is made to feel entirely at home." In 1898 the Andersons' daughter inherited the house, enlarged it, and renamed it Spring Park Inn. Because of its proximity to the Carolina, Western, and Knoxville Railroad, the inn attracted guests from all over the region. Nearby the Paris Mountain Hotel Company opened the Altamont Hotel in 1890. The twenty-three-room inn boasted daily stagecoach service from Greenville.

In spite of the spectacular views from its wrap-around porches, the hotel closed in 1898.[43]

After World War I the popularity of many of the upcountry's resorts gradually began to wane. The development of the automobile and "swift modern highways" as well as better rail connections and the lure of more exotic locations now easily accessible probably had much to do with this slow decline. Local lore suggests that during Prohibition, the Glenn Springs Hotel became a center for the sale and consumption of alcohol. One local historian explained that after several prominent citizens of the community had complained that the clubhouse had become "nothing more than an open bar-room," local police conducted a raid there that "resulted in a charge against the manager of maintaining a nuisance. Officers confiscated 'many bottles of beer, a small quantity of whisky, together with packs of cards, poker chips, and other supposed gambling effects.'" The hotel was condemned in the 1930s, and it burned to the ground on July 26, 1941.[44]

Resort hotels played important roles in the economic and social development of the South Carolina upcountry. Tourism investment in the state's western counties created employment and spurred the development of a transportation infrastructure. New communities sprang up around many of the hotels and were accompanied by the schools, churches, and stores needed to serve local residents. Those communities survived even as the hotels closed and local residents found other ways to earn a living. Tourism did not die in the upcountry after the twentieth century, but other types of attractions eclipsed the area's resort hotels. Tourism remains an important sector of the upcountry economy as the region's business leaders follow the example of their nineteenth-century predecessors.

Notes

1. "Editorial from the Industrial Issue of the *Spartanburg Herald*, Nov., 1886," reprinted in Mrs. T. Sumter Means, *Glenn Springs, So. Ca: Its Location, Discovery, History, Personal Sketches of Its Habitues, What It Will Cure, &c.* (Spartanburg, S.C.: Trimmier's Printing Office and Bookstore, 1888), 30, copy in Kennedy Genealogical and Local History Room, Spartanburg County Public Library, Headquarters Branch, Spartanburg, S.C.

2. Richard D. Starnes, *Creating the Land of the Sky: Tourism and Society in Western North Carolina* (Tuscaloosa: University of Alabama Press, 2005); Richard D. Starnes, ed., *Southern Journeys: Tourism, Heritage and Culture in the Modern South* (Tuscaloosa: University of Alabama Press, 2003); Stephanie Yuhl, *A Golden Haze of Memory: Tourism and the Making of Modern Charleston* (Chapel Hill: University of North Carolina Press, 2005).

3. For general upcountry history, see Philip N. Racine, *Seeing Spartanburg: A History in Images* (Spartanburg, S.C.: Hub City Writers Project, 1999); Walter Edgar,

South Carolina: A History (Columbia: University of South Carolina Press, 1998); Archie Vernon Huff Jr., *Greenville: The History of the City and County in the South Carolina Piedmont* (Columbia: University of South Carolina Press, 1995).

4. For more on the role of resorts as markers of status, see Thomas A. Chambers, *Drinking the Waters: Creating an American Leisure Class at Nineteenth Century Mineral Springs* (Washington, D.C.: Smithsonian Institution Press, 2002), xvii–xviii, 85. For more on the role of mountain resorts in linking lowcountry and western counties of southern states, see Starnes, *Creating the Land of the Sky,* 4.

5. Lawrence Fay Brewster, *Summer Migrations and Resorts of South Carolina Low-Country Planters* (New York: AMS Press, 1947), v, 5–35, quote on 5; Charlene Boyer Lewis, *Ladies and Gentlemen on Display: Planter Society at the Virginia Springs, 1790–1860* (Charlottesville: University of Virginia Press, 2001), 60.

6. Brewster, *Summer Migrations,* 53–57.

7. Ibid., 58–59.

8. Ibid., 62; Racine, *Seeing Spartanburg,* 97; ad for Merchants' Hotel in *Health Resorts of the South* (Boston: George A. Chapin, 1893).

9. Cindy S. Aron, *Working at Play: A History of Vacations in the United States* (New York: Oxford University Press, 1999), 3; John F. Sears, *Sacred Places: American Tourist Attractions in the Nineteenth Century* (New York: Oxford University Press, 1989), 3–9, quote on 4. The literature on the history of tourism is growing. In addition to the works of Aron, Sears, Starnes, and Yuhl, other recent works include Dona Brown, *Inventing New England: Regional Tourism in the Nineteenth Century* (Washington, D.C.: Smithsonian Institution Press, 1995); Marguerite Shaffer, *See America First: Tourism and National Identity, 1880–1940* (Washington, D.C.: Smithsonian Institution Press, 2001); A. K. Sandoval-Strausz, *Hotels: An American History* (New Haven, Conn.: Yale University Press, 2007); Susan Sessions Rugh, *Are We There Yet? The Golden Age of American Family Vacations* (Lawrence: University Press of Kansas, 2008).

10. Brewster, *Summer Migrations,* 54, 60, 64, 71; Means, *Glenn Springs, So. Ca,* 24–25.

11. Brewster, *Summer Migrations,* 61.

12. Sandoval-Strausz, *Hotels,* 88; Aron, *Working at Play,* 17.

13. Sandoval-Strausz, *Hotels,* 88.

14Aron, *Working at Play,* 17–19; John Bell, quoted in Lewis, *Ladies and Gentlemen on Display,* 62. The scholarly and popular literature on mineral springs resorts is plentiful. Some examples include Lewis, *Ladies and Gentlemen on Display*; Charles B. Firestone, *Bubbling Waters* (New York: Robert M. McBride, 1938); *Health Resorts of the South* (Boston: George A. Chapin, 1893); Stan Cohen, *Historic Springs of the Virginias: A Pictorial History* (Charleston, W.Va.: Pictorial Histories, 1981); Tracy J. Revels, *Watery Eden: A History of Wakulla Spring* (Tallahassee: Friends of Wakulla Springs State Park, 2002); Janet Mace Valenza, *Taking the Waters in Texas: Springs, Spas, and Fountains of Youth* (Austin: University of Texas Press, 2000); Gene Fowler, *Crazy Water: The Story of Mineral Wells and Other Texas Health Resorts* (Fort Worth: Texas Christian University Press, 1991); Chambers, *Drinking the Waters.*

15. Sandoval-Strausz, *Hotels,* 92.

16. Ibid., 90–91; Chambers, *Drinking the Waters,* 29.

17. Works Progress Administration, *History of Spartanburg* (Spartanburg, S.C.: Spartanburg Branch, American Association of University Women, 1940), 49.

18. Montague McMillan, *Limestone College: A History, 1945–1970* (Gaffney, S.C.: Limestone College Press, 1970), 1–5; Brewster, *Summer Migrations,* 82–84.

19. Huff, *Greenville,* 92–93, 209; Lydia Dishman, "A Healthy Departure," *Town* 1 (July 2011): 36.

20. Aron, *Working at Play,* 24–26; Sandoval-Strausz, *Hotels,* 88–90; Lewis, *Ladies and Gentlemen on Display,* 175–86.

21. Chambers, *Drinking the Waters,* 85.

22. Means, *Glenn Springs, So. Ca,* 20.

23. Ibid.; Racine, *Seeing Spartanburg,* 36.

24. Racine, *Seeing Spartanburg,* 36; Glenn Springs Historic District National Register of Historic Places Application, Vertical Files, Kennedy Genealogical and Local History Room, Spartanburg County Public Library, Headquarters Branch, Spartanburg, S.C.; Means, *Glenn Springs, So. Ca,* 22. Racine says that Glenn purchased the house in 1816, but other sources say 1826.

25. Glenn Springs Historic District National Register of Historic Places Application; Jennifer Walker, "The Glenn Springs Hotel," unpub. paper, ca. 1998, 8–9, Vertical Files, Kennedy Genealogical and Local History Room, Spartanburg County Public Library, Headquarters Branch, Spartanburg, S.C.; J. B. O. Landrum, *History of Spartanburg County* (1900; repr., Spartanburg, S.C.: Reprint Co., 1985), 443–45; Vernon Foster and Walter S. Montgomery Sr., *Spartanburg: Facts, Reminiscences, Folklore* (Spartanburg, S.C.: Reprint Co., 1998), 278; Glenn Springs Hotel Register, 1893–94, Kennedy Genealogical and Local History Room, Spartanburg County Public Library, Headquarters Branch, Spartanburg, S.C.; Means, *Glenn Springs, So. Ca,* 19.

26. Brewster, *Summer Migrations,* 78–80; Bruce W. Eelman, *Entrepreneurs in the Southern Upcountry: Commercial Culture in Spartanburg, South Carolina, 1845–1880* (Athens: University of Georgia Press, 2008), 10; Means, *Glenn Springs, So. Ca,* 23.

27. Means, *Glenn Springs, So. Ca,* 24; Brewster, *Summer Migrations,* 80.

28. Means, *Glenn Springs, So. Ca,* 25; Thomas W. Chadwick, ed., "The Diary of Samuel Edward Burges, 1860–1862," *South Carolina Historical Magazine* 48 (July 1947): 141–63, quote on 163.

29. Huff, *Greenville,* 209.

30. Means, *Glenn Springs, So. Ca,* 25.

31. Aron, *Working at Play,* 43–47; Sandoval-Strausz, *Hotels,* 112.

32. Aron, *Working at Play,* 49; Sandoval-Strausz, *Hotels,* 111–12; Chambers, *Drinking the Waters,* 185; Sears, *Sacred Places,* 209. For more on the New South movement in South Carolina, see Edgar, *South Carolina,* 425–28. For more on tourism as an element of New South boosterism, see Starnes, *Creating the Land of the Sky,* 10.

33. *Spartanburg City and County, SC: Their Wonderful Attractions and Marvellous Advantages as a Place of Settlement and for the Profitable Investment of Capital*

(Spartanburg, S.C.: Cofield, Petty and Co., Printers, 1888), quotes on 15, 28, 17; J. W. Simpson, *Spartanburg City and Spartanburg County, South Carolina, 1903* (Nashville: Brandon Printing, 1903), 19.

34. Walker, "Glenn Springs Hotel," 9.

35. Ibid., 10; Means, *Glenn Springs, So. Ca,* 26. Similar accounts were reprinted from W. H. Gaines in the *Augusta Chronicle* (27–28), Col. Thomas F. Greneker in the *Laurensville Herald* (28–29), and Maj. John P. Kinard in the *Newberry Herald* (29). Bagatelle was a table game resembling billiards.

36. Walker, "Glenn Springs Hotel," 12.

37. Ibid., 9–10.

38. Glenn Springs Hotel Register, 1891–93, Kennedy Genealogical and Local History Room, Spartanburg County Public Library, Headquarters Branch, Spartanburg, S.C. For more on Moore and Crawford, see Thomas Moore Craig, *Upcountry South Carolina Goes to War: Letters of the Anderson, Brockman, and Moore Families, 1853–1865* (Columbia: University of South Carolina Press, 2009).

39. Glenn Springs Hotel Register, 1891–93.

40. Ibid.

41. Slave Census, Spartanburg Co., 1860, copies held in Kennedy Genealogical and Local History Room, Spartanburg County Public Library, Headquarters Branch, Spartanburg, S.C., pp. 497, 499; Glenn Springs Historic District National Register of Historic Places Application. John Z. Zimmerman also farmed in the Glenn Springs community, and he lived in a large Greek revival home there. In 1860, some years after he sold the hotel, he still owned ninety-two slaves, suggesting that most of his enslaved workforce did not work at the hotel. See Slave Census, Spartanburg Co., 1860, pp. 185, 187.

42. Simpson, *Spartanburg City and Spartanburg County,* 36; "White Springs Lithia Hotel," brochure, n.d., located at the Kennedy Genealogical and Local History Room, Spartanburg County Public Library, Headquarters Branch, Spartanburg, S.C.; Henry Gardner Cutler, *History of South Carolina,* vol. 4 (Chicago and New York: Lewis, 1920): 214–15.

43. Huff, *Greenville,* 209.

44. Walker, "Glenn Springs Hotel," 14; Glenn Springs Historic District National Register of Historic Places Application; Foster and Montgomery, *Spartanburg,* 311–12, 492; "Famed Hotel at Glenn Springs Razed by Fire," *Spartanburg Journal,* July 27, 1941, 1.

"Education has Breathed over the Scene"

Robert H. Reid and the Reidville Schools, 1857–1905

Timothy P. Grady

On Friday, October 14, 1859, Thomas Vernon, editor of the *Carolina Spartan*, had a chance to visit the new town of Reidville, located some fifteen miles southwest of Spartanburg, South Carolina. His report captured, with wonder, the remarkable progress of a new community that had, at its heart, a dream of educational achievement. "Two years ago," he reported, "the native forest trees covered the spot." Yet in just that short time, "Presto! change! Education has breathed over the scene, and we now behold school edifices of substantial structure and high art finish—commodious for the present and long into the future." He continued describing the scene, saying that the "female school building is arranged with consummate judgment, and furnished with every adjunct essential to thorough instruction." While, he claimed, the male school was less imposing than the building for the female school, it was still "a handsome building, and arranged with special regard to comfort and convenience."

Each of the schools contained classrooms that were appointed with "splendid Philosophical Apparatus, perfect in all its appliances." The library and reading rooms were lined with cabinets containing "a series of beautiful painted and engraved glass diagrams of celestial phenomena for the magic lantern, illustrative of astronomical science, and similarly prepared diagrams for illustrating animal physiology." Along the walls of each school, "a long series of Philosophical Charts, explaining at a glance every form, line, and angle known to mathematics and the physical sciences, with globes, maps, &c." A boardinghouse and home for younger girls was run by Mrs. Sarah Stone, the grandmother of the women's teacher, Sarah Butler. Here "all the domestic arts and christian [*sic*] virtues [were] enforced by motherly example and sisterly affection."

According to the report, a dozen families were making Reidville their home, and more were planning to move there in the near future. The homes, it was claimed, were "new and elegant dwellings, several rivaling any of [Spartanburg's] boasted mansions." Overall, Vernon declared, "how cheering is this to the public-spirited gentlemen who projected this improvement." He foretold a long, bright future for Reidville and questioned what could hinder "a progress commensurate with the largest expectations of the liberal founders? The neighborhood is wealthy. The erection of a hotel is in agitation. The Sulphur and Chalybcate [*sic*] Springs will draw guests and visitors, and the travel now setting in that direction will be much increased." Indeed what could possibly happen to prevent the future greatness of the Reidville schools and the growth of the surrounding community?[1]

That grand future never came to pass. Despite the high hopes expressed by the visiting reporter, the ambitious dreams of those "public-spirited gentlemen" and the idealistic vision of the man who led the project, the Reverend Robert H. Reid, these schools would vanish into history slightly less than fifty years after their establishment. Still, the story of the Reidville schools yields valuable insights into the course of upcountry history through the last half of the nineteenth century. In this story of failure one can gain a deeper understanding of the social, economic, and educational changes that reshaped the region during this period.

The Reidville schools were founded at the crest of a wave of educational endeavors that would leave a lasting imprint on South Carolina's academic community in the surviving institutions of higher education that are synonymous with the upcountry today. It was in the decades before the Civil War that institutions such as Furman, Wofford, Limestone, Newberry, and others were begun, many by local leaders of religious denominations such as the Baptists, Methodists, Lutherans, and in the case of the Reidville schools, the Presbyterians. As such, the Reidville schools shared a great deal with those institutions in terms of its founding, goals, organization, and curricula in the early years of its operation. The key difference between those successful institutions and the Reidville schools over the long term was simply one of adaptation. While the others adapted to the changes in the region during the late nineteenth century and thus survived, the Reidville schools, by and large, failed to do so, though not always a result of a lack of effort. By the last decade of their existence, the schools had become parochial in nature, serving only the needs of a small handful of nearby residents with long ties to the cherished institutions. In 1905, nearing the end of his long life and only recently retired from an active involvement with the schools, Reverend Reid along with the trustees consented to the incorporation of the schools into the Spartanburg public school system. The grand dream ended, but their story echoes many aspects of the overall story of

Portrait of Robert H. Reid, late nineteenth century.
Courtesy of the Spartanburg County (S.C.) Historical Society.

the South Carolina upcountry during this period. In it one learns more of the region's intriguing past.

The story of the Reidville schools and the community that evolved around them began with their primary founder, Robert Hardin Reid. Reid, the son of Andrew Reid, a prominent Presbyterian elder in Anderson County, South Carolina, was born on July 17, 1821. Realizing his son's potential, Andrew Reid ensured that he received a private education locally in preparation for college. At the age of twenty-one, Robert Reid left Anderson for South Carolina College, the predecessor of the University of South Carolina, where he completed his studies with honors in 1846. At his graduation Reid was chosen to give the valedictory address to the assembled students, faculty, families, and distinguished guests, among whom sat Wade Hampton II, commonly referred to as Colonel Wade Hampton. Colonel Hampton was the father of Wade Hampton III, who would become a noted Confederate cavalryman and politician. Reid's speech was of such power and eloquence that it caught the attention of Colonel Hampton, who reportedly told one of Mr. Reid's friends, "That man should go to Germany for a few years to carry on his studies. I will furnish all the money needed."[2]

Despite the possible offer, Reid entered the Theological Seminary at Columbia, South Carolina, where he completed his studies in 1850. Pointing to an interest in both religious instruction and education, Reid took the steps necessary to become licensed to preach by the Presbytery of South Carolina two years before completing his seminary training in order to serve as chaplain for the Barhamville Collegiate Institute, a college preparatory school near Columbia. After his graduation from the seminary, Reid left Columbia to serve a two-year stint as minister at the Presbyterian Church in Anderson, South Carolina. His real opportunity, however, came in late 1852 when he accepted an offer to become the minister of the prestigious Nazareth Presbyterian Church in Spartanburg County beginning in January 1853.[3]

For Reid, the post at Nazareth proved transformative, and he soon found the occasion to use his position to great effect. From his position Reid would quickly evolve into a leader in educational and religious endeavors in the county. In terms of prominence, the leadership of Nazareth Church was perfectly suited to allow Reid this opportunity. The church began as the Tyger River Congregation, which linked the original mid-eighteenth-century Scots-Irish settlements of the district that spread out along the three branches of the Tyger River through their common bond, a strong Calvinist Presbyterian faith. Several years later, in 1765, the original meetinghouse for the congregation, renamed Nazareth, was built near today's existing structure at a central point close to the Middle Tyger River, making it the region's oldest religious organization. By the time of Reid's appointment, the church membership had grown large enough to spur the creation of four other Presbyterian churches in the Spartanburg District, for which he served as the sole minister for the first several years.[4] The Nazareth post represented a respected position in the community and gave Reid immediate entry into the realm of the intellectual, economic, and political elites of the area.[5]

On January 1, 1857, for his New Year's Day sermon, Reverend Reid took to the pulpit of Nazareth Church to speak to his congregation of his desire to improve the Tyger River region to keep up with the progress of Spartanburg Township. That progress by 1857 was pointing to a new direction for the future of Spartanburg District, and he, even as a relative newcomer, wanted to be a part of it. That future lay in education. By 1857 many of Spartanburg's elites were throwing their time, money, and efforts behind the creation of educational institutions. In 1850 the Reverend Benjamin Wofford left a bequest of one hundred thousand dollars for the founding of a college to be associated with the Methodist Church. Wofford College opened its doors in 1854 and by 1857 was entering its third year and attracting a healthy number of students. While the school had not, as of yet, generated enough tuition revenue to support its costs, it was progressing steadily, and the community leaders and alumni were firm in their resolve to keep the institution growing as the linchpin of the up-and-coming town.[6]

In the 1850s Spartanburg was a community with big dreams and grand ambitions. Already in the first half of the nineteenth century, Spartanburg farmers were joining their upcountry colleagues in participating in more market-oriented crop production along with their traditional focus on self-sufficiency. Cotton became more and more a part of their agricultural pursuits, with corn, wheat, and oats representing other marketable crops grown by market-savvy farmers eager to supplement their incomes. While the region's farmers expanded their production, Spartanburg Township experienced rapid growth as merchants, bankers, lawyers, manufacturers, and others relocated to the town looking to take advantage of the rising economic and political power of the upcountry as a whole. Textile mills, ironworks, and gristmills were among the numerous projects that attracted entrepreneurs and investors locally and from abroad. In 1849 efforts began among community leaders to attract local investment and state support that would, ten years later, bring the first railroad cars steaming into town as part of the Spartanburg and Union Railroad. Spartanburg was emerging as a center of commerce and culture to go along with its growing political power as part of the larger upcountry. Educational endeavors such as Wofford were simply part of a larger trend of advocacy that was gripping the elite class. As the historian Bruce W. Eelman put it, "this developing professional class advanced programs designed to fulfill their vision of a stable, law-abiding, educated community of productive commercial farms with improved transportation routes to markets in all directions and an important industrial sector."[7]

The founding of Wofford College, to rival the college in Columbia, was the most ambitious of the educational ventures in Spartanburg District that had been launched in the years immediately preceding Reid's New Year's Day sermon. Many others were started to try to provide access to elementary and college-preparatory education since the public school system in the state, started in 1811 under the so-called "Free School Act," had largely failed. With the state and local governments unable to provide educational access, most of the effort of providing schooling for children of all ages fell to private individuals and, more commonly, private institutions styling themselves "academies." These academies largely served the children of the higher social strata of their individual regions, and many served as sources of pride for their communities and were symbols of growth and future promise for the leading citizens typically involved in their founding. The earliest school in Spartanburg District, for example, was the Minerva Academy. Founded by the congregation of Nazareth Church, the Minerva school served children in the region into the first couple of decades of the nineteenth century just as the village of Spartanburg was taking shape. The Greenville Academy, started in 1819, began its classes for the boys and girls in that region when the village of Greenville boasted barely four hundred citizens and before it had an organized church.[8]

From these early beginnings academies in the upcountry proliferated, and by the 1850s numerous schools populated the region and Spartanburg District. In the Spartanburg region established institutions included the Bethel Academy in Woodruff, the Glenn Springs Academy in Glenn Springs, and the Poplar Springs Academy and Pine Grove Academy in the Tyger River area, both of which would be replaced by the Reidville schools. The New Prospect Academy near modern Inman, South Carolina, was run by the Reverend John G. Landrum, who also served as the minister of the New Prospect Baptist Church in the same area. In the village of Spartanburg several different schools served the larger population in the immediate vicinity and reflected the greater demand for education in their diversity of organizational structure. The Odd Fellows' School in town offered classes for children of all ages, including primary education as well as departments that specialized in the typical college-preparatory disciplines typical of the traditional academy. Catering to those of a more martial spirit, the St. John's Classical and Military School added a basic military regimen and training to the classical education of the academy.[9]

Women were included in the quest for education in the upcountry and in the Spartanburg District in particular. While some of the academies operating in the rural outskirts of the district offered mixed classes that could be accessed by interested young ladies, the majority of the smaller academies tended to cater to men alone, as women's education was geared more toward the arts and music as well as history, languages, and classics. Given that the accepted role for women at the time concentrated on the responsibilities of wife, mother, and household, women's education concentrated on subjects that would produce females who would be pleasant companions, proper social models of modest decorum and refinement, and mothers to guide their offspring in assuming their own proper roles in republican society. Curricula at most schools for women offered education in English, history, geography, botany, and chemistry. Beyond this basic education, most schools added moral and mental philosophy with the purpose of providing an acceptable religious and social structure around which a proper lady could understand how to use her knowledge in a proper social context.[10]

By the 1850s young women in the district interested in progressing beyond an elementary education had only a few options from which to choose. In the village of Spartanburg young women could attend the Spartanburg Female Academy, begun in 1837 and run by J. Wofford Tucker. Tucker, one of the intellectual leaders of the community in the 1850s, served as an early trustee of Wofford College before he moved west in 1858. The Female Academy in its early years would alternatively be called the Spartanburg Female Seminary and, in 1854, the Spartanburg Female College. The college would continue operating, with a short pause during the Civil War, until the late 1870s, when it would close its doors because of financial difficulties. The second major choice of women interested in education was located in the northern part of Spartanburg District in the village of Gaffney. Here in 1846 the Reverend Thomas Curtis and his son, the Reverend William Curtis, began the Limestone Springs Female High School in a former hotel built to access the nearby springs and racetrack, both of which had attracted a sizable tourist traffic. This school would operate successfully until the Civil War. After a decade-long hiatus, the school reopened in 1881 as the Cooper-Limestone Institute, later renamed Limestone College. For women south of the Spartanburg District, the Greenville Female Academy operated until 1854, when it was supplanted by the Greenville Baptist Female College, a forerunner of coeducational Furman University.[11]

The rash of new schools and academies in the Spartanburg District is not surprising given the context of educational changes occurring nationwide, though the South as a whole was decades behind other regions' developments. By the 1850s the United States was well into what historians such as Carl F. Kaestle have termed the common-school reform movement. During the first half of the nineteenth century, in areas outside the South, pioneers in education such as Horace Mann and Henry Barnard led reformers in using government action to provide for better access to education for all, higher standards in teacher training, better curricular classification, and other accomplishments. But while advocates and opponents existed everywhere for this cause, as Kaestle demonstrated, "the systematization of state-sponsored common schooling prevailed in the Northeast and the Midwest, while in the antebellum South, the reformers never quite mustered the political and economic support necessary to establish free common schools." That movement awaited southerners after the Civil War and would be accomplished only in fits and starts. Ironically, Robert H. Reid would involve himself deeply in that cause as well. Still, in Spartanburg, as in much of the rest of the South before the war, private academies and schools led the way in educational access. As such, Reid's efforts were simply among many confirming the trend rather than setting a new course of action.[12]

In 1856, with the growth, energy, and intellectual enthusiasm of the Spartanburg District as his backdrop and the influence and authority lent to him by his position as minister of the Nazareth Church, Reid began to develop an idea to capitalize on both to create two schools and a community around them that would reshape the Tyger River area and provide a model for educational achievement and enlightenment for the entire region. Through late 1856 Reid deliberated with several prominent members of Nazareth Church and, with their support, began composing a special sermon to bring the matter to the congregation at large. He chose January 1 of the following year to bring his idea into the open.[13]

In his New Year's Day address to the congregation in 1857, Reid laid out his case for two schools. The first was to be an academy to prepare young men for entry into Wofford, South Carolina College, or other institutions of higher education such as Davidson College or Columbia University. The second was to be a female high school to prepare women with the necessary knowledge and skills to fulfill their future roles as wives and mothers. His plan entailed soliciting a donation of land from among the wealthy landowners of the Tyger River region and then raising ten thousand dollars to provide for the construction of the needed facilities and the purchase of supplies. Reid pointed to the common heritage and outlook of the congregation, "their Scotch-Irish ancestry,—in all their history and everywhere the staunch friends of schools and colleges" throughout the country. Additionally, he claimed, the "notable decline of Presbyterianism in this region" had largely left "the education of our children to other denominations." It was not so much that it was bad that Landrum had staked a claim to Baptist leadership of elementary and secondary education in the district or that Wofford had shown the way for the Methodists to lead in higher education with the establishment of Wofford College. Rather, since Presbyterians had been among the first settlers of the region, Reid argued that they should step forward to reclaim their historic role as leaders in the community and in the education of the young.[14]

The assembled congregation greeted with relish Reid's challenge to regain their place in education in Spartanburg. A meeting was called for the following Sunday, January 7, to discuss the idea. As that meeting commenced, Col. Samuel N. Evins, a former state representative, militia officer, and head of one of the most prominent families in the area, took charge of the meeting, introducing the general idea and speaking strongly in his support of the project. There followed a convincing show of support by the heads of some of the most influential families in the area: Gen. Joel S. Miller, Maj. David Anderson, and the brothers James and Anthony Wakefield. The collected leaders of the congregation quickly united behind the concept of schools to serve as a focal point for the area. A committee, headed by Reid, was hastily put together to field the offers of support and seek out land for the new schools.[15]

The committee's work went quickly, and within a month several offers of land were made by the largest landholders of the congregation, with some offering multiple potential sites: "Col. Evins and Gen. Miller offered fifty acres of land on the road between them, Gen. Miller and Mr. Samuel Switzer one hundred acres at Flint Hill, Mr. Thomas Miller, Col. Evins, and Mr. Graac West one hundred acres near the Popular [*sic*] Spring, Mr. David Anderson one hundred acres at the Drummond Springs, Mr. J. and A. W. Wakefield hundred acres and the use of the powder or sulfur springs." The last site proved to be the unanimous winner after the committee had finished assessing each potential location. It was close enough to Nazareth Church for relatively easy travel; was conveniently located between the two largest towns in the area, Spartanburg and Greenville; and offered access to a mineral spring that could potentially draw tourists who could aid the economy of the new community to be formed around it. In all, the chosen location at what was then referred to as Wakefield Springs seemed to be perfect, and the committee voted unanimously to draw up an agreement with the Wakefield brothers for "such lands . . . as will afford suitable Building sites for both Institutions, as well as the Building up of a Town, with a perpetual right to the use of the Powder Springs."[16]

With the land in hand, the trustees appointed a building committee to survey the property for suitable building sites. After laying out the boundaries, a location for the female school was selected "on an eminence in the western portion of the school Land, and for the male school on an eminence in the Eastern portion of said land." A street was laid out in a straight line between the two schools, and in a nod to the grand and glorious dreams of the founders of the two schools, the street was planned to be one hundred feet wide to accommodate large processions and ceremonies. Over the next few months monetary donations were received and plans were drawn for the buildings that would house the two institutions. When the subject of names for the schools was raised as late as May 1857, the thirty-member board of trustees voted overwhelmingly to name both the new community and the schools that would be at its heart in honor of the young minister whose energies had united them in the grand design. The town became Reidville, and the schools were announced as the Reidville Male and Female High Schools. By the middle of 1857, the ten-thousand-dollar goal for fund-raising was met and a contract signed with Gen. J. W. Miller to construct the needed buildings. Planning began for the inaugural academic year to begin in early 1858.[17]

As news of the new schools spread, many of the more community-minded people in the Spartanburg District took the time to write glowing messages of support that the editor of the *Carolina Spartan,* Thomas Vernon, was only too glad to publish. Earlier efforts to support the Limestone Female High School,

*Tin-type image of the Reidville Female College, circa 1880s. Courtesy of the
South Caroliniana Library, University of South Carolina, Columbia, S.C.*

Spartanburg Female College, and Wofford College had been prominently mentioned by the paper and its subscribers.[18] Articles written by local supporters of
education, though not affiliated directly with the new Reidville project, began
to laud the importance of education in the area and to defend the prominent
role of the various Protestant denominations and ministers in bringing the various schools into being. One article noted that "such establishments of learning,
though they may originate with denominations . . . should be hailed by every
community and district as harbingers of good—fountains of intellectual light—
sources of blessing innumerable."[19] Another, focusing more specifically on the
Reidville venture, pointed to the great need for schools in that region, lauded
the money raised and the perfection of the location, and pointed out what was
seen as the true strength of the schools, "a reserve of a whole neighborhood of
patriotic and intelligent citizens, who can command five times that amount
[ten thousand dollars], if necessary, and who will do it rather than not succeed;
failure is impossible—success is a fixed fact."[20]

Tin-type image of the Reidville Male High School, circa 1880s. Courtesy of the South Caroliniana Library, University of South Carolina, Columbia, S.C.

With funds coming in and buildings under construction, all that remained necessary was to find an instructor to take primary charge of the students for the first session with the understanding that Reverend Reid and others would assist in the instruction. The Reverend Thomas E. Davis, a Presbyterian minister from just across the state line in Rutherfordton, North Carolina, was chosen as the principal of the male classical school. In March 1858 the doors of the Reidville Male High School opened with nine young scholars, though for the first six weeks the school was forced to operate in a small local building that had served as an impromptu schoolhouse for local children before the arrival of the new institutions. By the end of the session, thirty-eight students had enrolled in the school, promising numbers for its first, hastily organized effort. Of those thirty-eight, at least seventeen were young ladies, showing a healthy demand for the services of the female high school, which would not be ready to begin independent operation until the beginning of the following year.[21]

By the end of 1858 both schools had been completed, as were buildings adjacent to and along Main Street. These buildings would serve as a boardinghouse for young ladies attending the female high school from a distance, quarters for the teachers, and various stores and homes of private individuals whose owners had taken advantage of a private auction of town lots held in late 1857 to add money to the schools' endowment as well as to attract residents interested in becoming part of a thriving community in the future. As the female school was being organized for its first full academic year, teachers were found to teach there under the leadership of Reid, who accepted the role of principal and instructor of intellectual and moral philosophy as well as logic and rhetoric.[22] A young, local physician, Dr. John C. Oeland, who also served early on as secretary and treasurer of the board of trustees, was enlisted to teach natural sciences. A Greenville resident, Mrs. Sarah Butler, was hired to become the instructor in English, grammar, history, geography, and arithmetic. Butler's grandmother Sarah Stone was hired to take charge of the boardinghouse and would soon assume the title of "Matron of the School." As the second year opened, the enrollment of the male school alone increased to thirty-eight, and enrollment at the female school rose to numbers described as "twice ten or more" in a report on the first grand commencement held in July to celebrate the first full year of the schools' operation.[23]

On Thursday, July 7, 1859, the Reidville schools' first full academic year was brought to a close with a grand commencement that attracted an eager crowd of observers from around the district. They were treated to readings from student essays, exhibitions and examinations of the students judged by august committees, speeches given by Reverend Reid and Dr. Oeland, and a keynote speech on the importance of a classical education in the society of the time given by the Reverend Thomas A. Hoyt of Abbeville, South Carolina. The examination committees gathered to test the students on their attained knowledge reflected the extended and local connections Reid had managed to establish around the district since his arrival at Nazareth. Rev. John Landrum served as the chair of the female school committee, and Dr. Charles P. Woodruff acted in the same capacity for the male school. Both reported that the students "gave not only unmistakable evidence of sound and thorough instruction on the part of the teacher, but evidence of industry and application on their own part." Overall the day was a splendid success, and the participants, students, families, teachers, and supporters alike came away with a great sense not only of accomplishment but also of great promise for the future. As one attendee reported in the local newspaper, while the school was less than two years old, "yet it [has] its noble scholastic buildings, its surrounding edifices, its throngs of happy pupils, its corps of well-selected instructors, and its first 'Commencement Day.'" Was it any wonder, he continued, that all were certain of the "glowing predictions and fervid good wishes respecting its onward and upward fame, its increasing growth, and its widely-extended beneficial influence"? Robert Reid's dream had come true, and with such an auspicious beginning, the Reidville schools seemed certain to continue their progress without interruption.[24]

The advent of the Civil War brought a turn in the fortunes of the Reidville schools. That conflict and the rapid economic and educational changes that began during Reconstruction would leave an indelible imprint on the region and lay a course for education in the upcountry that would leave institutions such as the Reidville schools increasingly at a competitive disadvantage. While the founder and supporters of the schools adapted and innovated in an intense struggle to stay credible, it would prove a futile effort.

On Saturday, November 24, 1860, the leading men of the Spartanburg District came together to deliberate the question of secession in response to the election of Abraham Lincoln and to appoint representatives to the December 17 convention in Columbia called by the state legislature. Religious leaders and those who had led the way in education for the district took their place among the wealthy landowners and businessmen who dominated the politics of the towns and districts. Rev. John Landrum was elected as president of the assembly. Among the many serving in the capacity of vice president were Robert Reid, Rev. William Curtis of the Limestone Female High School, and Harvey Wofford, the executor of Benjamin Wofford's will and a founding trustee of Wofford College. Professor Jonathan W. Carlisle of Wofford College, who had given the keynote address at the opening ceremony of the Reidville Female High School, was appointed as one of six secretaries to the assembly. When the meeting concluded, a slate of six representatives was unanimously elected to travel to Columbia in support of secession. Given the importance of education, Landrum, Curtis, and Carlisle were chosen as three of the six. Just weeks later they and their colleagues from around the state took South Carolina to war.[25]

The Civil War had a devastating effect on Spartanburg District and on the upcountry as a whole. In terms of its influence on education, the drain on the numbers of young men in the region caused numerous schools to close their doors because of a lack of pupils, shortage of tuition funds, unavailability of teachers, or some combination thereof. Despite the hardships, however, and unlike other schools such as the Odd Fellows' School, the New Prospect Academy, and others, the Reidville schools not only survived but also served admirably as the unifying force for the community around the Tyger River region that its founder and supporters had envisioned from the beginning.

Throughout the war, enrollments at Reidville remained at smaller, though still viable levels. The enrolling class at the male school in the spring of 1861 totaled thirty-nine young men, a level comparable to that of the prewar classes. Just as in the prewar years, the enrollees continued to reflect a largely local character as fifteen of the students called Reidville home and were drawn from the children of local families in the area. Sixteen of the remaining students were

from the larger Spartanburg District with residences largely in nearby Cash-
ville, Woodruff, Glenn Springs, and Poolesville. Despite the local flavor of the
student body at large, the school's reputation, or perhaps that of Robert Reid,
had grown sufficiently to attract eight students from other parts of the state.
Young men from as far away as Charleston, Orangeburg, and Laurens and from
relatively close Greenville enrolled in the school for an education despite the
turmoil of the conflict.[26]

Still, while the early enrollment was healthy for the still-new school and reflected a growing reputation, the war did begin to affect the schools' enrollment
sufficiently to show that Reidville was not immune to the effects felt by many
other institutions. In March 1861 a local resident, Nancy Moore Evins, wrote to
one of her sons, Thomas Moore, that enrollment at the schools was "not large,
the male is near thirty and the female numbers 33." The fact that the schools'
enrollment, the male part at least, had never had a class larger than the thirty-
nine total enrollees of the spring session that year might have made her observation a commentary on the dramatic decrease rather than one taking notice of an
abnormally small class.[27]

The drop in enrollment became the norm through the rest of the war. Class
size remained in the twenties or lower, at least on the male side, for the next
eight years, reaching its nadir at a meager thirteen students in the fall of 1866
amid the disastrous aftermath of the war and the beginnings of Reconstruction.
Records for the female side are unavailable, but a similar drop in enrollment is
likely.[28] Unlike most of the schools in the area, the Reidville schools were fortu-
nate to have sufficient support from local citizens to refrain from closing their
doors. This showed the resolve and stubbornness of area residents to refuse to
lose the schools they had so recently gained. This fact also showed the relative
wealth and resources available to the Reidville area, second only to the town of
Spartanburg. Spartanburg showed its doggedness and ingenuity in coming up
with ways to keep the doors of Wofford College open by operating a high school
for the general community during the war-time years.[29]

The trustees of the Reidville schools, similarly, turned to charity to keep
a steady supply of students coming in and to draw sympathetic support that
would prove invaluable to keeping the institutions afloat. Toward the end of the
war, from 1863 through the first years of the postwar Reconstruction, the schools
began to open their doors to the orphans of the war for no charge. Advertise-
ments and personal fund-raising sought to supply an ongoing fund to provide
for these unfortunates. Reid, in his personal appeals, called on the good citizens
of the upcountry to provide for "the poor Orphans of the brave defenders of
our lives and property . . . [that have] claims upon our generosity and liberal-
ity, urged by every sentiment of Patriotism and Religion." In 1866, to support
the ongoing cause, the principal of the male school, Rev. W. B. Carson, called

on local planters, short on funds, to donate "so much wheat, corn, beef, pork or bacon . . . to be applied to the boarding of such indigent young men." This effort succeeded, as in every year through the first few of the 1870s, the numbers of male children whose names did not match those of their listed guardians, and therefore were out of the care of their parents, increased dramatically. Although no specific number can be ascertained, at least some must have been taking advantage of this generous offer.[30]

As the Civil War ended, the upcountry was caught in the same social and economic upheaval that gripped most of the rest of the South. While Spartanburg had escaped the physical destruction of the war, the momentous numbers of dead and wounded, an economic collapse, the mental burden of a lost war and occupation, and social and political upheaval gripped the population of Spartanburg District. The effect on the Reidville schools was visible to all in the dramatic drop in students until 1869. More dramatic and more worrisome in the long term than the lack of students, though, was the loss of the large endowment that had powered the schools to such rapid and impressive results from their inception. Just as many wealthy and influential individuals and institutions had done in the early years, the trustees of the schools had invested their funds in Confederate bonds that had promised high returns to those willing to do their patriotic duty in support of their country. With the defeat of the Confederacy, the bonds had become largely worthless and the invested funds were lost. For the small village of Reidville and the institutions at the heart of it, this loss of support was but the first challenge of many brought about by the economic and demographic changes that Spartanburg County experienced during the next few decades.[31]

To most historians, Spartanburg in the decades following the Civil War can be seen as a prime example of the rise of the New South. During these decades the South as a whole underwent drastic changes as outside investors and local leaders combined efforts to expand transportation links between key cities through railroads as new industries such as textiles, logging, and tobacco flooded into the region. The resulting economic and social transformation completely revamped many economically depressed regions, giving new energy and enthusiasm to many proponents of this change. In many ways Spartanburg underwent exactly this type of evolution. Conversely not all residents in Spartanburg County were such hard-core enthusiasts for change, and many who lived in Reidville could be counted among these holdouts. Though town leaders did make one half-hearted effort to attract investment in a railroad line early in the postwar years, by and large the residents of Reidville began to revel in the quiet simplicity of their lives and to promote that removal from the hustle and bustle as a benefit of attending their schools. In the contrast between the dynamic entrepreneurship and energy of Spartanburg and the more conservative, almost perverse reveling in quiet simplicity of Reidville, one can see in microcosm what the historian Don Doyle has demonstrated in larger, better-known urban centers in the South such as Atlanta and Charleston. According to Doyle, "Atlanta embodied the raw young power of the New South and was, to all appearances, unimpeded by the dead hand of the past." Charleston, on the other hand, "seemed content to languish in the backwaters of the New South." While the parallels are imperfect, it is still possible to say that during this time Spartanburg County experienced a similar evolution: the town of Spartanburg rose to prominence, while small, remote Reidville was destined to be a simple backwater community in decline.[32]

The first and most dramatic of the changes that reshaped Spartanburg County was the expansion of the railroad during the late 1860s and 1870s. In those years local leaders in the county attracted investors in railroad projects that sought to link South Carolina railroad lines nationally via existing pre–Civil War railroad hubs in the upcountry at Anderson, Greenville, and Spartanburg.[33] While the prewar railroads had linked these towns to Charleston, the plans in the 1860s and 1870s sought to use railroad lines running through Spartanburg to link Atlanta to Richmond via Charlotte through a railroad line nicknamed by supporters the "Atlanta and Richmond Air-Line." Once this project was completed in 1873, other projects that followed would eventually extend the existing railroad line from Columbia westward to Asheville and beyond as well as develop a spur line southeast to Greenwood, South Carolina. Spartanburg became the hub city of the upcountry, and this economically valuable transportation network attracted commerce and industry, especially textiles, to take advantage of the cheap and abundant cotton grown in the area.[34]

In the excitement and competition during the planning for the so-called "Air-Line" railroad, the citizens of Reidville began to experience the decisions that would set their community and their schools on a path of decline. When the planning for the Atlanta-to-Charlotte leg of the railroad got under way in 1868, many of the civic leaders of Spartanburg and Greenville Counties began to petition the railroad officials to choose their counties as the best route for the project. As this was being determined, small communities between the two larger county seats came together to pitch their own towns to railroad executives seeking local investment to offset the cost of the enterprise. In Reidville attendees at a local meeting on December 5, 1868, unanimously resolved that "the Air Line Railroad . . . is an enterprise . . . which the people of the upper Counties" were deeply interested in attracting. A three-person committee headed by Robert Reid was appointed to write to the company and seek to have Reidville considered as a potential route. The town of Woodruff followed suit with a competing offer in the following months. Both attempts, however, proved futile as the company, on the basis of more promising geographic surveys and other communities' equal willingness to invest money in the project, chose to run the route from Spartanburg to Greenville through an area several miles north of Reidville referred to as Duncan's.[35]

When the effort to attract the railroad to Reidville failed in the late 1860s, there was a shift in the attitudes of the local residents. Whereas before they had been willing to compete for the benefits of a railroad, now residents began to emphasize the quiet simplicity of the town and chose publicly to shun the perceived ills that came with the faster-paced life of the larger towns. In letters written to local newspapers after the loss of the railroad to Duncan's, there was a definite tendency to try to contrast the town of Reidville with its larger and growing rivals, focusing on the town's moral virtue and peacefulness. One writer, in 1875, described Reidville as "a beautiful little town . . . happily under a moral influence." The writer went on to point out that there were "no dram shops here, neither indeed can be." While a small selection of five stores of various kinds provided the necessities of life, the true selling point of the town was the fact that "so quiet is our little town, . . . it has not been deemed necessary to build a guardhouse" for law enforcement. Another anonymous writer sought to portray the quiet and rural setting as an integral part of the advantages of the educational institutions at Reidville. "At Reidville," the report claimed, "you have some advantages not enjoyed elsewhere [in] building up an institution." The location was rural, surrounded by large and prosperous farms, and "healthy, within two hundred yards of a good Sulpher [*sic*] spring." In addition, when combined with the quiet and modest setting, the costs of living and education were inexpensive compared to those of other places; one advertisement went so far as to claim that the female school was "not only one of the best, but one of the cheapest institutions in the county."[36]

With the concerted effort to keep the life of Reidville simple came an economic and political conservatism that strongly resisted efforts to continue the railroad extensions in Spartanburg. When the campaign included a proposal to pass a countywide tax assessment to support the new Spartanburg-Asheville railroad project in competition with rival plans in Greenville and Anderson, voters from the Reidville precinct opposed the idea. One voter expressed the sentiments of most other residents of the area when he stated that "we are not ready in this part of our native and beloved county to vote for any more taxes to build railroads." When the proposal was put to the test, voters in the Reidville precinct overwhelmingly opposed the proposal, with just over 83 percent of the electorate rejecting the project. However, they were overruled by Spartanburg voters, who favored the new tax, giving Spartanburg leaders the backing for the eventual construction of the railroad.[37]

Eventually three separate railroads crisscrossed the county, each completely bypassing the town of Reidville. Nearby the town of Woodruff benefited from the extension of the railroads from Spartanburg to Laurens County. The resulting investments in new textile factories by Spartanburg County led an economic boom that resulted in towns along the railroads in the county exploding in size and economic strength. Existing and new entrepreneurs poured money into new textile factories, resulting in overall investment and value in Spartanburg's textile mills increasing almost six times from 1870 to 1882.[38] The resulting population growth in the mill towns along the railroads caused a significant demographic shift, which by the 1880s began to reshape the political and economic landscape of the county. Some of the new urban areas leaped to prominence over the areas that had, by choice or by happenstance, been bypassed by the railroad expansion. A good example of this rapid rise in political fortunes is seen in the evolution of the once small town in northern Spartanburg County known earlier as Limestone Springs. When the Air-Line railroad chose this community as the route to Charlotte, the line rapidly grew in size, eventually far eclipsing its earlier importance. In 1875 the town was renamed Gaffney, and when, in 1897, the South Carolina legislature created Cherokee County, Gaffney was named its county seat.[39]

A similar population shift occurred in southwestern Spartanburg County, as seen in the changes wrought by the railroads in Reidville, Woodruff, and Duncan. Before the railroads, Woodruff and Reidville were relatively equal in size and prosperity. Of the two communities, Woodruff was the larger and was, relative to Reidville, bigger and better established by 1860.[40] That year the Woodruff postal district boasted some 400 residents compared to only 160 for the entire Reidville postal district. Yet it should be remembered that this was only three years after the town of Reidville had been founded, while the area around Woodruff had been actively farmed for decades. Duncan at the time was not even large enough to be eligible for a post office. After fifteen years Reidville had grown to be a prosperous community, so much so that by 1872, in the election in which Reid relinquished his position as school commissioner, 185 men voted as opposed to 244 in Woodruff, showing the relative equality of the immediate areas in terms of white, male populations. Duncan still did not merit a polling place.[41]

By the late 1870s and early 1880s the railroads provided a rapid impetus toward population growth for both Woodruff and Duncan. Woodruff in particular showed rapid growth over this time period. From 1874 to 1886 the town of Woodruff's population exploded, growing from some 150 persons to 1,650 as railroad activity expanded. As many as six passenger trains passed through the town daily, and thousands of tons of cotton were being shipped for local farmers annually. The area around Duncan grew as well, though in its case the majority of growth came just over the line in Greenville County, where Greer Station was incorporated as a town in 1874 and continued to grow in a rapid fashion through the late nineteenth and early twentieth centuries. By 1876 not only had

Duncan been given its own election district, but also total voters in that precinct outnumbered those in Reidville by over one hundred votes.[42]

The railroads' reshaping of the Spartanburg County landscape was only the most obvious of changes wrought by the economic boom of the New South era. As the town of Spartanburg began to grow in size and prosperity, an increasing amount of attention began to be paid to the quality and availability of educational opportunities within the town limits. Most notably, and most devastating for Reidville, was the cause of higher education for women in Spartanburg and in the nation as a whole. From 1855 on, the solution to the need for higher education for women in Spartanburg had largely been the Spartanburg Female College, which operated until 1872. The school, however, had never been able to shake a questionable reputation because of a lack of funds, rapidly changing instructors, and the larger issue of whether a proper southern lady truly needed an education beyond that available at a private seminary or high school. Given these factors, it is not surprising that many believed the demand for a proper education for women could be met by the existing institutions found closer to home in Reidville, Limestone Springs, Greenville, and other communities. The turning point in the debate over women's education came with the end of the Civil War as many Americans began to redefine the need for higher education regardless of gender.[43]

The evolution of women's higher education after the Civil War began with the founding of a string of high-powered women's colleges enabled by large endowments to build facilities, hire the necessary faculty, and develop strong curricula that could rival the best that male universities in the North had to offer. Beginning with Vassar in 1865 and followed by Smith and Wellesley, both founded in 1875, the new women's colleges challenged traditional concepts of a women's education by offering intellectual experiences second to none. The push for similar institutions in the South soon followed, with Spartanburg leading the way. In 1875 the *Carolina Spartan* editor H. L. Farley wrote an editorial bemoaning the poor state of women's education in the area. While noting the quality and importance of Wofford College for men, he proposed that "Spartanburg is also about the best location in the State for a Female College, and the removal of the one formerly here was a serious loss to the community." He called on the town leaders to fix the problem, proclaiming strongly that "we cannot long remain without one, and hope to see . . . the deficiency supplied in some way."[44]

Farley's despair over the lack of a "Female College" is slightly ironic in that Robert Reid had sought to address that vacancy with his Reidville women's school just a few months before the closing of the Spartanburg Female College three years before. In the fall of 1871 the decision had been made by the trustees to rename the school Reidville Female College, and it began the spring term under its new name. The name change had two benefits for the Reidville schools and the local community. First, it sought to take advantage of the lack of an alternative higher educational opportunity for young women in the county. Additionally, since Reid at the time was also serving as the public school commissioner for the county, the institutional change allowed some of the more advanced students to serve as instructors for the local children, which also served as part of the educational process for young ladies who hoped to work as teachers after graduation.[45]

The problem for the Reidville Female College in answering the calls for a "Female College" was that it had recently been a female high school. The trustees had not been able to match the lofty change in name with an equally lofty change in facilities, educational resources, and additional professors of high repute. The change in name therefore did not in the minds of most residents of Spartanburg allow Reid to compete with the quality of education now available at northern institutions such as Vassar, Smith, and Wellesley. To the modern and forward-looking population of Spartanburg, the change did nothing to meet the need for women's higher education in the upcountry. Editorials and private letters to local newspapers decried the failure of Spartanburg leaders to meet that growing need. In one particularly blunt editorial in 1879, the *Carolina Spartan* editor Charles Petty derided the failure of local female colleges such as those at Reidville and Limestone to grow beyond their finishing-school standards. Simply put, Petty stated, the "ridicule resting on 'girl graduates' and their scholastic attainments may be counteracted [only] by giving them an opportunity in a well-equipped college. This high education for girls is demanded by the times." That demand was met in Spartanburg just three years later when a group of local leaders in the fields of education, religion, and industry gathered under the leadership and support of Dexter Edgar Converse to engineer the development of Converse College. The rallying of the residents of the recently chartered "city" of Spartanburg meant that Converse would be the first of a string of southern women's colleges, such as Sophie Newcomb in Louisiana, Agnes Scott in Georgia, and Randolph-Macon in Virginia, that would answer the South's calls for women's higher education.[46]

For the Reidville Female College, the introduction and almost instantaneous credibility of Converse College was an insurmountable obstacle to attaining similar success. Where Converse had money, facilities, and the accessibility of a rapidly growing city around it, Reidville's schools had the peace and quiet of farms and the increasingly diminishing economic wherewithal of the local village of Reidville. Simply put, rustic Reidville could not effectively compete for young women desiring a true college education over the more cosmopolitan Spartanburg and its well-endowed competitor institution. The female college continued to decline in enrollments through the 1880s, a situation made worse as a result of increasing competition from the newly organized Cooper-Limestone

Institute, which in 1881 took the place of the Limestone Springs Female High School, as well as from the more conveniently located and better regarded Converse College. Over time the school began to serve only the immediate area around Reidville rather than having the wider geographic draw of which, in earlier decades, the college had been able to boast. This situation was echoed in the male school, though to a less dramatic degree.[47]

A final blow to the Reidville schools came from a slowly increasing focus on free public education accessible to all children, white and black, that was begun in earnest with the new state constitution ratified in 1868. The new mandate called for a public education system that would racially integrate white and black students and be supported by local taxes to be supplemented by state funds. Resistance to the idea of breaking down racial barriers, as well as widespread distrust and resentment of the state government that during Reconstruction was dominated by freedmen and white Republicans, caused Spartanburg white people to balk at the increased taxes and refuse to allow the implementation of the new system of education. When Robert Reid won the election to fill the new role of county school commissioner, he led the resistance to an integrated school system, though he did attempt unsuccessfully to convince local leaders to agree to the new tax levies, hoping thereby to improve the access to education in the county for white students. Throughout Reconstruction white elites around the state fought the idea of integrated public schools, and throughout the state they were never actually implemented. Adding to the problem, county leaders largely fought the new education system through the 1870s because of white distrust of the state government, apathy on the part of many lower- and middle-class parents over the benefits of a formal education, and the involvement of many county leaders in ongoing educational endeavors that benefited from the traditional reliance on private institutions to meet the educational needs of the county.[48]

In Spartanburg the resistance to the public school system actually served to benefit local academies such as those in Reidville for a short period. Starting under Reid in his role as school commissioner and continuing through the early 1880s, the solution to education became a confusing blend of public and private institutions that allowed commissioners to provide private institutions with taxpayer funds that were then used to reduce or replace tuition fees for local children. This resulted in the common practice of including nominally private institutions such as the Reidville schools in the count of "public schools" for the purposes of satisfying the new state mandates for public education. As an example, when Reid reported in 1869 to the state superintendent of education Justus K. Jillson that there were twenty-nine public schools in Spartanburg County, sixteen of those were privately operated and charged tuition. As noted earlier, students at the Reidville Female College used this system to gain teaching experience as well as to add to institutional funding. Not until the 1880s, when the county public school system had begun to be organized and professionalized sufficiently to meet the needs of its citizens, did people slowly begin to abandon the old system to the detriment of the private academies.[49]

Facing these challenges grew increasingly difficult by the late 1880s as the Reidville schools, the trustees, and the local community suffered a series of crises that, combined with the larger demographic and educational problems, served to put the schools on the final road to failure. On January 18, 1887, the male school building burned, devastating the already struggling school, which had never fully recovered from the loss of the original endowment during the Civil War. The economic setback may have been less than the emotional blow to Robert Reid, who after thirty years of service to the schools was confronted with yet another hardship from which to recover. The *Carolina Spartan* published a sympathetic account of the fire in which it extended the "profoundest sympathies . . . to the aged President of the Board of Trustees . . . [knowing] that the best energies of his life have been spent in founding up and sustaining the schools of Reidville." Arrangements were quickly made to move the classes to other quarters, and long-term accommodations were found in the female college. Unfortunately, by the time the money was raised to rebuild the male school, the female college was struggling with a crisis of enrollment.[50]

In early 1888 the principal of the female college, Joseph Venable, reported to the trustees that the school had not attracted sufficient students to maintain operations without additional support. To assist in the emergency, trustees asked Robert Reid to intervene directly and assume the role of associate principal for the remainder of the year. Unable to reconcile the situation or resenting Reid's interference, Venable chose to leave the school before the end of the year, and the decision was made to forgo another session for the school in early 1889. Over the next few years the schools struggled to recover their footing. A new administration under Mr. A. Spencer was begun in 1889, and the catalog and instructional methods of the school were revised in an effort to reestablish the schools' creditability. The catalog asserted proudly, for all who cared to request a copy, that the school, "under a recent reorganization . . . now offers all the facilities for a liberal education which can be expected in those institutions ranking next to the university." To what extent the claim was true is unknown, as little information on the curricular changes survives, but it did not have the desired effect. In 1892 both the male and female schools were united under Spencer's leadership to conserve funds. By this time resources were lacking to hire additional administrators or instructors, and consolidation was the only choice. So overwhelming were the struggles to help the schools recover that on April 3, 1892, in order to focus solely on the schools, Robert Reid submitted his resignation as pastor of Nazareth Presbyterian Church, a post he had held for almost forty years.[51]

By the 1890s the struggles of the Reidville schools were such that even the loyal backing from Reidville residents was insufficient to rescue them. Not only was the community experiencing a long, slow decline in terms of population, but in addition economic conditions in the state were such that farm prices had collapsed and small rural farmers were struggling. The economic hardships of the 1880s and 1890s resulted in the formation of populist groups such as the Grange and the Farmers, which attempted to influence state political leaders to support farmer-friendly legislation. In an indication of the hardships faced by the farmers in the Reidville region, they were some of the first in Spartanburg County to organize their local Grange after the end of Reconstruction. This shows the level of interest in attempting to better the economic conditions for small farmers in the area. Other communities would quickly follow their example. Still, despite their efforts, by the late 1890s the economy of Reidville was struggling, the schools were suffering from low enrollments, and the prospects for the future seemed uncertain.[52]

The end of an era came in 1898 when Robert Reid, increasingly frail with age and sensing the perilous state of the schools, offered his resignation as president of the board of trustees. After initially refusing his offer, in 1899 the trustees agreed to his stepping down from his post. He was succeeded by his son, the Reverend Benjamin Palmer Reid. Robert Reid's forty-two-year tenure as head of the Reidville schools came to a close, and at the turn of the twentieth century the trustees were unable to turn the schools around. Some new solution for the schools had to be found, and it came from the Spartanburg public schools, of which Reid had served as the first inspirational leader when they were organized in 1868.[53]

With Robert Reid gone, the trustees and their new leader turned to the growing public school system to provide a final solution to the struggles of the Reidville schools. Those free public schools, since their beginnings, had continued to grow and evolve into credible providers of elementary and secondary education. In 1902, to better match the growing acceptance of the public school system across the state, the trustees agreed to drop the status of the female college to that of a high school, modeling its curriculum and instruction on that commonly used in the state-sponsored schools around Spartanburg. Then, when confronted with the passage of a new tax on the citizens of the local school district in the Reidville area to support the free public schools in the area, the trustees approached the district school board with an offer to merge the two systems. In early 1905 an agreement was reached between the trustees of the Reidville schools and the school district to rent the building used by the female school and to combine the remaining students of the Reidville Male and Female High Schools with the new Reidville Graded School beginning in the fall of that year. In the spring of 1906, one academic year later, the first

graduation ceremony of the Reidville public schools was held and Reid's academies officially came to an end. It was the passing of an era, though in a way
the public school that exists on the site of the former female college, Reidville
Elementary School, continues the educational visions and aspirations of Reid,
the trustees, and all the supporters and former students of the original schools.
Touring that school, which proudly displays the artifacts and images of its predecessors and their founder, one can see that the history and legacy of the original Reidville schools rest in good hands.[54]

Less than a year after the graduation of the first public school class in Reidville, in February 1907 Robert H. Reid died at the age of eighty-six. His passing
was mourned in an obituary in the *Spartanburg Daily Herald,* which lauded
his long life of service in which he was devoted to "the betterment of his fellow
man . . . and untiring in his labor in religious and educational work."[55] That
his death followed so soon on the heels of his schools' demise is an ironic historical footnote on the story of the institutions that had, for so long, represented
his crowning achievements. The Reidville Male and Female High Schools were
the products of their time. They were institutions modeled on the standards and
academic theories of their day and were considered shining examples, in their
heyday, of the right way to educate the young. That their founding would so
soon be followed by the Civil War was simply one of the vagaries of fate. But in
the economic and social transformations that followed that conflict, even the
idealism and loyalty of the schools' patrons failed to avail the schools against the
hardships they faced. By 1900 they were anachronisms that could no longer slow
the wheels of progress that eventually caused their closure. Even so, the story of
the Reidville schools is instructive, as in their founding, their growth, and their
eventual decline one can see the passage of time and its effects on the continu-
ously evolving upcountry.

Notes

I would like to thank Jean Anderson of the Reidville Historical Society; Palmer Burchstead, great-grandson of Rev. Robert H. Reid; and the staffs of the South Caroliniana
Library of the University of South Carolina and the Sandor Teszler Library at Wofford
College for their invaluable assistance. I would also like to thank Claudia and Emily,
my wife and daughter for their love and support throughout.

  1. *Carolina Spartan* (Spartanburg, S.C.), October 10, 1859, not paginated.

  2. "Rev. R. H. Reid Dead; His Long Service Ended," *Spartanburg Daily Herald,* February 5, 1907; J. B. O. Landrum, *History of Spartanburg County* (Spartanburg,
S.C.: Reprint Company, 1900, 1985), 503; F. D. Jones and W. H. Mills, eds., *History of the Presbyterian Church in South Carolina since 1850* (Columbia: Published for
the Synod of South Carolina by the R. L. Bryan Company, 1926), 352. For Wade

Hampton II and Wade Hampton III, see Robert K. Ackerman, *Wade Hampton III* (Columbia: University of South Carolina Press, 2007).

3. Landrum, *History of Spartanburg County,* 503.

4. Readers will note that the terms "county" and "district" appear in this chapter in reference to Spartanburg and other places in the state during this period. In South Carolina the term "district" was the most commonly used until the passage of the South Carolina Constitution of 1868, when the term "county" replaced it. As this chapter spans both periods, the terms will be used interchangeably, with "district" more common in the early sections and "county" replacing it in later sections.

5. Vernon Foster and Walter S. Montgomery Sr., *Spartanburg: Facts, Reminiscences, Folklore* (Spartanburg, S.C.: Reprint Co., 1998), 33, 125; Landrum, *History of Spartanburg County,* 503–4; *Spartanburg (S.C.) Herald-Journal,* September 12 and 19, 1937.

6. David Duncan Wallace, *History of Wofford College, 1845–1949* (Nashville: Published for Wofford College by Vanderbilt University Press, 1951), 27–65. For Wofford College, see also Doyle Boggs, JoAnn Mitchell Brasington, and Phillip Stone, eds., *Wofford: Shining with Untarnished Honor, 1854–2004* (Spartanburg, S.C.: Hub City Writers Project, 2005).

7. See Bruce W. Eelman, *Entrepreneurs in the Southern Upcountry: Commercial Culture in Spartanburg, South Carolina, 1845–1880* (Athens: University of Georgia Press, 2008), 9–87, quote on 16.

8. *Spartanburg (S.C.) Herald Journal,* September 12 and 19, 1937; Lewis P. Jones, "History of Public Education in South Carolina," in *Public Education in South Carolina,* ed. Thomas R. McDaniel (Spartanburg, S.C.: Published for Converse College, 1984), 12.

9. *Spartanburg (S.C.) Herald Journal,* September 12 and 19, 1937; *Carolina Spartan,* April 24, 1856, December 17, 1857.

10. *Carolina Spartan,* January 8, 1857. For a good case study of a female academy in the upstate of South Carolina, see Judith T. Bainbridge, "A 'Nursery of Knowledge': The Greenville Female Academy, 1819–1854," *South Carolina Historical Magazine* 99, no. 1 (January 1998): 6–33. For women's higher education in the South, see Christie Anne Farnham, *The Education of the Southern Belle: Higher Education and Student Socialization in the Antebellum South* (New York: New York University Press, 1994).

11. Landrum, *History of Spartanburg County,* 71–77; *A History of Spartanburg County: Compiled by the Spartanburg Unit of the Writers' Program of the Works Projects Administration in the State of South Carolina* (1940; repr., Spartanburg, S.C.: Reprint Co., 1976), 109; Bainbridge, "Nursery of Knowledge," 6–8, esp. n5. For a history of Furman University, see Robert N. Daniel, *Furman University: A History* (Greenville, S.C.: Furman University, 1951); Alfred S. Reid, *Furman University: Toward a New Identity* (Durham, N.C.: Duke University Press, 1976).

12. See Carl F. Kaestle, *Pillars of the Republic: Common Schools and American Society, 1780–1860* (New York: Hill and Wang, 1983), 104–35, quote on 105–6.

13. Robert H. Reid, "The History of Reidville High School—The Name of Donors and the Sums Given," scrapbook compiled by Robert H. Reid held by the South Caroliniana Library, Manuscript Library, University of South Carolina, Columbia, pages not numbered.

14. Ibid.

15. Ibid.; Records of the Trustees of the Reidville High Schools, 1857 (accessed from copies transcribed by Ms. Jean Anderson, Reidville Historical Society, and digital copies provided by Mr. Palmer Burchstead, great-grandson of Rev. Robert H. Reid); Landrum, *History of Spartanburg County,* 254–56, 518;

16. Records of the Trustees of the Reidville High Schools, 1857.

17. Ibid.; *Carolina Spartan,* June 11, 1857, June 18, 1857, July 16, 1857.

18. Landrum, *History of Spartanburg County,* 315–18; *Carolina Spartan,* January 22, 1857, January 29, 1857.

19. *Carolina Spartan,* April 16, 1857.

20. *Carolina Spartan,* August 13, 1857.

21. *Carolina Spartan,* January 7, 1858; Register of the Reidville Male High School, 1858, original manuscript held at Sandor Teszler Library, Wofford College, Spartanburg, S.C.

22. The first session ended in July 1858 after only one session. The first full academic year began in August 1858, and the second session began in February 1859 and ended in July of that year.

23. *Carolina Spartan,* August 13, 1857, December 16, 1858, January 27, 1859; Register of the Reidville Male High School, 1859.

24. *Carolina Spartan,* July 14, 1859.

25. *Carolina Spartan,* November 29, 1860; Walter Edgar, *South Carolina: A History* (Columbia: University of South Carolina Press, 1998), 351–52.

26. Register of the Reidville Male High School, 1861.

27. "Nancy Moore Evins to Thomas John Moore, March 4th, 1861," in *Upcountry South Carolina Goes to War: Letters of the Anderson, Brockman, and Moore Families, 1853–1865,* ed. Tom Moore Craig (Columbia: University of South Carolina Press, 2009), 41.

28. Register of the Reidville Male High School, 1861–69.

29. Wallace, *History of Wofford College,* 74–76.

30. Records of the Trustees of the Reidville High Schools, 1863; *Carolina Spartan,* September 22, 1864, December 20, 1866; Register of the Reidville Male High School, 1864–75.

31. Records of the Trustees of the Reidville High Schools, November 16, 1863; *Carolina Spartan,* August 1, 1861, April 26, 1866; *Greenville (S.C.) Enterprise & Mountaineer,* April 4, 1888; Boggs et al., *Wofford,* 7–9.

32. Don Doyle, *New Men, New Cities, New South: Atlanta, Nashville, Charleston, Mobile, 1680–1910* (Chapel Hill: University of North Carolina Press, 1990), xv. For a general history of the New South, see Edward L. Ayers, *Southern Crossing: A History of*

the American South, 1877–1906 (Oxford: Oxford University Press, 1995). For the rise of Spartanburg, see Eelman, *Entrepreneurs in the Southern Upcountry.*

33. Edgar, *South Carolina,* 283.

34. Eelman, *Entrepreneurs in the Southern Upcountry,* 163–73.

35. *Carolina Spartan,* December 24, 1868, August 15, 1869, September 9, 1869. For the new school system and the new South Carolina state constitution, see Edgar, *South Carolina,* 385–94.

36. *Carolina Spartan,* December 16, 1874, April 21, 1875, January 19, 1876.

37. *Carolina Spartan,* May 12, 1875, July 9, 1875.

38. Eelman, *Entrepreneurs in the Southern Upcountry,* 181.

39. Ibid., 175.

40. "Duncan's" was the name of the railroad community that would later be shortened to Duncan, South Carolina. The community that benefited in that immediate area would later become Greer, South Carolina. For the sake of convenience, Duncan will be used rather than Duncan's.

41. Woodruff and Reidville entries, Spartanburg District, 1860 United States Census, Series M653, Roll 1226, HeritageQuest online, http://persi.heritagequestonline .com/hqoweb/library/do/census/results/image?surname=Reed&series=8&state=23& county=Spartanburg&countyid=859&hitcount=2&p=1&urn=urn%3Aproquest%3 AUS%3Bcensus%3B9093010%3B55289329%3B8%3B23&searchtype=1&offset=0 (accessed February 12, 2011); *Carolina Spartan,* October 24, 1872.

42. Hannah Barton Irby, *Woodruff: An Historical View* (Woodruff, S.C.: Self-published by Hannah Barton Irby, 1974), 20; "Official Returns of Spartanburg County, 1876," *Carolina Spartan,* November 15, 1876.

43. *Spartanburg (S.C.) Herald Journal,* September 12 and 19, 1937; Farnham, *Education of the Southern Belle,* 120–45.

44. Lillian Adele Kibler, *The History of Converse College* (Spartanburg, S.C.: Published by Converse College, 1973), 28; *Carolina Spartan,* February 3, 1875.

45. *Carolina Spartan,* January 18, 1872, December 17, 1875; W. W. Dixon, "Interview of James E. Coan," in *WPA Life Histories: Manuscripts of the Federal Writers' Projects, 1936–1940,* available at U.S. Library of Congress digital archives, http://memory .loc.gov/ammem/wpaintro/wpahome.html (accessed February 12, 2011).

46. *Carolina Spartan,* June 25, 1879, July 30, 1879; Kibler, *History of Converse College,* 28–52.

47. *Carolina Spartan,* July 22, 1881, Register of the Reidville Male High School, 1880–95; Landrum, *History of Spartanburg County,* 71–77.

48. Edgar, *South Carolina,* 387–97; Eelman, *Entrepreneurs in the Southern Upcountry,* 189–201.

49. Eelman, *Entrepreneurs in the Southern Upcountry,* 193. For the evolution of the Spartanburg Public School System, see Ella Poats, *Spartanburg County School District Seven: The First Ninety-Eight Years* (Columbia, S.C.: Published by the R. L. Bryan Company, 1982).

50. *Carolina Spartan,* January 26, 1887; *Greenville (S.C.) Enterprise & Mountaineer,* April 4, 1888.

51. Records of the Trustees of the Reidville High Schools, 1888; catalog of the Reidville Female College, 1889, 9; Register of the Reidville Male High School, 1892–93; *Spartanburg (S.C.) Herald-Journal,* August 7, 1938.

52. *Carolina Spartan,* February 19, 1879; Edgar, *South Carolina,* 427–52.

53. Records of the Trustees of the Reidville High Schools, 1898–99.

54. Fred Carol Ellenburg, "A History of Reidville Private High Schools, Reidville, South Carolina" (master's thesis, Appalachian State Teachers College, 1963), 81–82.

55. "Rev. R. H. Reid Dead."

Prelude to Little Bighorn

The Seventh U.S. Cavalry in the
South Carolina Upcountry

Andrew H. Myers

Our hearts so stout have got us fame,
For soon 'tis known from whence we came,
Where're we go they dread the name,
Of Garryowen in glory

    Quoted in Elizabeth B. Custer, *Following the Guidon,* 1890

Compared to other organizations of the United States Army, the Seventh Cavalry has attained an unusual prominence in the American memory. The regiment's fame stems largely from its 1876 defeat at the Battle of Little Bighorn, which occurred less than two weeks before the nation's centennial. Reenactments of Custer's Last Stand, several Hollywood films, and thousands of books and articles have enshrined the Seventh within the public imagination. The regimental song—an Irish quickstep called "Garryowen"—has become one of the most recognizable tunes associated with the armed forces.

Less well-known is the role played by the Seventh Cavalry in the South Carolina upcountry. From 1871 to 1873 its troopers served in the Palmetto State as part of a federal effort to crush the Ku Klux Klan. Military histories of the regiment and its leaders tend to minimize or overlook this episode in favor of events on the Great Plains.[1] Books about Reconstruction and the Klan focus on high-ranking officers or southern civilians.[2] Although the Seventh appears in writings about domestic insurrection and counterinsurgency, those concentrate on legalities and politics.[3]

The ordinary soldiers who served in the upcountry have meanwhile remained faceless, which is regrettable considering the important human dimension they add to the story. Like their brothers and sisters in Vietnam, Iraq, and

Afghanistan, they gave flesh and blood to government policies. Their priorities frequently diverged from those of their officers, but their actions—for better or worse and on multiple levels—directly shaped the hearts and minds of local civilians. In his pioneering social history of the Confederate army, Bell Wiley said that "the doings of common soldiers have usually served as a hazily sketched backdrop for dramas featuring campaigns and leaders."[4] The same holds true for the "Bluecoats" assigned to the upper reaches of South Carolina during the early 1870s. Here they will take center stage.

1865: Cavalry Operations in the Upcountry during the Civil War

The Civil War had shown the utility of mounted forces in the upcountry, the part of the Palmetto State that stretches westward beyond the fall line of the coastal plain. The cities of Cheraw, Camden, and Columbia lie on this boundary of river rocks and sand hills marking the end of the lowcountry and the start of the piedmont. Farther to the northwest, rivers and streams cut through rolling hills that in many places grow to mountains near the borders of North Carolina and Georgia. Infantrymen of the nineteenth century could fight well on this kind of ground, but they could not move quickly. Cavalry could.

The primitiveness of the upcountry's railroad system added to the difficulty of the terrain. All of the tracks going into the region branched out of Columbia. They terminated at Yorkville, Spartanburg, Greenville, Abbeville, and Walhalla. None linked the towns to each other. Only one line went into North Carolina, and only one went into Georgia. None crossed the Appalachian Mountains. Three incomplete tunnels built by the Blue Ridge Railroad marked a failed effort to connect to Tennessee during the 1850s. In 1863, when Gen. James Longstreet's corps was shifted from Virginia to reinforce southern defenses at Chickamauga, a direct rail route across the upcountry did not exist. Confederate troop trains required extra time to skirt its edges. Tracks would not traverse the upper piedmont to Atlanta until 1873 or go over the mountains until the end of the decade.[5]

The lack of infrastructure had the benefit of sparing the area from the war's worst ravages. Most notably Gen. William T. Sherman's army stayed in Georgia on the opposite bank of the Savannah River during its 1864 march from Atlanta to the sea. Only in early 1865, after these soldiers reached the coast and the Union logistics base at Hilton Head, did they move into South Carolina. Even then they remained close to the fall line after capturing Columbia.

A cavalry division consisting of approximately twelve regiments organized into three brigades screened Sherman's left flank. It made the deepest penetration of the upcountry to occur during the 1865 Carolinas campaign. Led by Gen. Judson Kilpatrick, part of this force tried to capture the gunpowder factory at Augusta and textile mill at Graniteville. Confederate cavalrymen under

Joseph Wheeler thwarted this effort on February 11 at the Battle of Aiken. Thereafter Kilpatrick's men kept a safer distance to Sherman's main body. They burned civilian houses and took away food as they swept through the districts of Lexington, Newberry, and Fairfield.[6] They also cut a major economic artery by destroying the railroad bridge over the Broad River at Alston. Despite these losses, the upcountry emerged comparatively unscathed.

Mounted Union troops made subsequent forays into this part of South Carolina when they helped hunt for Jefferson Davis. On April 19, 1865, a detachment from the Twelfth Ohio Cavalry slowed the rebel president's flight by burning the railroad bridge over the Catawba River that connected Columbia to Charlotte near Nation's Ford. These soldiers were part of a division under the control of Gen. George Stoneman that had spent the previous month wrecking Confederate logistics and undermining civilian morale in western Virginia and North Carolina. Upon learning that Davis had crossed the Catawba by boat and was making his way over the upper piedmont, Stoneman sent cavalrymen into South Carolina. One of the brigades went through Spartanburg. The other two swept through Greenville before fighting a skirmish near Anderson that marked some of the war's last exchanges of gunfire. The three brigades followed Davis out of the state into Georgia, where other Union forces captured him a few days afterward.[7]

1865–72: Struggles of the Infantry during Reconstruction

During Reconstruction the first federal troops to perform occupation duty in the upcountry were infantrymen from the Fifty-sixth New York and Twenty-fifth Ohio as well as the Thirty-third Regiment of U.S. Colored Troops. Some of the men had horses—and they had the support of a few contingents from the First Ohio Cavalry Regiment—but the majority of troops moved on foot or by train.[8] The latter mode of transportation was limited, ironically, by the wrecked railroad bridges at Alston and Nation's Ford. Infantrymen had difficulty countering guerrillas such as Manse Jolly, who ranged on horseback across the upper valley of the Savannah. A Confederate veteran, Jolly had sworn to avenge the deaths of his brothers who had died in the war. He became a folk hero among local white people in the process. At the town of Pickens, he fatally shot a white lieutenant of the Thirty-third U.S. Colored Troops. "Take me if you can," he told Lt. Col. Charles Tyler Trowbridge after brazenly confronting the regimental commander one morning at his headquarters in Anderson. According to Trowbridge, the renegade then spurred his horse and sped away.[9]

Jolly later participated in the murders of three soldiers from the First Maine Infantry Battalion, which replaced the Thirty-third. Lt. Col. Calvin S. Brown, its commander, also recognized the limitations of foot soldiers. As he reported in October 1865: "Humanity and the integrity of the Government demands that more troops be forwarded at once—a battalion of Cavalry in addition to the present force is actually needed. We do all we can with our present force but can not do all that can be done with an ample force of mounted men."[10]

Soldiers of the Fifteenth Maine Infantry Regiment had similar experiences in the valley of the Broad River, where the Seventh Cavalry would operate. Capt. Henry A. Shorey had overall responsibility for five companies of soldiers in that area. There they encountered vigilante groups that presaged the Ku Klux Klan. He said that "these lawless bands were then known as 'Slickers'" and that they "were thoroughly organized and mounted, and were perambulating the country at night, terrorizing the negroes." Shorey viewed James G. Fernandez of Union County as one of the worst culprits.[11]

Having limited numbers and mobility placed the federal troops at a considerable disadvantage. Shorey said that "with infantry soldiers less than fifty men to a county, and these thirty and forty miles from other military support, we were hardly in sufficient force to warrant us being especially pugnacious." He said that guerrillas in both Unionville and Spartanburg had "audaciously ridden into the villages and fired upon our soldiers in the street."[12]

The infantrymen compensated with aggressiveness and increased numbers. Army forces in Shorey's area doubled from five companies to ten. Commanders received "absolute power in the premises, including the right to confiscate property, burn buildings, arrest and imprison suspected parties, etc.; much, of course, being left to the discretion of that officer." They began offering reward money. Acting on a tip, federal soldiers hunted down Fernandez and killed him. They also jailed many whom Shorey called "leading citizens."[13]

Comparable efforts in the Anderson area failed to capture Manse Jolly, who fled the state to Texas, but they did result in the arrests of three other local civilians for killing the three First Maine soldiers. A military tribunal convicted the trio and sentenced them to death after widely publicized hearings in Charleston. Although President Andrew Johnson saved the southerners from the gallows, the episode demonstrated the resolve of local military authorities.[14]

The strategy of massing infantrymen in the upcountry became less practicable as volunteers were mustered out of service and replaced with smaller numbers of Regular Army companies from the Sixth U.S. Infantry, Eighth U.S. Infantry, and Fifth U.S. Cavalry Regiments.[15] Troop strength in South Carolina dropped during 1866 from 7,408 in January to 4,850 in April to 1,506 in October.[16] The reductions did not end there, however. Cuts to the size of the Regular Army and a growing need for soldiers to fight Indians in the West depleted available forces on the Atlantic coast.

The withdrawal continued despite signs of new unrest. During April 1868 the Klan advertised meetings in the *Yorkville Enquirer*. Its appearance coincided with approval of a new state constitution that gave African Americans

Locations of Seventh Cavalry Troops, March 1871–April 1873

Troop	March 1871	April 1871	May 1871	June 1871	July 1871	August 1871
A	Louisville, Ky.	Elizabethtown, Ky.	Elizabethtown, Ky.	Elizabethtown, Ky.	Elizabethtown, Ky.	Elizabethtown, Ky.
B	Unionville, S.C.	Unionville, S.C.	Unionville, S.C.	Unionville, S.C.	Unionville, S.C.	Unionville, S.C.
C	Chester, S.C.	Chester, S.C.	Chester, S.C.	Rutherfordton, N.C.	Rutherfordton, N.C.	Rutherfordton, N.C.
D	Mt. Vernon, Ky.	Mt. Vernon, Ky.	Mt. Vernon, Ky.	Mt. Vernon, Ky.	Mt. Vernon, Ky.	Mt. Vernon, Ky.
E	Spartanburg, S.C.	Spartanburg, S.C.	Spartanburg, S.C.	Spartanburg, S.C.	Spartanburg, S.C.	Spartanburg, S.C.
F	Louisville, Ky.	Louisville, Ky.	Louisville, Ky.	Louisville, Ky.	Meridian, Miss.	Meridian, Miss.
G	Ft. Lyon, Colo.	Ft. Hays, Kans.	Columbia, S.C.	Sumter, S.C.	Sumter, S.C.	Atlanta, Ga.
H	Ft. Hays, Kans.	Ft. Hays, Kans.	Nashville, Tenn.	Nashville, Tenn.	Nashville, Tenn.	Nashville, Tenn.
I	Bagdad, Ky.	Bagdad, Ky.	Bagdad, Ky.	Bagdad, Ky.	Bagdad, Ky.	Bagdad, Ky.
K	Yorkville, S.C.	Yorkville, S.C.	Yorkville, S.C.	Yorkville, S.C.	Yorkville, S.C.	Yorkville, S.C.
L	Ft. Wallace, Kans.	Ft. Wallace, Kans.	Ft. Wallace, Kans.	Ft. Wallace, Kans.	Ft. Wallace, Kans.	Ft. Wallace, Kans.
M	Ft. Hays, Kans.	Ft. Hays, Kans.	Louisville, Ky.	Darlington, S.C.	Darlington, S.C.	Darlington, S.C.

Locations of Seventh Cavalry Troops, March 1871–April 1873 (continued)

Troop	September 1871	October 1871	November 1871	December 1871	January 1872	February 1872
A	Elizabethtown, Ky.	Elizabethtown, Ky.	Elizabethtown, Ky.	Elizabethtown, Ky.	Elizabethtown, Ky.	Elizabethtown, Ky.
B	Unionville, S.C.	Unionville, S.C.	Spartanburg, S.C.	Spartanburg, S.C.	Spartanburg, S.C.	Spartanburg, S.C.
C	Rutherfordton, N.C.	Rutherfordton, N.C.	Rutherfordton, N.C.	Rutherfordton, N.C.	Rutherfordton, N.C.	Rutherfordton, N.C.
D	Columbia, S.C.	Yorkville, S.C.	Chester, S.C.	Chester, S.C.	Chester, S.C.	Chester, S.C.
E	Spartanburg, S.C.	Spartanburg, S.C.	Spartanburg, S.C.	Unionville, S.C.	Unionville, S.C.	Unionville, S.C.
F	Meridian, Miss.	Meridian, Miss.	Louisville, Ky.	Louisville, Ky.	Louisville, Ky.	Louisville, Ky.
G	Atlanta, Ga.	Columbia, S.C.	Spartanburg, S.C.	Spartanburg, S.C.	Spartanburg, S.C.	Spartanburg, S.C.
H	Nashville, Tenn.	Nashville, Tenn.	Nashville, Tenn.	Huntsville, Ala.	Huntsville, Ala.	Nashville, Tenn.
I	Shelbyville, Ky.	Shelbyville, Ky.	Shelbyville, Ky.	Shelbyville, Ky.	Shelbyville, Ky.	Shelbyville, Ky.
K	Yorkville, S.C.	Yorkville, S.C.	Yorkville, S.C.	Yorkville, S.C.	Yorkville, S.C.	Yorkville, S.C.
L	Winnsboro, S.C.	Yorkville, S.C.	Yorkville, S.C.	Yorkville, S.C.	Yorkville, S.C.	Yorkville, S.C.
M	Darlington, S.C.	Spartanburg, S.C.	Yorkville, S.C.	Unionville, S.C.	Unionville, S.C.	Unionville, S.C.

Locations of Seventh Cavalry Troops, March 1871–April 1873 (continued)

Troop	March 1872	April 1872	May 1872	June 1872	July 1872	August 1872
A	Elizabethtown, Ky.	Elizabethtown, Ky.	Elizabethtown, Ky.	Elizabethtown, Ky.	Elizabethtown, Ky.	Elizabethtown, Ky.
B	Spartanburg, S.C.	Spartanburg, S.C.	Spartanburg, S.C.	Spartanburg, S.C.	Spartanburg, S.C.	Spartanburg, S.C.
C	Lincolnton, N.C.	Lincolnton, N.C.	Lincolnton, N.C.	Lincolnton, N.C.	Lincolnton, N.C.	Lincolnton, N.C.
D	Opelika, Ala.	Opelika, Ala.	Opelika, Ala.	Opelika, Ala.	Opelika, Ala.	Opelika, Ala.
E	Unionville, S.C.	Unionville, S.C.	Unionville, S.C.	Unionville, S.C.	Unionville, S.C.	Unionville, S.C.
F	Louisville, Ky.	Louisville, Ky.	Louisville, Ky.	Louisville, Ky.	Louisville, Ky.	Louisville, Ky.
G	Spartanburg, S.C.	Spartanburg, S.C.	Spartanburg, S.C.	Spartanburg, S.C.	Spartanburg, S.C.	Laurensville, S.C.
H	Nashville, Tenn.	Nashville, Tenn.	Nashville, Tenn.	Nashville, Tenn.	Nashville, Tenn.	Nashville, Tenn.
I	Shelbyville, Ky.	Shelbyville, Ky.	Shelbyville, Ky.	Shelbyville, Ky.	Shelbyville, Ky.	Shelbyville, Ky.
K	Yorkville, S.C.	Yorkville, S.C.	Yorkville, S.C.	Yorkville, S.C.	Yorkville, S.C.	Yorkville, S.C.
L	Yorkville, S.C.	Yorkville, S.C.	Yorkville, S.C.	Yorkville, S.C.	Yorkville, S.C.	Yorkville, S.C.
M	Unionville, S.C.	Unionville, S.C.	Unionville, S.C.	Unionville, S.C.	Unionville, S.C.	Unionville, S.C.

Locations of Seventh Cavalry Troops, March 1871–April 1873 (continued)

Troop	September 1872	October 1872	November 1872	December 1872	January 1873	February 1873
A	Elizabethtown, Ky.	Elizabethtown, Ky.	Elizabethtown, Ky.	Elizabethtown, Ky.	Elizabethtown, Ky.	Elizabethtown, Ky.
B	Spartanburg, S.C.	Spartanburg, S.C.	Spartanburg, S.C.	Spartanburg, S.C.	Spartanburg, S.C.	Spartanburg, S.C.
C	Lincolnton, N.C.	Charlotte, N.C.	Charlotte, N.C.	Charlotte, N.C.	Charlotte, N.C.	Charlotte, N.C.
D	Opelika, Ala.	Opelika, Ala.	Montgomery, Ala.	Opelika, Ala.	Opelika, Ala.	Livingston, Ala.
E	Unionville, S.C.	Unionville, S.C.	Unionville, S.C.	Unionville, S.C.	Unionville, S.C.	Unionville, S.C.
F	Louisville, Ky.	Louisville, Ky.	Louisville, Ky.	Louisville, Ky.	Louisville, Ky.	Louisville, Ky.
G	Laurensville, S.C.	Laurensville, S.C.	Laurensville, S.C.	Laurensville, S.C.	Newberry, S.C.	Newberry, S.C.
H	Nashville, Tenn.	Livingstone, Ala.	Nashville, Tenn.	Nashville, Tenn.	Nashville, Tenn.	Nashville, Tenn.
I	Shelbyville, Ky.	Shelbyville, Ky.	Shelbyville, Ky.	Lebanon, Ky.	Lebanon, Ky.	Lebanon, Ky.
K	Yorkville, S.C.	Yorkville, S.C.	Yorkville, S.C.	Yorkville, S.C.	Yorkville, S.C.	Yorkville, S.C.
L	Yorkville, S.C.	Yorkville, S.C.	Yorkville, S.C.	New Orleans, La.	New Orleans, La.	New Orleans, La.
M	Unionville, S.C.	Unionville, S.C.	Unionville, S.C.	Oxford, Miss.	Oxford, Miss.	Oxford, Miss.

Locations of Seventh Cavalry Troops, March 1871–April 1873 (continued)

Troop	March 1873	April 1873
A	Louisville, Ky.	Dakota Territory
B	Memphis, Tenn.	Dakota Territory
C	Memphis, Tenn.	Dakota Territory
D	Memphis, Tenn.	Fort Snelling, Minn.
E	Memphis, Tenn.	Dakota Territory
F	Louisville, Ky.	Dakota Territory
G	Memphis, Tenn.	Dakota Territory
H	Louisville, Ky.	Dakota Territory
I	Louisville, Ky.	Fort Snelling, Minn.
K	Memphis, Tenn.	Dakota Territory
L	New Orleans, La.	Dakota Territory
M	Memphis, Tenn.	Dakota Territory

Source: Regimental Returns, National Archives

Grave located at the Episcopal Church of the Nativity, Union (formerly Unionville), South Carolina. The inscription reads, "Sacred to the memory of Alpheus E. Cushman, Late Farrier, Troop B, 7th U.S. Cav., who departed this life May 20th, 1871, Age 22 Years . . . Erected as a tribute of respect by his late Comrades."

unprecedented freedom and political power. With the help of black voters, an Ohio native named Robert Scott won election as governor of South Carolina. Scott was a Union army veteran who had spent three years as head of the S.C. Freedmen's Bureau. Other white northerners won seats in the legislature, as did more than seventy African Americans. White southerners responded with violence, murdering several legislators during the summer of 1868.[17]

Although military officials investigated some of these incidents and dutifully made reports, the outflow of troops continued. Two companies of the Fifth Cavalry ended their two-year tour of duty in South Carolina during September 1868. The remaining five companies of the Sixth Infantry left in February 1869. By the end of the decade, approximately four hundred federal soldiers remained in the state. All of these men belonged to the Eighth Infantry, which had three companies in Columbia and two in Charleston. They were replaced during October 1870 by an equivalent number of infantry companies from the Eighteenth Regiment.[18]

With no thanks to the U.S. Army, the tide of violence in South Carolina subsided. Wade Hampton III deserved the lion's share of credit. On October 23, 1868, he made a widely publicized call for peace. He and other white people then tried to work within the new constitutional framework by creating a political opposition group that could draw African Americans away from the Republicans by providing an alternative to the Democrats. They called themselves the Union Reform Party. Regardless of whether their offers of racial reconciliation were made in good faith or not, the effort failed. African Americans remained overwhelmingly loyal to the party of Lincoln. Scott and many other incumbents handily won reelection in 1870.[19]

The governor's victory—as well as his decision during the run-up to the election to create fourteen companies of black militiamen and arm them with rifles—sparked a renewed insurgency in the upcountry. On the day following the 1870 elections, white people in Laurensville fired guns into the armory, confiscated weapons from black troops who had come to aid a constable, and fanned out into the countryside searching for Republicans. The mob killed nine people.[20] Although a company of the Eighteenth had gone to Laurensville to monitor the polls, the federal troops ultimately provided no protection because the violence did not begin until after they left town. A black party tried to call them back, but white people thwarted the attempt. The infantrymen remained unaware of the situation until after they reached Columbia.[21]

An even bloodier series of incidents occurred in Union County. At the end of December 1870, a group of black militiamen had been accused of murdering a one-armed Confederate veteran in the course of stealing his barrel of whiskey. White vigilantes made two separate raids on the local jail, forcibly removed the suspects, and hanged or shot a total of ten African Americans. The culminating lynching took place on February 12.[22] The U.S. Army's reaction came four days too late. On February 16 a company of the Eighteenth left the state capital for Unionville. On February 24 the garrison at Charleston sent another company to Yorkville.[23] The latter was delayed in Chester after Klansmen sabotaged the railroad line.[24]

1873: The Seventh Cavalry Arrives

Recognizing the need for greater tactical mobility, the War Department authorized transfer of the Seventh Cavalry from the Military Department of the Missouri to the Military Department of the South. The latter encompassed seven former states of the Confederacy and was commanded by Gen. Alfred Terry.[25] Although the regimental headquarters of the Seventh moved to Louisville, Kentucky, it did not exercise tactical control. It instead provided administrative and logistical support to its companies. Terry issued the orders positioning units. Operational reports went through his staff rather than through the regimental commander.

Seven companies (also called troops) of the Seventh initially were sent to the Palmetto State. All of them came through Columbia on trains before riding into the piedmont by rail or horseback. The first group—Troops B, C, E, and K—arrived in March 1871 and went respectively to Unionville, Chester, Spartanburg, and Yorkville. By June they had been joined by Troop G in Sumter, Troop L in Winnsboro, and Troop M in Darlington. The regiment's other five companies—Troops A, D, F, H, and I—went to Alabama, Tennessee, and Kentucky.[26]

The Eighteenth Infantry contributed five more: C/18 at Yorkville, H/18 at Chester, I/18 at Laurensville, and K/18 at Newberry. The Third Artillery, which had a primary mission of defending the port of Charleston, sent its Battery I to Spartanburg, where it worked with the lone Company D of the Second Infantry.[27] In sum, the number of federal troops in South Carolina more than doubled during 1871 with a total of 1,030 soldiers at eight posts. The preponderance of them focused their efforts on the upcountry.[28] The dismounted infantrymen and artillerists often guarded detainees. When federal marshals asked for a posse to help serve arrest warrants, they normally received a detachment of cavalrymen.

Constituted in 1866 after the Civil War ended, the Seventh Cavalry had spent the entirety of its existence to this point on the frontier, where its soldiers helped protect settlers and railroad workers from Indians. The most significant battle in which the regiment participated was an 1868 victory over the Cheyenne near the Washita River. It also attracted publicity in 1870 after two of its troopers engaged in a gunfight at a Kansas saloon with Wild Bill Hickok.[29]

George Armstrong Custer, the officer most closely associated with the Seventh, did not accompany the soldiers who went to the Palmetto State.[30] He spent most of this period in Kentucky and had little direct involvement with activities in South Carolina. The only Custer stationed in the upcountry was George's younger sibling Thomas, who held a lieutenancy in Company M and would later die with his brother. Another officer better known for his involvement out West was Maj. Marcus Reno, who would subsequently face questions about his performance at Little Bighorn. He served as the post commander at Spartanburg.[31]

Maj. Lewis Merrill had similar responsibilities in Yorkville. He would likely be remembered for his actions there even if he had fought in the 1876 battle, which he did not. Merrill had experience countering guerrillas in Utah and Arkansas. He also possessed a deep knowledge of the law and the ability to deal with politicians. He used this background to advantage in the upcountry. The intelligence he gathered, reports he submitted, and coordination he made with various officials placed him at the center of events pertaining to the Ku Klux Klan. In addition he provided a valuable source of information about the lives of his soldiers in the descriptions he wrote for his reports.[32]

Troopers, Sergeants, and Company Officers

The Seventh resembled the rest of the army in that it contained many immigrants. A roster of 917 men assigned in 1876 lists 129 troopers from Ireland. Germans followed closely with 127. As Germany was not unified as a country until 1871, most of the men identified themselves as belonging to the member states from which they had come, such as Bavaria, Baden, Hanover, Prussia, and Württemberg. Other immigrants hailed from Canada, Denmark, England, Italy, France, Norway, Poland, Scotland, and Spain. The largest proportion of native-born soldiers came from the states of New York, Pennsylvania, and Ohio; they numbered 101, 80, and 61 respectively.[33] Although the list is of people assigned to the regiment after it returned from the South, the demographics differ little from a 74-man sample taken from the 1870 census of men identifiable as Seventh Cavalry troopers.[34] None of the soldiers was African American.[35]

Each of the regiment's twelve companies contained an average of 73 men assigned with about 60 actually present. The number of deserters averaged 2.3. Most of the other absent soldiers were taking leave or performing detached duty. Not all of those present could do their jobs as troopers. Some were sick or under confinement. These averaged 3.7 and 3.0 men respectively. The bulk of the unavailable soldiers, however, were assigned "extra" or "daily" duty. The former applied to those taken temporarily from their companies to support the post by working as clerks, guards, laborers, nurses, or cooks. The latter applied to those tasked to perform similar functions within their companies. Consequently the present-for-duty strength was usually fewer than 50.[36]

The preponderance of the men held the rank of private. Noncommissioned officers (NCOs) served as their first-line supervisors. A company normally had about fifteen of them.[37] They included six or seven sergeants and three or four corporals as well as company support specialists such as quartermasters, blacksmiths, farriers, teamsters, saddlers, buglers, and artificers. These NCOs usually started their careers as privates and earned promotion from the ranks. Most of those who came to South Carolina had seen combat on the plains. Some, such as Sgts. Winfield Scott Harvey of Troop K and John Ryan of Troop M, had fought in the Civil War.[38] The most seasoned sergeant in the company was the first sergeant. He wore a distinctive diamond patch above the chevrons on his sleeves to indicate his status.

A captain was assigned to each company as commander. Although each one in the Seventh was a veteran of the Civil War, not all of them actively led their units. Edward Myers came to Spartanburg with Troop E, but he suffered from a lingering illness that led to his death on July 11, 1871. Michael Sheridan, the younger brother of Maj. Gen. Philip Sheridan and nominal commander of Troop L in Yorkville, served elsewhere as an aide-de-camp. Capt. John Tourtelotte of Troop G did the same, which probably worked out for the best given that he had last visited South Carolina as a member of Sherman's army.[39]

In the absence of a captain, the senior of the company's two lieutenants would take charge. Lt. Thomas M. McDougall commanded Troop E after the death of Myers. McDougall had earned a battlefield commission during the Civil War. Donald McIntosh, who led Troop G in place of Tourtelotte, had received a lieutenancy in 1867. A Canadian of Native American ancestry, McIntosh had grown up on various western posts and worked as a civilian clerk during the Civil War.[40]

Some of the lieutenants received their commissions from the U.S. Military Academy. They included Edward Settle Godfrey of Troop K, who had enlisted with the Twenty-first Ohio Infantry in April 1861 and served for three months before entering West Point. He would serve a long career that included receiving the Medal of Honor.[41] The other lieutenant of Troop K, John Aspinwall, was too young to have fought in the Civil War. He had entered West Point at the age of eighteen and graduated in 1869. While at Yorkville he snapped his tibia and fibula after falling from a horse. Major Merrill appointed Aspinwall to be the post adjutant.[42]

Quarters

Soldiers stationed in the upcountry normally camped on grounds close to railroads and the main civilian centers of population. John Ryan of Troop M said that when he and his comrades arrived in Darlington, they found "a beautiful knoll with a heavy growth of trees on it. We trimmed the branches off these trees about eight or ten feet about the ground, cut out the undergrowth and shrubbery, and fixed it up so that we had a very beautiful camp."[43] They drew water from a nearby stream.

Rose Hotel, York (formerly Yorkville), South Carolina. Officers and troopers of the 7th Cavalry occupied this building during the years 1871–73.

Ryan thought less highly of the bivouac site at Spartanburg, to which his company moved in October 1871. "It was on rather low ground and the water was not very good," he said.[44] It did, however, have one convenience in that a civilian sutler had set up shop at a tent where soldiers could purchase sundries. The sergeant preferred the arrangements at Unionville, where he moved in December 1871. He relished the irony that the property used by the company belonged to a man who had fought for the Confederate army. He nevertheless befriended the owner because—unlike other local southern veterans who usually emphasized their status as officers—this one took pride in having served as an enlisted man.[45]

Troopers in the encampments used A-frame tents that could shelter two to three men each. "An A tent is built in the shape of a wedge, a pole in each end and one ridge pole and it is spiked down at the bottom," Ryan said. "We had these tents erected on poles about two feet from the ground." The men fashioned bed frames using "saplings and barrel staves laid across them." Mattresses came from "oats and corn sacks filled with hay or straw and sewed together." The men dug trenches around the base of the shelters to divert rainwater and built frames to hold their rifles and sabers.[46] If time and lumber allowed, they made wooden floors. Having the tents off the ground in this way was especially beneficial during late November and early December 1871, when six inches of snow twice fell in Spartanburg.[47]

Many of the soldiers at Yorkville enjoyed indoor quarters. The men of Troop K occupied a brick building that had previously been the Rose Hotel. The infantrymen from C/18 lived in a wooden structure across the main street. Merrill said that renting the buildings from the owners cost "less than would be the wear and tear of the necessary canvas."[48]

Whether the companies stayed in or out-of-doors, officers lived apart from their men. The use of tents made this kind of segregation easy to accomplish in the field. At places such as Yorkville, officers found private dwellings or rooms at other hotels. In Spartanburg, Major Reno rented a house for his wife and son. Edward Bomar, whose father was mayor of Spartanburg, encountered Mrs. Reno on several social occasions and played regularly with her boy. During an interview given during the 1930s, Bomar shared his childhood memories of seeing captains and lieutenants residing at houses in his neighborhood.[49]

Horses

Cavalrymen defined themselves by their mounts and devoted considerable time, effort, and resources to caring for the animals. The Seventh Cavalry averaged sixty-three horses per company.[50] Each company had a blacksmith and a farrier. Both had the duty of ensuring that the horses had proper shoes. The latter differed in that he tended to have greater veterinary knowledge. The former dealt more with the actual metalwork.

At Yorkville the Rose Hotel adjoined a stable with sufficient room for Troop K to keep its mounts. After the soldiers of Troop L moved from Winnsboro during October 1871, the newcomers sheltered theirs at a facility on the opposite side of the street. A contractor supplied hay and grain, which was brought by rail and stored nearby in a rented warehouse.[51] Ryan said that at their various camps the soldiers tied their horses to a "picket rope" stretched between trees about forty feet in front of the tents. They "had one large tent erected for our forage and bales of hay and quartermaster's stores."[52]

Keeping the animals healthy was as important as keeping them fed. Ryan said that camping outdoors during the winter led to problems with snow blindness. Merrill reported that several of the horses at Yorkville had a contagious bacterial infection called "glanders." The major had the veterinary surgeon for the regiment at his immediate disposal.[53] Farriers shouldered medical responsibilities at the more distant outposts. One of these—a man of Scottish extraction named Simpson—treated the Bomar family's horse for an infection of botfly larva.[54]

Both Bomar and Ryan expressed concerns about the spread of equine influenza. In fact the cases they witnessed were part of an epizootic that swept across the entire country during late 1872. At Unionville the farrier supervised the application of feed bags filled with streaming wet hay to soothe the lungs of the sick animals. The treatment must have done some good since the companies there suffered far fewer losses of serviceable horses than did Troop C, which by that time had moved to Charlotte, North Carolina. In December 1872 that company reported the regiment's highest number, twenty-one, of unserviceable horses.[55]

Soldiers of the Seventh Cavalry helped spread the disease into the upcountry not only by riding into otherwise isolated pockets of the countryside but also by bringing additional horses into the region. Earlier during 1872 the regimental quartermaster had directed each company to send five men to Kentucky for the purpose of procuring replacement mounts. Ryan served as the noncommissioned officer in charge of one such detail and recorded the journey in his memoir.[56]

His perspective is revealing not only about horses but also because he brings into contrast the ways in which officers and enlisted men sometimes had conflicting views of reality. Although George Custer had no involvement with tactical operations in South Carolina, he did take an interest in the new horses for Ryan's troop because Thomas Custer also belonged to it. In addition, as a senior commander, George wanted each company to have similarly colored horses for ease of identification during battle. "We sent Tom's troop 24 very handsome black horses," the lieutenant colonel wrote to his wife: "'M' is to be mounted like 'D' on black."[57] Ryan had a clearer picture of the truth. "We then tried to make our company a black horse company but failed as we could not procure enough blacks," he said. "We then had three different colored horses in the company."[58]

Merrill too mentioned the new acquisitions from Louisville, but he did not seem concerned about their colors. He did not say anything about the flu either, but he did worry about glanders and said that he had approved the shooting of four new horses that had the sickness.[59] In this regard at least, the Yorkville commander indicated an awareness of the army's environmental impact on the surrounding community.

Death, Disease, Accidents, Burial, and Medical Care

Although the equine influenza virus of 1872 could not infect human tissue, other pathogens did. Typhoid and pneumonia were the biggest killers. At least fourteen cavalrymen died of disease while stationed in the upcountry, and eighteen when deaths at Darlington, Sumter, and Charlotte are counted.[60] Unionville had the highest number with four. Spartanburg and Yorkville followed with three each. Merrill reported that one of the latter became delirious from fever and tumbled to his death through one of the windows at the Rose Hotel.[61] The floor-level sills on the upper stories of this building bore an unfortunate resemblance to doors.[62]

Three other men at Yorkville fell through these same openings. None of them died, but one lost his leg.[63] Pvt. Edmund Waring of Troop H at Unionville enjoyed no such luck after a moving train amputated both of his legs; he died.[64] The only accidental death during military operations happened when Pvt. Charles Brown of Troop C drowned while trying to ford the Catawba River between Lincolnton and Charlotte.[65] Lt. John Weston of Troop L accidentally impaled himself with a saber while training at Yorkville, but he survived.[66]

One murder occurred. On April 11, 1872, George Hall of Troop M left the encampment at Unionville to go drinking with three other privates and Sgt. Charles Betzig. They went to the house of a local black laundress. For unknown reasons Betzig struck Hall in the head with a fence picket. The private died. Betzig deserted and was never apprehended.[67]

Human remains were not usually sent to next of kin. The Rose Hill Cemetery at Yorkville contains the graves of three soldiers from the Seventh Cavalry and five from the Eighteenth Infantry.[68] The body of Pvt. Adolphus E. Cushman of Troop B lies in Unionville at the Episcopal Church of the Nativity.[69] Ryan claims to have participated in the funerals of the six other cavalrymen who died at Unionville during 1872. He said that each received full military honors to include a riderless horse and the firing of gunshots over the grave. White-painted boards served as markers.[70]

The death toll was hardly unusual in a world without antibiotics and other modern medical marvels. It was low by most measures. Soldiers in South Carolina had better access to health care than did most civilians. Each post in the upcountry—to include the smaller, more remote ones—had a civilian physician or "assistant surgeon" from the U.S. Army Medical Corps. Larger posts such as Yorkville had hospital stewards assigned, and extra duty soldiers sometimes served as nurses. Ryan said that all of the men received smallpox vaccinations.[71] Records indicate also that the Office of the Surgeon General sometimes helped ensure the purity of the soldiers' food.[72] The main reason for having military doctors, of course, was to treat battlefield wounds. Thankfully for their health, the soldiers of the Seventh Cavalry did not participate in many gunfights during their time in the upcountry. None was killed in action.

All things considered, the men of the Seventh Cavalry had relatively few medical complaints. Companies stationed in the upcountry had an average of 3.27 sick men at any given time during their deployment. By comparison,

Soldiers of the 7th Cavalry and 18th Infantry buried
at the Rose Hill Cemetery, York, South Carolina.

troopers of the regiment located in other parts of the South had a rate of 4.23.[73] Merrill, who had few kind words for South Carolina, gave credit to the upcountry's weather for the relative lack of illness. He said, "The climate is very fine both winter and summer, and is as healthful and pleasant as any in which I have ever lived."[74]

Food

Having a varied, nutritious diet helped maintain wellness. The military quartermaster system supplied barrels of salted pork and flour. Other staples included coffee, sugar, salt, and lard. A list from February 1875 (albeit two years after the Seventh departed) indicates that soldiers at Yorkville had access to vinegar, Worcestershire sauce, gherkin pickles, salmon, oysters, raspberry jam, and condensed milk. Some of the food was obtained locally.[75] Merrill mentioned that he authorized the purchase of beef from nearby farmers.[76] Ryan said that African American civilians would sell fresh produce in season. The sergeant remembered that on one occasion the company purchased an entire wagonload of watermelons. The money to pay for the food came from the "Post Fund," which was replenished by the sale of horse manure and other locally generated sources of cash.[77] The companies at Yorkville supplemented what the army provided by planting and tending vegetable gardens.[78]

The post at Yorkville also had a bakery, which by December 1871 could produce 140 rations of bread at a time.[79] Men on extra duty served as cooks. Soldiers had to improvise at smaller posts such as Unionville. Ryan said that they started by digging a six-by-ten-foot square into the red clay of a stream embankment. "We built a brick front facing the stream and built a sheet iron top over this oven. Some of the men constructed a log house and chinked it up with this clay." One of the privates in the company had experience as a baker. He "turned out some fine bread, and it was a great treat for us, as we were accustomed to the government hard tack."[80]

Sometimes the men fed themselves through extralegal initiatives. Edward Bomar remembered that his father caught three soldiers stealing fruit from the family orchard. The elder Bomar held the soldiers at gunpoint and threatened to have them arrested. According to the son, "They begged for mercy and then after a fatherly lecture he sent them away in peace with all the peaches they could eat."[81]

However soldiers obtained rations, they needed a place to consume them. The men at Yorkville had room in their buildings for a dining facility. Ryan said that at Unionville "we also built a large mess hall of pine logs and chinked it up with the red clay which was taken from the embankment when the oven was dug out." They covered it with "a couple of large tarpaulins" and "had rough boards for tables and benches." He described it as "quite comfortable."[82]

Soldiers burned wood fires for cooking and heating. They purchased fuel from local civilians. Merrill complained that much of what they bought consisted of "green wood or half rotten windfalls." Presaging later generations of American military men in foreign lands, he attributed the situation to the laziness of the inhabitants. In his opinion the local civilians had "a want of energy and business tact."[83]

Clothing and Laundresses

Having adequate uniforms was a problem too. Soldiers of the early 1870s wore leftovers from the Civil War. Manufactured in haste by sometimes unscrupulous contractors, these garments were of notoriously poor quality. "The clothing is generally complained of, and with reason," said Merrill in an 1871 letter. "The working off the old supplies of the war, gives in many cases inferior clothing; far below the old standard."[84] Emptying government warehouses led to shortages of the most popular sizes. In a November 1872 letter, the post commander at Laurensville complained that the forty-three pairs of boots in sizes 8 and 9 that he had ordered for the men of Company G had failed to arrive. He said that "the Cavalry are going barefooted in consequence."[85] Such conditions lend credence to Merrill's assertion that "dissatisfaction with the quality and allowance of clothing" contributed to the desertions of some soldiers.[86]

Rather than replenish stocks, War Department leaders decided to introduce a new design that would be better suited for duty on the frontier. Most notably the "Swiss Coat" had pleats that allowed soldiers to add layers of clothing underneath for warmth. In a report written near the end of 1872, Merrill expected the complaints to "cease so soon as the new uniform is furnished."[87]

As with food, the men in the ranks found ways to improvise their shoes and clothes. One soldier in Ryan's unit had experience as a cobbler. He carried his tools with him and earned extra money by plying his civilian trade. Unfortunately for him, he wasted most of his gains on alcohol. Another cavalryman knew how to tailor clothes. He was assisted by his wife, who followed the company around the upcountry. Besides helping to sew, she baked pies to sell.[88]

Quite a few women washed clothes for soldiers. They did not belong officially to the armed forces, but they provided a vital service. Some, such as the African American woman whose house near Unionville became the scene of Private Hall's murder, were nearby residents. A great many others, though, were military wives who accompanied their husbands from post to post.[89] Troop B in Spartanburg had at least three such laundresses.[90]

Sergeant Harvey of Troop K expressed resentment at the treatment the women received while traveling by boat during the trip to South Carolina. He said, "With the officers' dogs and hay bags rolling there was no chance for soldiers' ladies and soldiers to sleep. The officers act very ungentlemanly on board the boat in showing respect to soldiers' wives, especially Maj. Merrill."[91] Some of the officers may have been discourteous, but most recognized the value of laundresses and/or spouses and took steps to foster their well-being. When Troop E moved from Spartanburg to Unionville during November 1872, the post adjutant ensured that they had rail transportation at government expense.[92]

Off-Duty Activities

Of course soldiers sought women for purposes besides laundry. According to Ryan, "It would be no unusual sight after taps . . . to see four or five men strike out from camp with a haversack containing loaves of bread, canned fruit, flour, etc. . . . They would take these things over to these shanties, where the women would cook this stuff. . . . They would have a good time and sometimes get drunk and in the morning before reveille roll call you could see them sneaking back to camp."[93]

The sergeant referred to the women involved as "grass widows." Not all of them were white. "I have known some of the men to go four or five miles from camp to some of these Negro cabins to have a good time," he said. "Sometimes some of these men would wind up in the guard house for being absent from roll call, also for leaving the camp without permission."[94] Whatever the race, comparatively few of these relationships endured. Ryan said that when his unit left Darlington for Spartanburg, "a good many of the boys in the company left their sweethearts behind them."[95]

Exceptions did occur. First Sgt. Edwin Bobo of Troop C married a local teenager, Annie Missouri, during 1872 while he was stationed with his unit at Lincolnton. They had two sons and remained together until Edwin was killed at Little Bighorn. A year or two later Annie married Sgt. Daniel Kanipe, a North Carolinian who had enlisted with the Seventh Cavalry at Lincolnton and was one of only a few members of his company to survive the 1876 battle.[96]

Similar connections were forged in Darlington. Charles Mooney, an Irish immigrant and the farrier for Troop M, married a local woman and took her with him. He came back after his enlistment expired and established a successful wagon-building company.[97] Mooney appears on the 1880 manuscript census for Darlington with his wife and two teenaged stepchildren.[98]

Ryan said that several soldiers stationed at Yorkville later returned as well. Merrill did not mention anything about such nuptials in his report. Rather he discreetly said that "the circumstances of easy access to whisky-shops, and being stationed in a village where close supervision of conduct is by no means easy, without undue attempt to restrain the men from recreation, contributed to more looseness of conduct than would be found at a military post or camp away from such surroundings."[99]

The troopers clearly had few qualms about interacting with local civilians. Ryan remembered a saloon in Unionville. "Our men used to frequent this place very often," he said. "I was in there myself on a few occasions." In fact he served at least once as a temporary barkeeper. "While I was quite a hand to dish out the lager beer to the boys, I was quite a poor hand at making change. . . . I think that for every ten cents that I took in for a glass of beer, the soldiers got about five glasses free."[100]

Business owners in Darlington lost even greater sums of money by extending credit to soldiers. The civilians had no way to collect the loans after Troop M moved to Spartanburg. Ryan remembered one soldier saying, "When the last bugle call was sounded in that camp to move, that probably settled the debts as far as they were concerned."[101]

Having soldiers nearby could be a mixed blessing. Cavalrymen came to the aid of civilians in Unionville to extinguish a fire that on March 15, 1872, destroyed two blocks of the town. Several soldiers risked their lives by going into a burning bank and helping to extract the safe. The owners had promised them a barrel of whiskey as a reward.[102] Unfortunately for the townspeople, the officers of the company took the liquor instead. "This was a great disappointment to the enlisted men and they vowed they would get square," said Ryan. Soldiers again were ordered to help when another fire broke out. This time the men dropped breakable items out the windows and pilfered "knives and razors, also a number of black hats."[103]

Thefts apparently occurred on occasion too. During November 1871 a group of soldiers from Troop E under the control of a U.S. marshal visited the houses of men who had already been placed under arrest and were being detained elsewhere. The soldiers informed the wives that their husbands would be executed in the morning. According to the local newspaper, the soldiers also made "sad havoc among fine dresses and toilet articles. . . . One of the ladies lost a fine gold watch and chain." The Unionville council conducted an investigation and made a formal complaint. The marshal thanked the townspeople for their promptness and expressed "in somewhat sarcastic terms, his regret that they had not been equally prompt in reference to other murderous and unlawful proceedings which had taken place."[104] Lt. Thomas McDougall, the acting commander of Troop E, apparently attributed the men's behavior to a "drunken spree" and offered no apology. The matter then went to Major Reno at Spartanburg, who recommended that the lieutenant undergo a trial by court-martial.[105] McDougall suffered no long-term negative consequences. He remained in command and had a long career with the regiment.

Soldiers were not responsible for every problem. Merrill said that in Yorkville "there has been no instance in which the folly and misconduct of the civilian have not been the original incentive in bringing about difficulty."[106] Ryan said that while staying overnight in Columbia some of his men were accosted by "a couple of village toughs" who "used some very insulting, profane and indecent language in regard to the blue uniform they had on and the flag that they represented." The "ex-Confederates" ganged up on two of the men. Ryan broke up the fight by knocking the ringleader unconscious with the butt of his .44 caliber Colt revolver.[107]

The Civil War remained a sore topic. Ryan remembered an altercation in which a civilian called one of the soldiers a "damn Yank." The cavalryman responded by making an unflattering comment about a portrait of Robert E. Lee that was hanging on the barroom wall. A fight ensued. According to Ryan, "the outcome of it was that one of our men drew his pistol from his holster and let a bullet fly, which demolished the beautiful picture." Significantly the local law enforcement authorities did not become involved. A Seventh Cavalry corporal with a group of other soldiers took the brawlers into custody.[108]

Many of the cavalrymen used their time to learn about Civil War history. Ryan had fought in the Battle of Secessionville and made a point of touring Fort Sumter while passing through Charleston. He visited spots where soldiers of Sherman's army had camped outside of Columbia, where they had burned Wade Hampton's mansion, and where the artillerists had positioned their cannon to shoot at the Statehouse. He made a special trip to Florence to see the prisoner-of-war camp for enlisted men. Harvey too seemed enthralled by the war. His diary contains multiple entries about the battlefields he passed in Chattanooga, Atlanta, and Columbia on his 1871 trip to Yorkville.[109]

Not all off-duty hours were spent away from camp. The post at Yorkville had a reading room.[110] Ryan said that the mess hall the men constructed at Unionville served a similar purpose. "They would generally lounge around in this room, and read what books or papers they had, or play cards, such as poker and Mexican Monte." Given the shortage of cash, the men often gambled using the pound of tobacco they received every month from the quartermaster.[111]

They also spent idle hours tossing people in blankets. Men would hold the sides taut and create a sort of trampoline. Sometimes the person in the center was a willing participant. Other times he or she was a hapless victim. Ryan remembered soldiers bouncing several African American civilians. He said, "Of course, this was not permitted, according to army regulations but our officers were not present and therefore they did not know anything about this."[112]

Harvey indicated in his diary that the soldiers of Troop K regularly played baseball. On the Fourth of July in 1871 "our troop again played a game of ball with Co. C of the 18th U.S. Infantry and Co. C beat. Some of our boys are on a drunk."[113]

Soldiers who missed roll call or allowed alcohol to interfere with their military duties could easily find themselves placed under arrest. The company commander had the power not only to confine men but also to impose more imaginative punishments, such as forcing them to carry heavy logs.[114] At Spartanburg and Yorkville the majors could hold garrison court-martials for more serious offenses. Sentencing a man to prison at Fort Leavenworth required a general court-martial. These occurred infrequently for the Seventh Cavalrymen in the upcountry during the period 1871–73. When they did, the parties involved went to Columbia.[115]

Bugle calls set the pace of life. In between reveille in the morning and taps at bedtime, the army had standard tunes for assembling to eat, seeing the doctor, listening to the first sergeant, receiving mail, assembling for training, and so forth. Music also served as a means of communicating while on the march or in battle, so every company had at least one trumpeter. Camps with multiple companies had larger musical ensembles. Edward Bomar said that in Spartanburg "there was a brass band, an army band, a fascinating, soul capturing band, which stayed somewhere in town and came out on the public square, at intervals, to play for the town; marvelous waltzes and old love tunes; oh yes! 'The Captain with his Whiskers' and 'Katie Darling' and 'Marching through Georgia' and the like."[116]

Training, Readiness, and Operations

A cavalry unit needed regular training to remain effective. Each man carried a .50 caliber, breech-loading Sharps carbine and a .44 caliber revolver. Firing either of these weapons, especially while mounted, required skill. Troopers also needed to practice fighting with their sabers.[117] In addition they had to know how to maneuver as a team. The U.S. Army had manuals spelling out the various movements.[118]

Ryan indicated that training was part of their routine. At Darlington "we had mounted drill, platoon and company drill in the forenoon, and in the afternoon we moved out about a mile from camp and drilled in a large field mounted." They did the same while at Unionville. Ryan said that these activities often attracted civilian spectators.[119] Similar exercises took place at Laurensville. The commanding officer there wrote in his January 1783 report: "Of the Cavalry— twenty drills were had of the 'School of the Platoon' mounted. Mounted drills were suspended November 23rd on account of the epidemic amongst the horses. The Recruits lately assigned to the company have been drilled twice a day (Sunday excepted) since December 13, in the 'School of the Trooper' dismounted."[120]

Readiness levels concerned officers such as Merrill. Although he predicted that the Ku Klux Klan would reassert itself if soldiers were withdrawn, he believed that continued provost duty would hurt tactical proficiency. However well organized, the drilling for new recruits in the upcountry was a poor substitute for experience on the plains. Officers too became rusty. Merrill said that "constant service with small commands and other circumstances which afford little time and no facilities for theoretical instruction, has tended to bring about a degree of satisfaction with low professional attainments."[121]

Indeed the level of alertness appeared to decrease over time. Harvey's diary focused on the Klan to a greater extent when he first arrived at Yorkville in March 1871 than it did when he was discharged six months later. His concern climaxed on June 12 after he heard that the group was planning to attack the post. "Our troops laid on their arms ready to receive them but they are too big of a coward to come and let us see them," he wrote. "I suppose they will not bother us any more." He wrote a few days later that the "K.K.K. have gone into North Carolina."[122]

One company of the Seventh Troop C, was sent into the Tarheel State that same month. It moved from Chester to Rutherfordton, where approximately one hundred Klansmen had conducted a raid on the town jail during the night of June 11.[123] Troop C would spend six months there before shifting subsequently to Lincolnton, Dallas, and Charlotte.

Whether they were stationed in North or South Carolina, the primary mission of the Seventh Cavalry troopers was to serve in "posses" rather than to defend its posts. In 1870 Congress had passed the Enforcement Act, which prescribed criminal penalties for individuals who interfered with federal elections. The range of offenses was expanded through legislation passed in February and April 1871. Federal marshals served arrest warrants. Cavalrymen provided protection for the lawmen and helped with apprehension.[124]

The problem lay in gathering sufficient evidence to bring formal charges. The Klan operated in secret, and few people were willing to testify openly about it. Consequently federal troops had relatively little to do. They could help local officials with matters of state law, but only upon official request. Soldiers also escorted federal revenue agents making raids on illegal alcohol distilleries. Moonshining was especially prevalent in the mountainous "Dark Corner" near the Greenville County town of Gowansville. According to Reno, cavalrymen from the Spartanburg garrison conducted multiple missions in this area without success.[125]

Soldiers pursuing bootleggers and Klansmen sometimes caused problems with local civilians by stealing food. Reno's explanation for this practice again demonstrates the social distance within the ranks. "It frequently happens that the escorts are kept out by the Marshalls beyond the time, for which they are rationed and complaint has been made that the men helped themselves to forage and provisions," the major reported. "I've no doubt in cases where the men have gone under a Sergeant this may have occurred, although they received the strictest orders in regard to this matter, but an enlisted man cannot be made to appreciate the responsibility attaching to this kind of duty."[126]

Unlike American troops in, say, Vietnam, Iraq, or Afghanistan, U.S. soldiers in the South Carolina upcountry did not conduct operations with the military forces of the local government, which in this case meant the predominantly black militia. Nothing in the official records of Merrill or Reno indicates that they gave equipment, armaments, ammunition, training, advice, or assistance to that organization, and Ryan did not mention such either.

Harvey's diary too is silent on this issue, but his does suggest how duty in the upcountry could change personal prejudices about race. As he moved from Kansas to South Carolina, the blacksmith seemed fascinated by African Americans, but he seemed to view them more as objects than people. "Plenty of niggers and lots of fun," he wrote in Chattanooga. "We made them dance and jump and sing." Atlanta also had "plenty of niggers." He began ascribing emotions to them after he reached Yorkville. "Plenty of niggers and all scared to death," he wrote. "We have some trouble with the niggers," he said later that spring, hinting that, for better or worse, he was establishing individual relationships. By summer they had become "negroes" to him.[127]

Ku Klux Klan activity waned as Harvey had his change of heart. At the Yorkville post headquarters, Merrill remained persuaded that the calm was illusory. He focused his efforts on interviewing witnesses, soliciting information, and learning as much as possible about the Klan. He began sending detailed reports about the group to General Terry, who forwarded the materials farther up the chain of command until they reached Congress, which in turn tasked an investigative subcommittee to visit South Carolina during July and August.[128]

Based on the information that came to light, President Ulysses S. Grant decided in October to suspend the writ of habeas corpus in nine South Carolina counties, eight of which were in the upcountry.[129] Federal authorities would have the power to imprison people indefinitely without pressing charges. Witnesses presumably would be more willing to testify if the suspect were in jail or under bond. Soldiers helped U.S. marshals round up more than a thousand people.[130]

The methods used resembled the "cordon and search" tactics described in more recent U.S. Army field manuals.[131] Ryan described one operation that involved about sixty mounted men: "We surrounded this place at daylight in the morning and our orders were to allow everybody to go in, but nobody to go out. At daylight the U.S. marshal, who was with us and held warrants for certain parties in that town, immediately proceeded to the center of the town, accompanied by a couple of commissioned officers and a detail of enlisted men."[132]

Sometimes the raids involved larger forces. On another occasion, while Ryan was stationed at Spartanburg, his company received orders one afternoon to prepare to go on a mission after dark. They would leave by horseback at midnight. Battery I of the Third Artillery and Company E of the Eighteenth

Infantry would depart by train. They timed their movements so that they would converge on the target area at daylight the next morning. "We immediately surrounded this town, put pickets on every road leading into the town, and had orders to allow nobody out of the town but anyone that wished to enter could," Ryan said. "After this place was surrounded thoroughly, our officers and marshals with detachments immediately advanced into the village and made numerous arrests."[133]

The sound of thundering hooves or a knock on the door could strike fear in civilians and render them more cooperative, but the noise could also serve as a warning. To prevent anyone from escaping, soldiers positioned themselves to the rear of the objective. Civilians who tried to flee would thus be flushed into the arms of waiting captors.[134] The situations often required greater tact than force. Mothers, wives, and children were understandably upset to have husbands and fathers taken away by strange men with guns. Allowing a suspect to say good-bye or put a brief affair in order bought potential goodwill. Treating mothers, wives, and daughters with respect prevented the kinds of rebellion that the British had brought upon themselves during the American Revolution in this exact part of the country.[135] By the same token, soldiers had to overcome their sense of delicacy to apprehend men who tried to use women as shields.[136]

Stealth could help too. Ryan described several instances where fugitives built ingenious hiding places from which they could fight back. The sergeant preferred to avoid direct confrontations by catching his opponents unaware or sleeping. In order to find one suspect who had fled across the state border into Georgia, he dressed in civilian clothes to follow the man's wife and child as they traveled by train to visit him.[137]

The work did not end at the moment of apprehension. Cavalrymen had to herd their captives back to a holding facility near or at one of the outposts. The local jail served this purpose in the town of Unionville. Although the local sheriff remained in charge, soldiers pulled duty as guards.[138] At Yorkville, Merrill housed detainees in tents and surrounded them with infantrymen from the Eighteenth Regiment.

Violations of the Ku Klux Klan Act required trial in a federal court. The nearest one to the upcountry was in Columbia. Military authorities sent trainloads of prisoners there. Ryan performed escort duty as the sergeant in charge of one such detail. He said, "I had a couple of my guards stationed at each end of the car inside the doors."[139]

The work of these soldiers was largely for naught. Prosecutors indicted about thirteen hundred detainees, but the effort fell short because the federal government did not devote the resources necessary to bring the cases to trial. Less than a tenth of the men accused were convicted, and most of those pleaded guilty. Charges against the remainder were dismissed.[140]

1873: Return to the Plains

The Seventh Cavalry began leaving South Carolina in December 1872 when Troop M received instructions to go to Mississippi.[141] Most of the others departed for Tennessee and points westward during March 1873. The infantrymen left the state or withdrew to Columbia. By September an infantry company at Yorkville and another at Newberry were the only federal forces left in the up-country. Both belonged to the Eighteenth Infantry.[142]

Troop strength remained stable until July 1876, when a massacre of black militiamen took place in the Aiken County town of Hamburg. The entire Eighteenth Infantry came to the state during the summer to monitor an increasingly violent political campaign. The resulting election contributed to a national impasse over the presidency and a dispute within South Carolina over the governorship. After the Compromise of 1877 put Rutherford Hayes in the White House, the new president withdrew all federal occupation forces. The soldiers of the Eighteenth Infantry went north to quell a railroad strike. Wade Hampton "redeemed" the state for white people. Reconstruction ended, and no U.S. cavalry came to rescue it.[143]

Notes

The author would like to thank Susan Thoms of the Spartanburg County Public Library Kennedy Room and Paul Harrison of the Old Army Records Section of the National Archives and Records Administration (NARA) for their assistance with the research for this chapter.

1. In a seventeen-page article about the Seventh written in 1892, Ernest Albert Garlington devotes two sentences to the two years spent in the South; see E. A. Garlington, "Seventh Regiment of Cavalry," in *Army of the United States: Historical Sketches of Staff and Line with Portraits of Generals-in-Chief,* ed. Theodore F. Rodenbough and William L. Haskins (New York: Maynard, Merrill, & Co., 1896), 251–67. Garlington, who received the Medal of Honor for actions during 1890 at Wounded Knee, was a native of Newberry, South Carolina. He was attending the University of Georgia and West Point during the time the Seventh Cavalry was occupying his hometown. In a more recent book, the historian Thom Hatch calls the duty in the South "inglorious" and devotes a single sentence to the episode; see Thom Hatch, *The Custer Companion: A Comprehensive Guide to the Life of George Armstrong Custer and the Plains Indian Wars* (Mechanicsburg, Pa.: Stackpole Books, 2002), 53–54.

2. Richard Zuczek, *State of Rebellion: Reconstruction in South Carolina* (Columbia: University of South Carolina Press, 1996), 88–117; Michael J. Martinez, *Carpetbaggers, Cavalry, and the Ku Klux Klan: Exposing the Invisible Empire during Reconstruction* (Lanham, Md.: Rowman and Littlefield, 2007); Jerry L. West, *The Ku Klux Klan in York County, South Carolina, 1865–1877* (Jefferson, N.C.: McFarland & Company,

2002); Allen W. Trelease, *White Terror: The Ku Klux Klan Conspiracy and Southern Reconstruction* (New York: Harper, 1971).

3. Mark Moyar, *A Question of Command: Counterinsurgency from the Civil War to Iraq* (New Haven, Conn.: Yale University Press, 2009), 33–61; Robert W. Coakley, *The Role of Federal Military Forces in Domestic Disorders, 1798–1878* (Washington, D.C.: U.S. Army Center of Military History, 1988), 310–13; James E. Sefton, *The United States Army and Reconstruction, 1865–1877* (Baton Rouge: Louisiana State University Press, 1967), 213–35.

4. Bell Wiley, *Life of Johnny Reb: The Common Soldier of the Confederacy* (Baton Rouge: Louisiana State University Press, 1978), 13.

5. "South Carolina—Railroads," http://www.carolana.com/SC/Transportation/railroads/home.html (accessed January 15, 2013); Frederick A. Eiserman, "Longstreet's Corps at Chickamauga: Lessons in Inter-Theater Deployment" (master's thesis, U.S. Army Command and General Staff College, Ft. Leavenworth, Kansas, 1971), Combined Arms Research Library Digital Library, http://cgsc.cdmhost.com/cdm4/item_viewer.php?CISOROOT=/p4013coll2&CISOPTR=1647&CISOBOX=1&REC=14 (accessed January 15, 2013). Scott Reynolds Nelson argues in *Iron Confederacies: Southern Railways, Klan Violence, and Reconstruction* (Chapel Hill: University of North Carolina Press, 1999) that the development during the early 1870s of a railroad connecting Atlanta and Charlotte was responsible for a spike in Klan violence and that President Grant suspended habeas corpus in this area to protect the interests of northern railroad investors who had political ties to the Oval Office. Nelson's thesis, though compelling, requires additional evidence.

6. Francis Sumner, "Graphic Account of the Perils and Sufferings of the Family during Sherman's March," in John Brown Carwile, *Reminiscences of Newberry* (Charleston, S.C.: Walker, Evans & Cogswell, 1890), 85–91; E. Don Herd Jr., *South Carolina Upcountry, 1540–1980: Historical and Biographical Sketches*, vol. 2 (Greenwood, S.C.: Attic Press, 1982), 444–68.

7. Chris J. Hartley, *Stoneman's Raid 1865* (Winston-Salem, N.C.: John F. Blair, 2010); Thomas Bland Keys, "The Federal Pillage of Anderson, South Carolina: Brown's Raid," *South Carolina Historical Magazine* 76, no. 2 (April 1975): 80–86; reports of Col. William J. Palmer, May 6 and May 12, 1865, in *Official Records of the War of the Rebellion*, series 1, vol. 49 (Washington, D.C.: War Department, War Records Office, 1897), 547–52; Frank H. Mason, "General Stoneman's Last Campaign and the Pursuit of Jefferson Davis," in *Sketches of War History, 1861–1865: Papers Prepared for the Ohio Commandery of the Military Order of the Loyal Legion of the United States*, vol. 2, ed. Robert Hunter (Cincinnati: Robert Clarke & Company, 1890), 21–43; Vernon Foster and Walter S. Montgomery Sr., *Spartanburg: Facts, Reminiscences, Folklore* (Spartanburg, S.C.: Reprint Co., 1998), 220–27; Herd, *South Carolina Upcountry*, 469–97.

8. For locations of infantry regiments, see *New York Times*, August 9, 1865; and Edward D. Culp, *The 25th Ohio Veteran Volunteer Infantry in the War for the Union* (Topeka, Kans.: George W. Crane & Company, 1885), 134–39. According to *Union Army*, vol. 2 (Madison, Wis.: Federal Publishing Company, 1908), 451, the First Ohio

Cavalry was dispersed across South Carolina and Georgia during the summer of 1865 until it was released from active duty that September. According to the *New York Times* article, the only company of the First Ohio in the vicinity of the upcountry was located in Columbia. A July 19, 1865, entry in the diary of Capt. Norris Crossman mentions twenty-five men from the First Ohio in Greenville. Crossman served in the Fifty-sixth New York Infantry, and his diary is in the archives of the South Carolina Historical Society, Charleston, S.C.

9. Charles Tyler Trowbridge, "Six Months in the Freedmen's Bureau with a Color Regiment," paper read before the Minnesota Commandery of the Military Order of the Loyal Legion, October 11, 1904, in Torrance et al., *Glimpses of a Nation's Struggle*, vol. 31 (St. Paul, Minn.: St. Paul Book and Stationery Co., 1909); Robert S. McCully and Manson Sherrill Jolly, "Letter from a Reconstruction Renegade," *South Carolina Historical Magazine* 77, no. 1 (January 1976): 34–40; Herd, *South Carolina Upcountry,* 387–443.

10. Lt. Col. Calvin S. Brown of the Third Sub-District, Western S.C., Anderson Courthouse, report to Brig. Gen. C. H. Howard, October 23, 1865; Records of the Assistant Commissioner for the State of S.C., Bureau of Refugees, Freedmen and Abandoned Lands, 1865–70, NARA Microfilm Publication M869, Roll 34; Freedmen's Bureau Online, http://freedmensbureau.com/southCarolina/scoperations3.htm. Accessed January 16, 2013.

11. Henry A. Shorey, *Story of the Maine Fifteenth* (Bridgeton, Me.: Press of the Bridgeton News, 1890), 168.

12. Ibid., 169.

13. Ibid.

14. McCully and Jolly, "Letter from a Reconstruction Renegade," 34–40; Herd, *South Carolina Upcountry,* 387–443.

15. George F. Price, *Across the Continent with the Fifth U.S. Cavalry* (New York: D. Van Nostrand, 1883); Clifford L. Swanson, *The Sixth United States Infantry Regiment, 1855 to Reconstruction* (Jefferson, N.C.: McFarland & Co., 2001); R. H. Wilson, "Eighth Regiment of Infantry," in *The Army of the United States: Historical Sketches of Staff and Line with Portraits of Generals-in-Chief,* ed. Theodore F. Rodenbough and William L. Haskins (New York: Maynard, Merrill, & Co., 1896), 511–25.

16. Sefton, *United States Army and Reconstruction,* 261.

17. Martinez, *Carpetbaggers, Cavalry, and the Ku Klux Klan,* 112; Zuczek, *State of Rebellion,* 58.

18. *Report of the Secretary of War* (Washington, D.C.: Government Printing Office, 1868), 370–517, contains testimony, affidavits, and other evidence pertaining to violence in South Carolina. For orders moving various units, see *Reports of the Secretary of War* for 1868, 1869, and 1870, all available on Google Books. With few exceptions the total numbers of soldiers listed in the War Department reports match those provided by Sefton, *United States Army and Reconstruction,* 261.

19. Zuczek, *State of Rebellion,* 76–78; Martinez, *Carpetbaggers, Cavalry, and the Ku Klux Klan,* 115–18.

20. Zuczek, *State of Rebellion*, 88–89; Martinez, *Carpetbaggers, Cavalry, and the Ku Klux Klan*, 119.

21. John A. Leland, *A Voice from South Carolina* (Charleston, S.C.: Walker, Evans & Cogswell, 1879), 51–64.

22. Zuczek, *State of Rebellion*, 90–91; Martinez, *Carpetbaggers, Cavalry, and the Ku Klux Klan*, 72–73.

23. *Report of the Secretary of War*, 1871, 62.

24. Trelease, *White Terror*, 366.

25. The states were Mississippi, Alabama, Tennessee, Kentucky, Georgia, Florida, and South Carolina.

26. The monthly "returns" of the Seventh Cavalry list the location of each troop. They also contain detailed numbers regarding personnel, by-name accountings of gains and losses, orders received, statuses of horses, and other information. The data were compiled at the regimental headquarters and handwritten onto printed forms. Copies are available on microfilm (Record Group 94, Series M744, Roll 71) at the downtown mall facility of NARA in Washington, D.C.

27. The senior officer of each military post submitted a monthly "return" to the commander of the military department to which he was assigned. He did this report in addition to the one for his unit that he sent to his regiment. This document contains a listing of every unit present at the post. The numbers regarding personnel tend to be less extensive than the ones sent to the regimental headquarters, and they do not provide by-name accountings of gains and losses, but they often contain brief narratives of significant events that occurred during the month. The collections of post returns for this part of the South are not as complete as the regimental returns. Copies are available on microfilm (Record Group 94, Series M-617, multiple rolls) at the downtown mall facility of NARA in Washington, D.C.

28. *Report of the Secretary of War*, 1871, 61–64. The total numbers match that of Sefton, *United States Army and Reconstruction*, 262.

29. Garlington, "Seventh Regiment of Cavalry," 251–67; Joseph G. Rosa, *Wild Bill Hickok, Gunfighter: An Account of Hickok's Gunfights* (Norman: University of Oklahoma Press, 2003), 114–23.

30. The commander of the Seventh Cavalry was Col. Samuel Sturgis. Although George Custer had held the rank of major general during the Civil War, he had reverted to his Regular Army rank of lieutenant colonel and was the second-most-senior officer of the regiment.

31. Susan H. Thoms, "Spartanburg's Civil War," *Carologue* 19 (Spring 2003): 10–17; Ronald H. Nichols, *In Custer's Shadow: Major Marcus Reno* (Norman: University of Oklahoma Press, 1999), 107–22.

32. Martinez, *Carpetbaggers, Cavalry, and the Ku Klux Klan*, 83–95; Lewis Merrill, "Report to Brigadier General Albert Terry," September 23, 1872, in *Report of the Secretary of War*, 1872, 85–91.

33. The 1876 roster was compiled under the supervision of John Doerner, chief historian at the Little Bighorn National Battlefield. The roster is posted online by the

Friends of the Little Bighorn, whose members support the battlefield, http://www
.friendslittlebighorn.com/7th%20Cav%20Muster%20Rolls.htm. Accessed January 16,
2013.

34. The 1870 sample comes from the manuscript population returns for a com-
pany-sized element of the Seventh Cavalry encamped along the Saline River in Ellis
County, Kansas (Series M593, Roll 434, page 2). The company to which these soldiers
belonged is unknown, but five of the names match with soldiers for Troop G on the
1876 roster. The only official muster rolls for the Seventh Cavalry available at NARA
are for Troop C. These are located in Record Group 391. Unfortunately none of
the men listed from Troop C appears on the 1870 census. The regimental returns for
the summer—also available at the National Archives—suggest that Troop C was in the
field and therefore not included in the enumeration.

35. African Americans wanting to join the U.S. Army during this period could
enlist in the Ninth or Tenth Cavalry or the Twenty-fourth or Twenty-fifth Infantry
Regiments.

36. The statistical data were generated by the author using monthly regimental
returns.

37. Mary Lee Stubbs and Stanley Russell Connor, *Armor-Cavalry, Part I: Regular
Army and Army Reserve* (Washington, D.C.: Office of the Chief of Military History,
1969), 20, 23.

38. Although parts of Ryan's memoirs were published as newspaper articles during
the early 1900s, the complete manuscript was not discovered until 2000. The historian
Sandy Barnard, who had previously written a biography of Ryan titled *Custer's First
Sergeant,* edited the manuscript and published it as two books: *Ten Years with Custer:
A 7th Cavalryman's Memoirs* (Terre Haute, Ind.: AST Press, 2001); and *Campaigning
with the Irish Brigade* (Terre Haute, Ind.: AST Press, 2001). The former book covers
Ryan's service in the upcountry during the 1870s, but the latter book is also of interest
to South Carolina historians because it details Ryan's participation in the 1862 Battle
of Secessionville near Charleston. The diary of Winfield Scott Harvey is located at the
Library of Congress in box 6 of the Edmund Settle Godfrey Papers. It begins in 1868
and unfortunately ends when Harvey's enlistment expired during September 1871 after
the sergeant had spent only six months at Yorkville.

39. Guy V. Henry, *Military Record of Civilian Appointments in the United States
Army,* vol. 1 (New York: D. Van Nostrand, 1873); *Records of Living Officers of the United
States Army* (Philadelphia: Lewis R. Hamersly, 1884); George W. Cullum, *Biographical
Register of the Officers and Graduates of the United States Military Academy from 1802 to
1867: Revised Edition with a Supplement Continuing the Register of Graduates to January
1, 1879* (New York: James Miller, 1879). Details of war-time service and speculation
about personality conflicts among Seventh Cavalry officers are plentiful within the
vast literature on Custer's Last Stand.

40. While at Spartanburg, McIntosh began using a notebook to record financial
transactions. The entries occasionally make reference to events in his life, but the document hardly qualifies as a diary. The notebook was discovered on the Little Bighorn

battlefield where McIntosh was killed. The original was stolen and destroyed. Fortunately, Daniel O. Magnussen had already made a transcript. The University of Denver Library, Colorado, has a copy.

41. The papers of Edward Settle Godfrey are located at the Library of Congress.

42. An entry in the Harvey diary dated June 1, 1871, details Aspinwall's injuries, as does an article in the *Yorkville Enquirer* for July 6, 1871.

43. Ryan, *Ten Years with Custer,* 137.

44. Ibid., 145. The campsite at Spartanburg was at a place called "Twitty's Grove" near Henry Street.

45. Ryan, *Ten Years with Custer,* 146. Ryan had a tendency to repeat himself. He tells the same story on p. 153. The campsite at Unionville is located behind the Grace United Methodist Church.

46. Ryan, *Ten Years with Custer,* 138.

47. Marcus Reno to the Adjutant General, Department of the South, December 15, 1871, NARA RG 393, Post of Spartanburg, Letters Sent, 1871–73, vol. 1 of 2.

48. Merrill, "Report to Brigadier General Albert Terry," 88.

49. Spartanburg District Office, Federal Writers Project, interview with Edward E. Bomar Sr. titled "What Happened When 'Yankees' Came to Town," Kennedy Room, Spartanburg County Public Library, Spartanburg, S.C.

50. The statistical data were generated by the author using monthly regimental returns.

51. Merrill, "Report to Brigadier General Albert Terry," 88.

52. Ryan, *Ten Years with Custer,* 147.

53. Merrill, "Report to Brigadier General Albert Terry," 87. The *Yorkville Enquirer* expressed concerns about glanders in its issue of September 19, 1872.

54. Bomar interview.

55. Ibid.; Ryan, *Ten Years with Custer,* 147. The regimental returns include numbers of serviceable and unserviceable horses. The *Yorkville Enquirer* reported on the local effects of the epizootic in its issues of November 7, November 14, and December 12, 1872.

56. Ryan, *Ten Years with Custer,* 138–40.

57. George Armstrong Custer to Mrs. Calhoun, 1871, in Marguerite Merington, ed., *The Custer Story: The Life and Intimate Letters of General George A. Custer* (New York: Devin-Adair, 1950), 242.

58. Ryan, *Ten Years with Custer,* 140.

59. Merrill, "Report to Brigadier General Albert Terry," 87.

60. The names and dates of deaths are listed on the monthly regimental returns. Aside from a few differences in spelling, this information correlates with the deaths described in Ryan, *Ten Years with Custer,* 150–51.

61. Merrill, "Report to Brigadier General Albert Terry," 86–87.

62. The Rose Hotel in Yorkville was still standing as of 2011. Although it has been renovated, the low windowsills match the ones in photographs of the windows taken during the 1870s. A Reconstruction-era photograph of about two dozen soldiers posing

on the porch of the Rose Hotel exists. A copy is located in Arnold Shankman et al., *York County, South Carolina: Its People and Its Heritage* (Norfolk, Va.: Donning, 1983), 57.

63. Merrill, "Report to Brigadier General Albert Terry," 86–87. For the June 6, 1871, entry for his diary, Sergeant Harvey described how a private named Winkelman was drunk, jumped through the window, and lost a leg as a result.

64. Ryan, *Ten Years with Custer,* 150. According to the regimental return, Waring died on February 26, 1872.

65. According to the regimental return, Brown died on March 10, 1872.

66. *Yorkville Enquirer,* October 17, 1872.

67. Ryan, *Ten Years with Custer,* 150–51. The regimental return for that month specifically references Betzig as having caused the death.

68. The Seventh Cavalrymen buried at Rose Hill are Adolphus Cash of Troop D, who died of disease on November 9, 1871; Samuel Brown of Troop L, who died of typhoid fever on July 8, 1872; and George H. Whittimore of Troop K, who died of disease on November 10, 1872.

69. According to the regimental return, Cushman died of disease on May 25, 1871. According to local lore, none of the other churches in Unionville was willing to accept the remains and the grave was intentionally placed in an isolated part of the cemetery. During the 1950s the obelisk over Cushman's grave was renovated as a gesture of reconciliation. See Allan Charles, *Narrative History of Union County, South Carolina* (Greenville, S.C.: Press Printing, 1997), 228–29.

70. Ryan, *Ten Years with Custer,* 151–52. Either Ryan misremembered or some of the bodies were exhumed and reinterred. The present grave of Pvt. Byron Stump, a new recruit who died of disease upon his arrival in Unionville during February 1872, is at the national cemetery in Florence, South Carolina. Similarly that of Edward Myers is located at the national cemetery in Wilmington, North Carolina. His tombstone identifies him by his brevet rank of colonel.

71. Ryan, *Ten Years with Custer,* 144–45.

72. "Proceedings of a Board of Survey Convened at Yorkville, S.C., May 21, 1872," NARA RG 393, Post of Yorkville, Proceedings of Boards of Survey.

73. The statistical data were generated by the author using regimental returns.

74. Merrill, "Report to Brigadier General Albert Terry," 87.

75. Company C of the Eighteenth Infantry remained at Yorkville for several years after the Seventh Cavalry departed. See "Certified List of Stores Sold to Officers and Enlisted Men at Yorkville, S.C. in the Month of February 1875," NARA RG 393, Post of Yorkville, Miscellaneous Records.

76. Merrill, "Report to Brigadier General Albert Terry," 88.

77. Ryan, *Ten Years with Custer,* 144, 154. Many of the entries in the McIntosh diary are for money spent from these funds.

78. Merrill, "Report to Brigadier General Albert Terry," 88.

79. "Proceedings of a Board of Officers convened at Yorkville, SC, January 3, 1872," NARA RG 393, Post of Yorkville, Proceedings of Boards of Survey.

80. Ryan, *Ten Years with Custer*, 152.

81. Bomar interview.

82. Ryan, *Ten Years with Custer*, 152.

83. Merrill, "Report to Brigadier General Albert Terry," 88.

84. Major Merrill to the Assistant Adjutant General, Department of the South, October 3, 1871, NARA RG 393, Post of Yorkville, Letters Sent, vol. 1 of 4.

85. First Lt. Joseph K. Hyer to the Inspector General at Columbia, S.C., January 7, 1873, NARA RG 393, Post of Laurensville, Letters Sent, vol. 1 of 2.

86. Merrill, "Report to Brigadier General Albert Terry," 86.

87. David Cole, "Survey of U.S. Army Uniforms, Weapons, and Accoutrements," U.S. Army training guide for Army Museum System's Basic Curatorial Methods Training, 29–30, http://www.history.army.mil/html/museums/uniforms/survey.html. Accessed January 16, 2013.

88. Ryan, *Ten Years with Custer*, 158.

89. Ibid., 150–51; Merrill, "Report to Brigadier General Albert Terry," 87.

90. Capt. William Falck of the Second Infantry to "the Agent U. R. R. McCoy," February 15, 1873, NARA RG 393, Post of Spartanburg, Letters Sent, vol. 2 of 2.

91. Harvey diary, entry dated March 16, 1871.

92. Post Adjutant to First Lt. Thomas Custer, November 9, 1871, NARA RG 393, Post of Spartanburg, Letters Sent, vol. 1 of 2.

93. Ryan, *Ten Years with Custer*, 159.

94. Ryan, *Ten Years with Custer*, 159.

95. Ibid., 145.

96. Daniel Kanipe, "A New Story of Custer's Last Battle," in *Contributions to the Historical Society of Montana* (Helena, Mont.: Independent Publishing Company, 1908), 277–83; Arthur C. Unger, *Custer's First Messenger!? Debunking the Story of Sergeant Daniel A. Kanipe* (El Segundo, Calif.: Upton and Sons, 2011); Richard Federici, "Sgt. Daniel Kanipe: McDowell County's Big Hero at Little Bighorn," http://www.mohicanpress.com/battles/ba04004.html. Accessed January 16, 2013.

97. Ryan, *Ten Years with Custer*, 145.

98. Manuscript Census Return for 1870, South Carolina, Darlington County, Darlington Township, p. 17, Series T9, Roll 1227, p. 52.

99. Merrill, "Report to Brigadier General Albert Terry," 86.

100. Ryan, *Ten Years with Custer*, 161.

101. Ibid., 144.

102. Ibid., 148–50.

103. Ibid., 150. The *Yorkville Enquirer* reported about the fire in its March 21, 1872, issue.

104. *Yorkville Enquirer*, November 16, 1871.

105. Major Reno to the Assistant Adjutant, Department of the South, November 14, 1871, NARA RG 393, Post of Spartanburg, Letters Sent, vol. 1 of 2.

106. Merrill, "Report to Brigadier General Albert Terry," 86.

107. Ryan, *Ten Years with Custer*, 156.

108. Ibid., 164.

109. Ibid., 137, 143; Harvey diary, entries for March 14, March 22, and March 23, 1871.

110. Merrill, "Report to Brigadier General Albert Terry," 87.

111. Ryan, *Ten Years with Custer*, 152–53.

112. Ibid., 137.

113. Sefton, *United States Army and Reconstruction*, 225; Harvey diary, entry for July 4, 1871.

114. Ryan, *Ten Years with Custer*, 146.

115. Harvey diary, entry for July 2, 1871. The men court-martialed were First Sgt. A. D. Johnson and Pvt. William Logue of Company K.

116. Bomar interview. The band likely belonged to the Eighteenth Infantry since the one for the Seventh Cavalry was stationed in Kentucky with the regimental head-quarters.

117. The U.S. Army had decided on these rather than the repeating Spencer car-bine in order to standardize ammunition with the infantry. Not until after leaving South Carolina would the men of the Seventh receive the Springfield Model 1873 rifle with the .45 caliber, copper-cartridge bullets that tended to jam and that might have contributed to the disaster in the West. The .44 caliber pistol did not yet use metal cartridges. See Stubbs and Connor, *Armor-Cavalry*, 24, 25. Ryan, *Ten Years with Custer*, 151 and 156, indicates that Ryan had a sharps carbine and a .44 caliber pistol.

118. Phillip Saint George Cooke, *Cavalry Tactics: Regulations for the Instructions, Formations, and Movements of the Cavalry of the Army and Volunteers of the United States* (Philadelphia: J. P. Lippincott, 1862). This manual remained in use for many years after the end of the Civil War.

119. Ryan, *Ten Years with Custer*, 138, 162.

120. First Lt. Joseph K. Hyer to the Inspector General at Columbia, S.C., January 7, 1873, NARA RG 393, Post of Laurensville, Letters Sent, vol. 1 of 2.

121. Merrill, "Report to Brigadier General Albert Terry," 87.

122. Harvey diary, entries for March 26, June 5, June 11, and June 12, 1871.

123. Trelease, *White Terror*, 342. Klansmen found ready sanctuary in the Tarheel State, especially the counties of Rutherford, Cleveland, Gaston, and Lincoln. Linked by the valleys of the Broad and Catawba Rivers, these areas shared a common cultural heritage as well as economic and social ties to the South Carolina upcountry. The best example of this linkage is the novelist Thomas Dixon Jr., whose book and play *The Clansman* became the basis for the film *Birth of a Nation*. Dixon grew up in Cleveland County near the town of Shelby. His father was a Baptist minister who belonged to the Ku Klux Klan. The younger Dixon would later dedicate *The Clansman* to his Uncle Leroy McAfee, who was a Klan leader in Yorkville. See Raymond A. Cook, *Thomas Dixon* (New York: Twain, 1974), 23–24.

124. Martinez, *Carpetbaggers, Cavalry, and the Ku Klux Klan*, 137.

125. Major Reno to Major J. H. Taylor, Assistant Adjutant, Department of the South, August 7, 1871, NARA RG 393, Post of Spartanburg, Letters Sent, vol. 1 of 2.

126. Major Reno to Major J. H. Taylor, Assistant Adjutant, Department of the South, October 15, 1871, NARA RG 393, Post of Spartanburg, Letters Sent, vol. 1 of 2.

127. Harvey diary, entries for March 21, March 23, March 25, March 27, May 4, June 5, June 15, and June 20, 1871.

128. The counties were Chester, Chesterfield, Fairfield, Lancaster, Laurens, Newberry, Spartanburg, Union, and York. With the exception of the second, all of these were in the upcountry. See Martinez, *Carpetbaggers, Cavalry, and the Ku Klux Klan*, 139–41.

129. Martinez, *Carpetbaggers, Cavalry, and the Ku Klux Klan*, 147–48. The first order misidentified Union County as Marion County. The error was quickly corrected.

130. Merrill, "Report to Brigadier General Albert Terry," 89.

131. U.S. Army Field Manuel 3–24.2, *Tactics in Counterinsurgency*, April 2009. The "cordon and search" technique used against the Ku Klux Klan differed from those used by the Seventh Cavalry during its most famous battles. At the Washita River in 1868, troopers of the regiment divided into smaller elements, surrounded their opponents during the night, and made simultaneous assaults from multiple angles at daylight. They employed similar tactics with less success at the 1876 Battle of Little Bighorn. See Ryan, *Ten Years with Custer*, 75, 289–90; and Elizabeth B. Custer, *Following the Guidon* (New York: Harper & Brothers, 1890), 39–40.

132. Ryan, *Ten Years with Custer*, 154. A well-used copy of one of the lists has been preserved in NARA, RG 393, Post of Yorkville, Miscellaneous Records.

133. Ryan, *Ten Years with Custer*, 146.

134. Ibid., 155, 156–57.

135. Ibid., 159.

136. Ibid., 157.

137. Ibid., 157, 159–60, 162.

138. Ibid., 148.

139. Ibid., 155.

140. Zuczek, *State of Rebellion*, 122.

141. Ryan, *Ten Years with Custer*, 164.

142. *Report of the Secretary of War*, 1873, 70. The regimental and post returns provide precise dates on which the various units departed and arrived. Six other companies from the Eighteenth manned the garrison at Columbia.

143. *Report of the Secretary of War*, 1876, 50–53, 61–63, 68, 79–81; Clarence C. Clendenen, "President Hayes' 'Withdrawal' of the Troops: An Enduring Myth," *South Carolina Historical Magazine* 70, no. 4 (October 1969): 240–50; Zuczek, *State of Rebellion*, 159–201.

"At present we have no school at all which is truly unfortunate"

Freedmen and Schools in Abbeville County, 1865–1875

Katherine D. Cann

The freedmen's eagerness for education after emancipation has become almost legendary; even the poorest willingly gave time, effort, and a share of their meager resources to the cause of education. This desire generated consternation among white people who struggled to adjust to the realities of the post–Civil War South. Was an education really necessary for freedmen? If so, how would such schools be financed? Who would provide leadership and direction? White and black leaders throughout the South answered these thorny questions and others in various ways. Abbeville County, South Carolina, once a hotbed of secessionism, provides a case study of the successes and failures of educating the freedmen in the chaotic and divisive era of Reconstruction.

Abbeville County in the nineteenth century stretched for miles along the banks of the Savannah and Saluda Rivers at the southeastern fringe of the upcountry. Small rivers, streams, and creeks flowing through the county contributed to the alluvial soil that is richer than the red clay so characteristic of much of the South Carolina upcountry. The first settlers included Scots-Irish Presbyterians and French Huguenots, who embraced the Patriot cause during the American Revolution. Idealistic and religious Presbyterians shaped a Utopian-style community in Cokesbury. Early in the century, before his emergence as a controversial national figure, John C. Calhoun practiced law in an office on Abbeville's town square.

French and German settlers came to Abbeville County hoping to make wine and produce silk, but cotton became the basis for the county's nineteenth-century wealth and aristocratic sensitivities. By 1859 two-thirds of white families owned slaves, who comprised two-thirds of the county's population. Near Calhoun's former law office is Secession Hill, where prominent white people voted to secede a month before the historic December 20, 1860, convention in Charleston. Five years later, as the Confederate death knell tolled, President Jefferson Davis and select cabinet members met for the last time near Secession Hill, at the home of Armistead Burke, before they fled south from Richmond. At the meeting, the Confederate leaders agreed to give up the cause.[1]

Robert E. Lee's surrender at Appomattox in April 1865 unleashed a storm of political and social disruption, violence, and uncertainty. Southerners struggled to make order out of chaos and to find their way in what seemed to be an alien landscape. The problems of the era as described by historians were legion. For the four million freed men and women of African descent, the new order brought both fear and hope. As the Reconstruction era began, many white people responded to the uncertainty by lashing out against the most vulnerable of southerners—the newly freed slaves.

During 1866 episodes of violence pitting white against black rocked Abbeville County. United States Lt. Col. John Devereaux, stationed at Hamburg on the Savannah River, wrote to his superiors that on most days freedmen appeared in his office claiming that "they are being driven off" by threatening and intimidating white people. Elbert MacAdams, a freedman, died in May when a white gang shot him and slit his throat.[2] In July, Reuben Golding, known as a desperate ruffian who was "much dreaded by people in the neighborhood," left Abbeville heavily armed and planning to go to Cokesbury to "shoot a Negro." His victim, A. Payton, had never been a slave and had lived in Canada and New York during the war. He had come home to South Carolina once the war was over, and local residents described him as a man of good character.[3] Other violent incidents against African Americans abounded during the period: a child removed from his home and forced to work for a white man; freedmen whipped by the Ku Klux Klan; freedmen intimidated when they attempted to cast ballots; a black carpetbagger and state senator murdered by the Klan.[4] In most cases the perpetrators were "unknown." Local officials made little, if any, attempt to ascertain the guilty parties, who never faced any type of judgment. W. F. DeKnight, a Freedmen's Bureau agent in Abbeville, noted that "the freedmen are safe nowhere," and their situation "is worse than bondage."[5]

The brutality against the freedmen stood in marked contrast to the upcounty's reputation as a place of education and refinement, home to attorneys and planters, and the location of several schools of note. Early in the century the renowned architect Robert Mills described Abbeville as "the original seat of learning in the upper country," where several educational options were available to white people. For example, Presbyterians, Methodists, and the Masons maintained schools at Cokesbury. At Due West the Associate Reformed Presbyterian Church established Erskine, the first church-related college in South Carolina. Willington Academy, sometimes considered "the most prestigious preparatory school in antebellum South Carolina," was by far the best-known educational institution in Abbeville County. Its reputation for preparing students to enter colleges such as Yale and Princeton attracted students from many parts of the country. John C. Calhoun and other prominent antebellum South Carolinians—Hugh Swinton Legare, James L. Pettigru, and George McDuffie— studied under Moses Waddel, the academy's founder. A casualty of the Civil War, Willington Academy closed in 1861.[6]

In short, the county had a distinguished educational heritage, and after the Civil War its white leadership generally accepted the notion of educating the freedmen and sometimes encouraged it. Better-educated white people generally frowned on "ignorant whites who will not try to educate themselves or their children [and] which endeavor to throw obstacles in the way of the education of the blacks." However, as Joel Williamson documents in *After Slavery*, their support of black schools rarely extended beyond providing minimal basic education.[7]

In a county such as Abbeville, where the ratio of freedman to white was 2:1, adjusting to a new social, economic, and political order raised perplexing questions, including the proper structure for educating the freedmen. Although white citizens of Abbeville County may have reluctantly accepted the inevitability of education for African Americans, their opinions on the topic varied. F. A. Conner, a respected white educator who lived near Cokesbury, echoed the views of other leading white southerners: "[We] wish to see [the freedmen] acquire property and education, and become happy and contented in their enjoyment."[8] Early in 1866 an anonymous resident of Due West suggested in a letter to the editor of the *Abbeville Press* that a comprehensive curriculum based on reading, writing, and the principles of arithmetic would ensure a consistent labor supply in the future. The freedmen had served the white people faithfully, he declared, and "they must do the principle part of the labor for years to come. If they know that we are trying to do something for their children in the way of education . . . they will labor the more assiduously, and pleasantly, and properly." Furthermore the writer believed that an educated black population would be better prepared to take Christianity to the "heathens" should the freedmen return to Africa, an idea that had gained some popularity.[9]

White people also viewed education as a deterrent to crime. Mary Elizabeth Moragne, a white schoolmistress near Little River, complained that there were "many children, once useful, now troublesome and noisy vagrants." Lester Walker, a Freedmen's Bureau agent who lived in the town of Abbeville, reported "200 children in this place, who are wandering around the streets with apparently nothing to do, and unless measures are so taken to enlighten them, they will be fed into crime and will have to suffer the consequences."[10]

African Americans were committed to education as a tool for racial uplift. A number of historians have found that slaves, for whom education was often forbidden, exhibited the desire to learn. James P. Anderson's work on education for black people in the South shows that the educational aspirations that began among the slaves continued in freedom. Even the most impoverished willingly sacrificed to obtain education for themselves and their children.[11] A delegate to the South Carolina Colored People's Convention in 1866 affirmed the importance of education to the freedmen's future: "Whereas, Knowledge is power, and an educated and intelligent people can neither be held in nor reduced to slavery, we will insist upon the establishment of good schools for the thorough education of our children."[12] The plaintive observation to Gov. Robert K. Scott that "at present we have no school at all which is truly unfortunate" exemplified the plight of the freedmen—a willingness to learn hampered by scant resources.[13]

Some of the early impetus for educating the freed people came from the federal government. Cognizant of the freedmen's almost legendary zeal for learning—and aware that their future depended on it—the United States government took steps to provide educational opportunities. Congress established the Bureau of Refugees, Freedmen, and Abandoned Lands in 1865 to aid the former slaves in the transition to freedom by acting on their behalf in the former Confederate states. The bureau attempted to bring some order to the confusion of the era by creating new social and economic relationships and establishing schools.

The Freedmen's Bureau, though widely disliked by white people, offered assistance in negotiating labor contracts, buying land, and determining fair wages. The bureau's work was invaluable to former slaves seeking a modicum of economic independence and stability. However, as W. E. B. DuBois noted, its most significant contribution to the freedmen's future was bringing to public attention the "planting of free schools among the Negroes, and the idea of free elementary education among all classes in the South."[14]

The Freedmen's Bureau's educational efforts, hampered by inconsistent regulations, changing attitudes, high staff turnovers, and lack of money, did not begin in Abbeville County until late 1867, and within a year its educational activity in the county had been significantly curtailed. Reuben Tomlinson, committed to reforming education in South Carolina, served as state superintendent of education under the bureau's auspices. He administered a haphazard organization over which he had little influence. Although some schools could be found in the upcountry, most of the fifty-six bureau schools in South Carolina were near the coast. The Freedmen's Bureau offered advice, located land for school buildings and sometimes built them, provided transportation for teachers, and collected information and statistics.[15]

Corruption among local Freedmen's Bureau employees in Abbeville County impeded the organization's effectiveness. In October 1867 the *Abbeville Press* reported that freedmen supported an educational subscription drive in Abbeville initiated by the local bureau agent C. L. Allen and urged white people to contribute to the fund to encourage racial harmony. Similar subscription drives occurred in the townships of Lowndesville, Greenwood, and Due West. Although a "considerable amount" reportedly was pledged, poverty assured that little would actually be collected.

Unfortunately for the freedmen, Allen proved to be a scoundrel who not only failed to establish a school but also damaged the bureau's local prestige when he left Abbeville for "parts unknown," taking the subscription money with him. His conduct embarrassed the Freedmen's Bureau, and Lester Walker, the agent to whom Allen had reported, remarked that only the exemplary behavior of a successor could restore respect for the Freedman's Bureau and its programs.[16]

Despite Allen's dishonesty, by April 1868 the bureau was operating a school in Abbeville. Walker's confident report on this school claimed that 270 pupils had enrolled. Agency officials expected the number to grow. The school building was in good repair. Equipped with books and a teacher, the school exceeded the bureau's "most sanguine expectations." Another bureau agent reported several small schools scattered throughout the county, mostly organized by locals and staffed by black teachers. Financial hardship, he thought, was the only obstacle to more schools established by the freedmen.[17]

W. F. DeKnight replaced C. L. Allen as the Freedmen's Bureau agent in Abbeville County and presented a much gloomier picture of the education system. He found that a purported night school never existed and that the day school desperately needed external financial support since the teacher could not collect the ten-cents-per-week tuition fee per student. The teacher, reportedly on the verge of "starvation," was all set to leave the school. DeKnight observed that one school near Abbeville was "being taught, as best it can be, by a colored man." The school at Harrisburg had neither books nor a teacher. At Due West a school building erected by local freedmen stood empty for lack of a teacher. Of four schools previously reported in the county, DeKnight could find no trace. He strongly recommended that the bureau establish another school and send teachers to the area, for he believed that a large number of freedmen would attend.

DeKnight found the general circumstances of the freedmen in the county disturbing. Their "moral and social status," he noted, "is far lower than I have witnessed it in many another locality, and everything possible should be done to lift them up out of the horrible and repulsive slough of degradation into which they have been left by the foul crime of slavery." The white people who seemed to support the freedmen's schools, DeKnight asserted, did so to maintain "forever their supreme control over [the freedmen and] would rather plunge them still deeper, [into oppression] than to extend a finger of help to rescue them." DeKnight was unpopular in Abbeville and worried that he might be "shot down by some drunken, if not by a sober scoundrel, even here in my own office." An observer at Calhoun's Mill, where the black population exceeded that of the white people by more than three to one, corroborated DeKnight's opinion of the white attitude. "The white people are much opposed to the enlightenment of the Colored Folk."[18]

Even before the Freedmen's Bureau embarked on its educational mission, many freedmen had begun to establish schools on their own initiative, an on-going process. Soon after the events at Fort Sumter in 1861, federal troops began occupying South Carolina's sea islands, home to thousands of slaves. There northern aid societies established schools, some of which survived the arduous Reconstruction process. In the upcountry, where the federal troop presence was smaller and came later, the situation was different. Such was the case in Abbeville County, where some freedmen quickly began to create educational opportunities. Heather Andrea Williams, in *Self-Taught: African-American Education in Slavery and Freedom,* uses a variety of primary sources to illustrate the freedmen's initiative in organizing schools.[19]

In Abbeville County, historically "noted for the liberal patronage of its institutions of learning," black and white church congregations joined the educational campaign, organizing and maintaining schools. Located in rural areas with limited resources, many of these schools were short-lived. At Turkey Creek Church, white locals built the school attended exclusively by the freedmen. The most ambitious undertaking of this nature in the county was in Cokesbury, a small village with a Utopian past and a prewar reputation as an educational center. There local freedmen financially supported a well-attended school. In 1870 the African Methodist Episcopal (AME) Church selected Cokesbury as the site for a freedmen's leadership school. Soon called Payne Institute, the school, financed primarily by two thousand dollars collected in tuition fees, enrolled 132 black students when it opened in 1870. In 1880 AME officials closed the school, moved it to Columbia, and changed the name to Allen University.[20]

A group of freedmen had organized a school near Mt. Carmel by 1867. The teacher, Nelson Joiner, a mulatto, had left Abbeville early in the war. He returned to teach and gained enough stature that he represented Abbeville County at the 1868 Constitutional Convention and in the state house of representatives. To impress local white people with the skills and knowledge of his students, Joiner organized a public examination and dinner in July 1867. During the examination the pupils "gave evidence of faithful instruction both in literature and morality." O. T. Porcher, a prominent minister and teacher, spoke to the crowd "in a spirit which could not fail to disabuse their minds of any error which teaches them the Southern white man is not a true friend to them."[21]

In 1868 delegates to the South Carolina Constitutional Convention, in what is often considered the most significant achievement of Reconstruction in South Carolina, wrote a document that authorized a statewide biracial public school system. A majority of the delegates were black and clearly recognized the social and economic advantages that would accrue with educational opportunity. The new constitution took effect almost immediately. Counties received state school revenue from a two-mill property tax and a poll tax based on attendance. Locally elected school commissioners allocated state funds and had the power to levy additional taxes.[22] The new public schools raised concerns among the white population of Abbeville about the school financing method, the freedmen's capacity for learning, the fear that schools would become political forums, and the possibility of racial mixing. Upper-class white people resented the expense that would fall on their shoulders as property owners. Wild exaggerations of the cost of the system appeared in the newspapers. Benjamin F. Perry, provisional governor of South Carolina immediately after the war ended, contended that implementing and maintaining a "free school system, for the education of the Negroes" would cost one million dollars annually. Unlike the prewar method of assessing property that placed the highest rate on merchants and bankers, the new method uniformly taxed all property at full value. In addition local educational administrative bodies as well as the General Assembly could levy taxes. The white general public worried about annual tax increases, fearing that taxing property owners to educate nonproperty owners would result in "the young [black people being] brought up in idleness under the show of education." School officials, elected by universal suffrage, could tax the minority property owners who may not have been equitably represented in the tax-levying body. People suggested various schemes to raise money for the schools. One individual proposed a fifty-cent head tax on all freedmen to support the schools. The Abbeville District Board of Trustees considered a capitation tax on all parents of school-age children.[23]

The question of school finance was paramount to the upper class, but surely all white people feared that the schools would become a forum for disseminating Republican propaganda. Northern teachers were automatically suspect. Rumors of large groups of freedmen gathered in the schools filled many whites with dread. Some perceived the public exhibitions, so popular among the black schools, as opportunities for "political harangues" rather than occasions to showcase educational improvement. In the opinion of a Due West resident, "If we refuse to take hold of this thing ourselves, it will be managed by those who have but little love for the white population of the South. . . . it will be a thousand times better that these schools should be under our own superintendence than that of strangers, whether enemies or not."[24]

White resistance to educating the freedmen began to wane as the Reconstruction process moved forward and economic and political concerns became paramount. At public meetings attended by the freedmen, local white people reportedly gave "honest advice and wise counsel" to the crowd, admonishing the freedmen "to eschew party politics, secret political leagues and all affiliation with unknown adventurers, [to exercise] the habits of industry and economy and . . . to cultivate harmonious relations with the white race." The *Abbeville Press and Banner* reported in 1871 that Bishop Richard H. Vanderhorst of the Colored Methodist Episcopal Church thought the freedmen near Chiles Cross Roads "appreciate very highly the interest their white friends have taken in their behalf." Sporadic protests against educating the freedmen occurred throughout South Carolina, but no determined effort to halt the creation of educational institutions for African Americans materialized.[25]

Former slaves in Abbeville County showed interest in the proposed system even before South Carolina voters, a majority of them freedmen, ratified the new constitution. In February 1868 a committee appointed to ascertain the degree of enthusiasm among the freedmen for both day and night schools found a number of adults and children who desired educational opportunities. The white northern overseer at a gold mine near Calhoun's Mills wrote that the freedmen there were "simple but honest. . . . They want the Gospel and secular education, but there [*sic*] extreme poverty stands in the way."[26]

Sixteen townships functioned as educational districts in the county. Black people outnumbered white people in all townships except Due West. In accordance with the new public school legislation, in 1868 Abbeville County voters elected Hutson J. Lomax, a delegate to the Constitutional Convention, as the county's first commissioner of public schools. White people of the county considered Lomax, a mulatto, a "well-behaved servant" who exhibited a "civil and respectful demeanor."[27]

By the end of 1869 at least nine public schools, most in poor condition, operated in Abbeville County. Of the three white schools, one had previously been a private school. Only 7 percent of the 314 students enrolled in the public schools were white. In the first year 4 percent of the total school-age population attended public schools. While 6 percent of the black children eligible to attend school took advantage of the new system, less than 1 percent of eligible white children did so. As county residents adjusted to the reality of public education, the figures changed significantly. By 1875, 5,387 pupils, about half the school-age population, attended the county's 154 public schools, with 71 percent of the overall student population made up of black people.[28]

Justus K. Jillson, a white Republican who had moved from Massachusetts to Kershaw County, served as South Carolina state superintendent of education throughout the Reconstruction era. He believed that "the education of *all* children of *all* classes and castes is indispensable to the highest and best welfare of the community." State law emphasized the fundamentals—alphabet, spelling, and reading and required instruction in English, United States history and government, and "good behavior." In addition to the basics, Jillson thought, art, music, and natural history should be integral elements of the curriculum. Some of the state's free schools offered more advanced subjects including mental arithmetic, geography, history, and the "higher branches," but few students of either race had the academic background to take advantage of them. In 1872–73 only 210 of the 4,481 public school students enrolled in these more advanced courses. Near the end of Reconstruction, a Greenwood citizen praised the public schools in his community for educating the students on the "broad basis of a pure and liberal education . . . .[accompanied by] a thorough uprooting and a complete revolution in the order of thinking."[29]

Although the number of public schools steadily increased after 1868, the state's strained economic condition required them to rely on tuition and contributions from private sources. While the 1868 Constitution mandated public schools, neither the Constitution nor state law offered regulations related to facilities, teachers, or supplies. Schools operated in whatever buildings were available. Many school districts failed to provide books, paper, or teachers. Near Bordeaux on the Savannah River, John Harmon allowed a black school to operate in a pine building for an annual fee of twenty-five dollars. The school's supporters in the neighborhood paid the rent. The wooden Fort Pickens School needed windows and benches. The school for white children at Lebanon Church met in a wooden building, owned by the church congregation, that had neither a chimney nor a roof.[30] The decidedly unacademic atmosphere of many schools must have made it difficult for even the most earnest pupil to learn.

To a large extent, the success or failure of education during this period depended on the quality of the teachers. The Reconstruction teaching corps, as examined in Ronald Butchart's *Schooling the Freed People,* consisted of a variety of men and women: both black and white, and native southerners and "Yankees." A few had been abolitionists, but others simply wanted jobs. Some came from the elite; others had neither status nor money. Some were well educated; others were not.[31]

Abbeville residents expressed divided opinions about teachers' qualifications. A resident of Due West argued that southern white teachers were the best choice to teach in freedmen's schools: "Many white persons teach in colored Sabbath schools and think it no disgrace, and why not in colored day schools? . . . The day is not far distant when many of our poor young men and women (and pray, who is not poor now?) would prefer to wield the birch over colored pupils than to toil in the burning sun, or stand over the washtub. Or the cooking stove." However, in some circumstances, he wrote, "black teachers could be found, who, for a very small compensation, could manage the schools for a year or two until better teachers, of the same class, could be procured."[32] At least one Abbeville County school commissioner, Thomas A. Williamson, a black man who served as a delegate to the Constitutional Convention, allegedly refused to accept any southerner, black or white, as a teacher. As time passed, more white people worried about the negative effect of northern teachers, fearing that their instruction would be political. One white resident opined in the local paper that "it is almost impossible for such teachers to avoid instilling into the minds of their pupils and their parents the bitter feelings so prevalent in the North against the South."[33]

White people in Abbeville County demanded that teachers exhibit good moral character. One group of trustees urged that school board members or prominent citizens attest to the character of all prospective teachers. To ensure their character, thought a resident of Due West, "all schools, whether taught by white or black[,] should be visited weekly by two or three judicious men of the neighborhood to see what sort of books are used, what sort of instructions are imparted, and whether the teachers are faithful or not."[34]

In 1869–70 all 12 public school teachers in Abbeville were native southerners; half of them were white and 10 were men. After 1870, in spite of the local newspaper's protestations, the number of northerners and the number of women employed as teachers increased. Of 92 teachers certified in 1873, 23 were black. The 18 women were deemed qualified to teach only grades one to three. The county commissioner's report to the state superintendent of education in 1875 showed 10 northerners and 62 women among the county's 163 teachers.[35]

The average teacher's salary of less than thirty dollars per month hardly compensated for the social opprobrium and personal danger that teachers of freedmen sometimes faced. Verbal and physical attacks on outsiders occurred more frequently than on native southerners. From the time he arrived in Abbeville, W. O. B. Hiott, a teacher at Liberty Hill School near the Savannah River, believed he was "in the land of [his] most enraged enemies." While acknowledging that many white citizens did not oppose his efforts to open a school, others were "cussing and threatening [his] certain disstruction [sic]," and he feared death at the hands of "those wretched enemies."[36] Concern for personal safety contributed to attrition among even the most dedicated and idealistic teachers.

Public celebrations continued to demonstrate students' progress. The festive occasions consisted of barbeque, music, and oratory. Often the county school commissioner, local trustees, the state superintendent of schools, or another prominent local citizen praised the students' achievements. The performance of black students in Calhoun Township prompted an onlooker to commend the participants who "generally stood a good examination in spelling and reading . . . and did credit to themselves in delivering their pieces of poetry and speeches." He observed that he had "every reason to believe that our public schools will improve."[37]

In 1872 Superintendent Jillson contended that educational success depended on the quality of local authorities and local cooperation. Although Jillson's idea

was sound, these circumstances could rarely be found. Incompetent and ignorant county school commissioners complicated the work of creating a public
school system. The Abbeville County Grand Jury indicted Thomas A. Williamson for malfeasance in office; the charge was dismissed. The grand jury also
called Williamson's successor, W. L. Presley, to appear. The presentment in February 1873 described Presley as an "honest, upright, and well-meaning official"
but noted concerns about his competence. As the jurors interpreted the law,
county school commissioners were required to qualify for first-grade teaching
and have a capacity for business. In his appearance before the jury, Presley stated
that he had attended school for only eighteen months, and when questioned
by a juror, he could not multiply 8 times 8. The grand jury's investigation also
revealed that the county board of examiners, of which Presley was a member,
had hired teachers whose moral character as well as knowledge of subject matter were questionable. The grand jury inquiry focused public attention on the
school commissioner and his office, but Presley was not removed from office.
He did not run for a second term.[38]

Many white citizens in Abbeville County were probably relieved when
J. F. C. DuPre, a white wholesaler and cotton broker, became the school commissioner in November 1874. DuPre seemed sincere in his desire to improve the
school system, and in less than a year the county grand jury found that DuPre's
office was in "very good order." The local newspaper called him "the right man
in the right place . . . [who] secured the best teachers and trustees that it was
practicable to obtain under the circumstances."[39] In a less racially charged time,
perhaps the same praise could have been given to the two black commissioners
who preceded DuPre. The election of a white commissioner may have influenced white attendance in public schools and accounted in part for the growing
number of white children who attended public school after 1875.

Complaints against the board of examiners and district trustees led the
Abbeville County Grand Jury to scrutinize the activities of trustees in several
school districts. In 1873 jurors criticized various school officials for failing to
maintain schools adequately and engaging in shady financial activities. Trustees often neglected to carry out their duties, such as enumerating school-age
children as required by state law, applying for textbooks, and holding district
meetings. Attempts to remove incompetent trustees caused friction and could
not easily be accomplished.[40]

Financial difficulties plagued the new school system from the beginning.
Superintendent Jillson, who had little authority over the public schools and
was little more than a data recorder, frequently chided the legislature for fail-
ing to fund the system adequately. The political corruption and thievery that
pervaded South Carolina during Reconstruction took its toll on the educational system. According to the historian Joel Williamson, at least one-fourth of

monies designated for South Carolina schools evaporated because of fraud and incompetence. In 1869 the superintendent recommended a minimum state appropriation of $125,000 for public schools statewide. The following year the legislature belatedly earmarked only $50,000 for the state's public schools. In 1871 the estimated minimum of state monies required by Abbeville County alone was $30,000.[41]

In his 1872 report to the General Assembly, Jillson demanded that the legislators make the free common schools "what they were intended to be, the great lever—power potent to raise the toiling masses from the darkness of ignorance up to the broad light of intelligence and usefulness." The legislature appropriated $300,000 for public schools in 1872, but none of it was dispersed. Although the value of taxable property in Abbeville was third highest in the state, the county's share of state funds, based on property tax, was relatively small and never sufficient to support the schools during the Reconstruction era.[42]

To augment the constitutionally required poll tax and property tax, the commissioners in each school district could impose an additional levy approved at an annual meeting of district voters. However, poverty and tax evasion hindered local tax collection. State law required county school commissioners to withhold the state appropriation from districts that did not adopt a local levy and redistribute their share to the districts that did. In June 1871 J. K. Jillson directed the Abbeville County district boards of trustees to seek voter approval for a tax of not more than three dollars for each child in the district between the ages of six and sixteen. Many of the voters' meetings that followed resulted in only a fifty-cent tax to be paid by each voter. The local levies for 1873 in Abbeville County varied from one to three mills per dollar of taxable property. Some districts, however, subscribed a specific sum ranging from two hundred dollars at Indian Hill to twenty-five hundred dollars at Abbeville. William Presley, the school commissioner at the time, dutifully indicated that he would withhold state appropriation for the coming year from the three districts where no tax was raised: Ninety Six, Cokesbury, and Due West.[43]

When schools reopened after the summer break in August 1874, nine of the county's sixteen school districts that failed to levy a tax that year did not receive a state appropriation. The trustees of those districts met with the county board of examiners to dispose of funds remaining from the preceding year. Subsequently trustees in two districts held meetings in their respective districts hoping to reopen the schools on schedule and retain the state funding. Voters approved a tax, and the schools opened. However, schools remained closed in the other districts.[44]

The total amount of money available to Abbeville County for school purposes in 1875 was $29,105, somewhat less than the $30,000 deemed necessary four years earlier and less than the previous year because of a decline in the number of school-age children. Local school district taxes accounted for almost half the total monies available (46 percent). The state appropriation equaled 37 percent, while the poll tax (less than $200, which was not collected) yielded 15 percent. Throughout the Reconstruction era, voters in Abbeville consistently contributed more in local taxes to education than did any other county except Charleston.[45]

Without state funds or adequate local revenue, Abbeville County state schools struggled to survive. Each year from 1869 to 1875 the state delayed forwarding the designated appropriation for Abbeville County. State law required schools to be open for nine months of the year if funds were available; they seldom were. For most of the Reconstruction era, schools in Abbeville County, as in most other South Carolina counties, were in session only about five months per year. Teachers grumbled at the state's failure to pay their low salaries and petitioned for back pay. Eventually, in 1875, the state adopted a special three-quarter mill tax to pay the back claims.[46]

Nearly all of the schools established during Reconstruction in South Carolina were primary and elementary schools. As the school population grew, the need for teacher training for black people became apparent. With a public school system in place, the benevolent societies that had given financial support to southern schools, including the American Missionary Society, expanded their work to include normal or teacher-training schools and colleges such as Hampton Normal, Agricultural and Industrial Institute in Virginia, Fisk in Nashville, and Avery Institute in Charleston. In Abbeville County the educational effort of the American Missionary Association (AMA) had lasting effects. Formed by a group of abolitionists in the mid-nineteenth century, the AMA embarked on a mission to support educating the freedmen in the post–Civil War era. The organization embraced the idea that, based on Christian principles, all Americans, regardless of race, were entitled to equal rights. The members of the association believed that "no race should be permanently dependent upon another for their own development." Education, they thought, was the key to an independent future.[47]

The AMA work began in Abbeville County in 1872, when the association assumed authority over a privately organized freedmen's school in the village of Greenwood. The story of this school, started by an idealistic young minister and a group of local black people, illustrates some of the challenges facing those who sought to bring education to the freedmen during Reconstruction. In November 1871 a theology student, C. A. Young, gave up a scholarship to Harvard Divinity School and, dedicated to teaching the freedmen, paid his own expenses to move south. With the backing of the local black community in the town of Greenwood, Young opened a school in a "pleasant . . . somewhat out of repair brick building" that was also used by the neighborhood Baptist congregation. The site had been the Hodges Institute, a Baptist boys' school founded in 1846. Two of the new school's trustees were black; the third was a white man.

Young faced much frustration as he attempted to get the school under way. Several squatter families on the grounds and in the building had damaged the property. The head of one of the squatter families was reportedly "a tolerably clever old man, but his grown-up sons who go in with him are noted as the worst of men. The old man could not get a house in the village simply because he had such a bad family." Young and some of the neighbors apparently persuaded the squatters to leave. To raise funds, Young rented out some of the property and intended to use the annual rent, fifty-five dollars in cash, to make repairs. The idealistic Young accepted only a small salary, thinking that "the People do not feel able to do but very little for the school." By the end of January 1872 about ninety students had enrolled in the school, which enforced "strict, military" discipline, but financial problems persisted. Young found collecting the rent for the land difficult, and many students could not pay even a modest tuition.[48]

Various benevolent groups showed interest in adopting the little freedmen's school. The AMA, a strong contender, was favored by Young, who hoped that the association would keep the institution "out of the hands of those who would use it for political purposes." The American Missionary Association took responsibility for the school in May 1872, and by fall it was known as Brewer School, named for Josiah Brewer, a missionary to Africa. The schoolroom had no heating source and contained only a "few backless benches." Students who were able paid a nominal fee, and the AMA began to make repairs that included painting, replacing broken windowpanes, erecting and repairing fences, rebuilding steps, and installing a new roof.

The school's success encouraged its board of trustees to endorse an AMA proposal to establish a "school of higher grade," and Brewer became a normal school in January 1873. However, it offered instruction only in the primary and intermediate grades. Rumors that the AMA sought only to "make money out of the people" did not seem to cause irreparable damage to the association's educational effort in the county; some students walked several miles to attend school. Still, enrollment declined from thirty in January to twenty-three in June. Most of those who left school were over sixteen, a pattern common in rural areas where spring planting required the labor of young men and women. Public exercises preceded the summer vacation and "delighted" the audience. The students' performance assured that the school would reopen in the fall.[49]

At Brewer, as in schools across the rest of the South, enrollment was erratic, and the school did not operate every day. Students left in the spring and fall for the planting and harvesting seasons. Money was always a problem. The low price of cotton made finding a tenant for the acreage difficult. Inevitably,

Brewer lost students to the public schools, and possibly to Payne Institute. By 1873 the AMA teacher lamented the lack of a "school worthy of the name" in the area and observed that "little interest is felt in education by either black or white in this part of the state." Some of the students left, he said, because "their money gave out and they were obliged to return to their home and labor."[50]

In addition to the school's standard curriculum, a campus chapel offered daily devotions, with a goal of imbuing Brewer students with Christian principles and moral guidance. A temperance society discouraged alcohol consumption in hopes that "God will bless us in our endeavors to promote the cause of temperance and virtue among this people."[51]

The school struggled in 1875–76 when the economic situation was worse than it had been since the war. Money was scarce. Prices were high, and merchants would trade only in cash. Students came to Brewer from all parts of Abbeville County and from neighboring counties as well. The teacher hesitated to turn them away, even when they could not pay even a nominal tuition. Enrollment decreased, and rumors suggested that the school would close. By fall of 1876, as the election approached, the teacher reported that the students had "nothing to pay with. The whites give little or nothing for getting their cotton picked out and they are giving work only to those who pledge to vote with them."[52]

J. D. Backenstose, the AMA teacher who succeeded Young, organized a Sabbath school that was more successful than the regular school. In its first month, five teachers taught forty pupils. As enrollment in the regular school decreased, the number of pupils in the Sabbath school increased.[53] For those who were forced to give up school, the Sabbath school offered a substitute and enabled students obliged to work in the fields to have some learning experience. After Reconstruction the AMA continued to support Brewer Normal School, and while it was not always prosperous, it did endure.

In Abbeville County the question of racial separation did not seem of great importance until late in the Reconstruction era. The possibility of racially mixed schools was rarely, if at all, acknowledged by most white people. Even those who publicly advocated a state educational system supported only racially separated institutions. The public school calendar, lasting from February to November, virtually excluded farmers, the occupation of most freedmen, and could be regarded as an attempt to perpetually bar many of their children from the public school system.[54] The freedmen were far more concerned with obtaining an education than attending mixed schools.

Gov. Robert K. Scott urged the General Assembly to provide at least two schools in each school district—one black, the other white. "I deem this separation of the two races in the public schools a matter of the greatest importance to all classes of our people." The long-term success of the public school system, the governor thought, depended on racial segregation.[55]

A public school commissioner in Edgefield County, bordering Abbeville County, echoed the governor's sentiments. He noted that black people were "universally in favor of separate schools" and recommended that fifty white and fifty black schools be established in each county. At least one of the Abbeville County school commissioners, William Presley, endorsed the conclusion reached by the state school board that "public sentiment was not yet ripe 'for mixed schools.'" In 1874 the *Press and Banner* printed an article from the *New York Times,* described as "the leading organ of the Republican Party." The article, which pointed out that mixed schools would endanger public education, proved to the white people of Abbeville that even those who professed to be the freedmen's best friends and most ardent supporters did not accept the idea of racial mixing.

In 1875 the trustees of Lethe School, a state-supported school for underprivileged white children in Abbeville County, considered whether or not to admit black students. The five-man board, two of whom were black, adopted a resolution that "mixed schools should be avoided . . . it is the judgment of the Board that it could never have been contemplated by [the founder] Dr. John de la Howe that the manual school provided for by his will should ever be a mixed institution."[56]

Before 1873 less than one-half the white school-age population patronized the public schools. However, as white people became accustomed to the idea of publicly supported education, they began to take advantage of the opportunities that the public schools offered. At the end of Reconstruction the number of public schools had grown to 130. School districts owned about one-fourth of the schools and rented some others. Other people owned 81 schools. The total students enrolled had reached 4,411, about two-thirds of them black.[57]

While the creation of educational opportunities for black citizens marked the Reconstruction era, those opportunities soon were curtailed. Federal educational activities were of short duration. Many of the benevolent societies lost interest. The triumph of the Redeemers in the 1876 election assured that the hopes of those who supported even a modicum of education for the freedmen would be dashed. The public school system for which many had seemed so hopeful in 1868 became rigidly segregated. Reduced state funding for the black schools ensured that for many, educational progress was agonizingly slow. Between 1880 and 1895 the state appropriation per black student decreased about 60 percent, and the segregated schools were deficient by almost any measure.

During Reconstruction a number of entities had offered a haphazard, underfunded school system. In addition to private schools organized by the freedmen and churches, the work of the Freedmen's Bureau and charitable organizations established a solid foundation upon which a public school system could be built. In the decades after Reconstruction, the public schools became the mainstay for all children in Abbeville County who wanted an education.

Notes

1. Walter Edgar, ed., *The South Carolina Encyclopedia* (Columbia: University of South Carolina Press, 2006), 1. Abbeville County in 2011 was much smaller as it lost land in the late nineteenth and early twentieth centuries when the General Assembly created Greenwood and McCormick Counties.

2. See www.freedmensbureau.com, /SC/SC2.html (accessed October 29, 2010); Records of the Assistant Commissioner for the State of South Carolina Bureau of Refugees, Freedmen, and Abandoned Lands, 1865–70, National Archives Microfilm Publication M869, Roll 34, "Reports of Murders and Outrages."

3. Records of the Freedmen's Bureau, "Reports of Murders and Outrages"; "Reports of Conditions and Operations," July 1865–December 1866.

4. Ibid.; Peggy Lamson, *The Glorious Failure: Black Congressman Robert Brown Elliott and the Reconstruction in South Carolina* (New York: W. W. Norton, 1974), 84.

5. Elizabeth Rauh Bethel, *Promiseland: A Century of Life in a Negro Community* (Philadelphia: Temple University Press, 1981), 276.

6. Edgar, *South Carolina Encyclopedia*, 2, 309, 1032–33, Robert Mills quoted on 2.

7. Martin Abbott, *The Freedmen's Bureau in South Carolina, 1865–1872* (Chapel Hill: University of North Carolina Press, 1967), 94; Joel R. Williamson, *After Slavery: The Negro in South Carolina during Reconstruction, 1861–1877* (Chapel Hill: University of North Carolina Press, 1965), 214; L. Walker to Maj. H. Neide, April 6, 1868, and L. Walker to Bvt. Maj. Edwin Deane, November 5, 1867, Records of the Freedmen's Bureau.

8. F. A. Conner, quoted in *Abbeville Press,* January 31, 1868. In 1869 the name of the local newspaper changed to the *Press and Banner.*

9. *Abbeville Press,* March 16, 1866.

10. Mary Elizabeth Moragne, unpub. typescript diary, 1867, South Caroliniana Library, University of South Carolina, Columbia; L. Walker to Bvt. Maj. Edwin L. Deane, November 5, 1867, Records of the Freedmen's Bureau.

11. James P. Anderson, *The Education of Blacks in the South, 1860–1935* (Chapel Hill: University of North Carolina Press, 1988), 9ff.; Alrutheus Ambus Taylor, *The Negro in South Carolina during Reconstruction* (Washington, D.C.: Association for the Study of Negro Life and History, 1924), 100; Henry Allen Bullock, *A History of Negro Education in the South from 1619 to the Present* (Cambridge, Mass.: Harvard University Press, 1967), 27.

12. Unidentified, quoted in Heather Andrea Williams, *Self-Taught: African American Education in Slavery and Freedom* (Chapel Hill: University of North Carolina Press, 2003), 78.

13. Samuel Johnson et al. to Gov. Robert K. Scott, August 12, 1868, Governor Robert K. Scott Papers, South Carolina Department of Archives and History, Columbia (the latter is hereafter cited as SCDAH).

14. W. E. B. DuBois, "The Freedmen's Bureau," 362, www.freedmensbureau.com (accessed January 23, 2011); Walter Edgar, *South Carolina: A History* (Columbia: University of South Carolina Press, 1998), 396.

15. Richard Zuczek, *State of Rebellion: Reconstruction in South Carolina* (Columbia: University of South Carolina Press, 1996), 273–75; Ronald E. Butchart, *Schooling the Freed People: Teaching, Learning, and the Struggle for Black Freedom, 1861–1876* (Chapel Hill: University of North Carolina Press, 2010), 31; Abbott, *Freedmen's Bureau in South Carolina,* 21; Williamson, *After Slavery,* 211.

16. Capt. C. R. Becker to Bvt. Maj. Edwin L. Deane, September 25, 1867, December 6, 1867, L. Walker to Maj. H. Neide, March 12, 1868, Records of the Freedmen's Bureau; *Abbeville Press,* October 25, 1867, January 24, 1868.

17. L. Walker to Maj. H. Neide, April 6, 1868, Records of the Freedmen's Bureau; Richard Taylor to Maj. H. Neide, May 9, 1868, Records of the American Missionary Association, microfilm mss., South Caroliniana Library, University of South Carolina, Columbia (hereafter cited as AMA Records).

18. Richard Taylor to Maj. H. Neide, May 9, 1868, and W. F. DeKnight to First Lt. William Stone, November 30, 1868, Records of the Freedmen's Bureau; Richard Taylor to "Dear Brother," February 14, 1868, AMA Records.

19. Williams, *Self-Taught,* 67–70ff.

Abbeville Press, September 7, 1865; Paul Knox, "The Development of Education in Abbeville County, South Carolina" (master's thesis, University of South Carolina, 1929); E. Don Herd Jr., *Mount Ariel–Cokesbury South Carolina: A Biography of an Upcountry Utopian Community,* vol. 3 (N.p.: privately published, 1979), 163; www .allenuniversity.edu; "Report of the State Superintendent of Education," in *Reports and Resolutions of the General Assembly of the State of South Carolina, 1869–70* (Columbia, S.C.: State Printer, 1870), 236. Hereafter cited as *Reports and Resolutions.*

21. Williams, *Self-Taught,* 80–93ff.; *Abbeville Press,* September 7, 1865, January 24, 1868; O. T. Porcher, quoted, August 2, 1867; Capt. C. R. Becker to Bvt. Maj. Edwin L. Deane, September 27, 1867, W. F. DeKnight to Maj. H. Neide, June 30, 1868, Records of the Freedmen's Bureau. Joiner had some problems with the white people of Abbeville County. Early in the war, some locals accused him of "tampering with the Negroes," forcing him to leave town. In 1868 the Ku Klux Klan chased Joiner from the county.

22. Francis B. Simkins and Robert H. Woody, *South Carolina during Reconstruction* (Chapel Hill: University of North Carolina Press, 1932), 434–36; Williamson, *After Slavery,* 219–24; Edgar, *South Carolina,* 386. South Carolina public schools operated according to temporary legislation until 1871, when the General Assembly passed more permanent regulations.

23. *Press and Banner,* October 2, 1868, March 16, 1866, March 27, 1868, November 12, 1873, November 19, 1873.

24. *Abbeville Press,* March 16, 1866; Moragne, diary, 13.

25. Abbott, *Freedmen's Bureau in South Carolina,* 93; *Abbeville Press,* August 23, 1867, Bishop Vanderhorst quoted, August 17, 1871.

26. Richard Taylor to "Dear Brother," February 14, 1868, AMA Records.

27. *Abbeville Press,* January 24, 1868

28. *Abbeville Press,* June 21, 1867, January 24, 1868; *Press and Banner,* May 1, 1872; Williamson, *After Slavery,* 224; *Reports and Resolutions,* 1869–70, 405–6, 421–22, 503,

1875–76, 460. The numbers reported by the state superintendent of education from 1867 to 1876 are not reliable and may not be accurate.

29. Lerone Bennet Jr., "South Carolina: Post Bellum Paradise for Negroes," *Ebony* 21 (January 1966): 116; *New York Times,* August 25, 1872; *Reports and Resolutions, 1872–73,* 262; *Press and Banner,* October 13, 1875.

30. Simkins and Woody, *South Carolina during Reconstruction,* 439; *Reports and Resolutions,* 1871–72, 86, 1875–76, 454; Monthly School Reports, 1870, in files of the State Superintendent of Education, SCDAH, 1870; W. O. B. Hoitt to Gov. Robert K. Scott, May 12, 1869, Scott Papers.

31. Butchart, *Schooling the Freed People,* xi and ff.

32. *Abbeville Press,* March 16, 1866.

33. Williamson, *After Slavery,* 370; Abbott, *Freedmen's Bureau in South Carolina,* 95; *Abbeville Press,* March 16, 1866. Butchart, in *Schooling the Freed People,* has found that few teachers were politically savvy enough to indoctrinate anyone they taught.

34. *Abbeville Press,* October 16, 1866; *Press and Banner,* November 1, 1873.

35. *Abbeville Press,* October 16, 1866, April 10, 1872, February 12, 1873, November 12, 1873; *Reports and Resolutions,* 1869–70, 406, 1875–76, 460; Moragne, diary, 13. For a comprehensive analysis of southern schoolteachers during Reconstruction, see Butchart, *Schooling the Freed People.*

36. W. O. B. Hiott to Robert K. Scott, May 12, 1869, Scott Papers; *Reports and Resolutions,* 1874–75, 372.

37. *Press and Banner,* July 27, August 10, 1871, August 13, 1873; Taylor, *Negro in South Carolina,* 101.

38. Abbott, *Freedmen's Bureau in South Carolina,* 90, 93; *Press and Banner,* October 20, 1870, March 6, 20, 1872, February 26, June 25, 1873.

39. *Press and Banner,* November 11, 1874; J. F. Dupree to J. K. Jillson, November 27, 1874, letters to state superintendent of schools, SCDAH. See *Reports and Resolutions* for enrollment statistics.

40. *Press and Banner,* August 13, October 22, 1873, November 3, 1875; *Reports and Resolutions,* 1875–76, 437.

41. Williamson, *After Slavery,* 266; *Reports and Resolutions,* 1869–70, 65, 1872–72, 92; Simkins and Woody, *South Carolina during Reconstruction,* 438.

42. *Reports and Resolutions, 1872–73,* 255, 273–74.

43. *Reports and Resolutions,* 1874–75, 359; *Press and Banner,* June 9, June 23, July 7, August 3, November 7, 1871, June 19, 1872, August 20, 1873; "An Act to Amend an Act Entitled 'An Act to Establish and Maintain a System of Free Common Schools for the State of South Carolina'" (hereafter cited as "An Act to Amend").

44. *Press and Banner,* June 10–August 12, 1874.

45. *Press and Banner,* April 23, 1873; *Reports and Resolutions,* 1872–73, 253–55, 74–75, 354–55, 75–76, 441.

46. Simkins and Woody, *South Carolina during Reconstruction,* 436; *Reports and Resolutions,* 1871–77; "An Act to Amend"; H. J. Lomax to Government School Commissioner, November 1868, in Teachers' Back Pay Claims, files of the state superintendent of education, SCDAH; *Press and Banner,* May 26, 1875.

47. Bullock, *History of Negro Education,* 31; Williamson, *After Slavery,* 223, 229; http://www.northbysouth.org/1998/edu/charleston/ama.htm (January 20, 2011). The American Missionary Association, a Christian organization formed in 1849, aimed to promote Christian missions both in the United States and in other parts of the world. See Bullock, *History of Negro Education,* 19.

48. C. A. Young to Rev. E. M. Cravath, January 1, 27, 1872, May 18, 28, 1872, July 15, 1872, Rev. W. B. Jones to Rev. J. D. Backus, January 12, 1872, H. Alexander to Rev. E. M. Cravath, December 16, 1871, James T. Ford to C. A. Young, April 18, 1872, L. L. Alexander to Rev. E. M. Cravath, December 16, 1871, AMA Records.

49. Allen B. Ballard, *One More Day's Journey: The Story of a Family and a People* (New York: McGraw Hill, 1984), 127; C. A. Young to E. M. Cravath, May 28, July 15, 1872, G. W. Rowe to Rev. E. M. Cravath, October 5, 1872, J. D. Backenstose to Rev. E. M. Cravath, January 16, June 30, 1873, Reports of Brewer Normal School, January–June 1872, AMA Records.

50. J. D. Backenstose to E. M. Cravath, November 28, 1872, December 13, 1873, May 2, 1872, AMA Records.

51. J. D. Backenstose to E. M. Cravath, April 5, 1875, AMA Records.

52. J. D. Backenstose to M. E.Strieby, October 31, 1876, AMA Records.

53. J. D. Backenstose to E. M. Cravath, November 13, 1872, December 6, 1872, J. D. Backenstose to M. E. Strieby, Reports of Brewer Normal School, January–June 1873, AMA Records; "Brewer Middle School," prepared by Greenwood School District 50, n.d., videocassette. Brewer became a segregated black school in 1925 when the American Missionary Association gave the property to the Greenwood School District. As of this writing, the property was still in use by Greenwood School District 50.

54. *Reports and Resolutions,* 1869–70, 48; Knox, "Development of Education in Abbeville County," 36; Williamson, *After Slavery,* 216.

55. Gov. Robert K. Scott, quoted in Williamson, *After Slavery,* 221.

56. Williamson, *After Slavery,* 222; *Abbeville Press,* July 17, 1868; *Press and Banner,* October 8, 1873, June 10, 1874, June 9, 1875.

57. *Reports and Resolutions,* 1874–75, 370, 373–74.

From Slavery to Freedom

African American Life in
Post–Civil War Spartanburg

Diane C. Vecchio

The end of the Civil War signaled a major transition in the lives of both black and white people in South Carolina and brought important changes to the economic and political structure of Spartanburg. For the nearly nine thousand Spartanburg slaves who were emancipated, freedom was met with exhilaration and trepidation. Similar to the rest of the South, white progress had been associated with white racial superiority in the upcountry, and the idea of African Americans' independence was met with hostility and despair by many white people, who reacted passionately fearing both economic competition and the elimination of their political freedoms.[1] The Civil War's outcome for black South Carolinians was a dramatic reorientation to the economic, cultural, and racial norms that had defined society since the colonial period. Armed with little more than the clothes on their backs, some freedmen and freedwomen sought jobs far away from the plantations they had grown up on, while others remained on the plantations but worked the land as free wage earners. Most black families worked the land as sharecroppers, while others eventually achieved economic independence through various forms of business enterprise. A large number of black men were employed as skilled workers, and most African American women worked as domestic servants and laundresses. Similar to those in other areas of the postbellum South, newly emancipated black people in Spartanburg created institutions that offered both spiritual and material support, particularly through the building of independent black churches and fraternal societies. More important, perhaps, African Americans established institutions of learning, which had been denied them as slaves. While black people in the upcountry struggled to adapt to a new social and economic order, their efforts were often stifled by racial violence perpetrated by the Ku Klux Klan. This chapter examines the experience of African Americans in Spartanburg, the county seat and the second-largest town in the upcountry, as they moved from slavery to freedom following the Civil War.

Spartanburg had its beginnings as a county in the first sessions of the post–Revolutionary War state legislature on January 1, 1782. The growth of the newly designated courthouse village of Spartanburgh (as it was spelled then) gauged in the first official United States census of 1790 showed that Spartan County's population was 8,800. Of that number 7,913 were white, 860 were slaves, and 27 were listed as free persons, not white. While fewer than 200 of the district's 1,204 households owned even a single slave, slavery had nonetheless been established early in the upcountry's history.[2]

In the early years of the county's development, slaves worked the various plantations in Spartanburg District. B. B. Foster owned forty-three slaves, who worked his cotton plantation near Glenn Springs; other slaves picked cotton on Thomas Williamson's plantation in Woodruff, where a splendid, Georgian-style home built in 1793 (now known as the Nicholls-Crook Plantation House) presided over one thousand acres.[3] Slaves were also an important source of labor at Walnut Grove Plantation,[4] located in south Spartanburg County, as well as the Price House in Woodruff, where twenty-eight slaves worked the two-thousand-acre plantation. Thomas Price, one of the county's earliest entrepreneurs, operated a store and post office located next to his house, and in addition he kept a "house of publick entertainment" that provided food, drink, and lodging to stagecoach travelers passing through the area.[5] The Glenn Springs Hotel, built in 1815 and enlarged in 1838, was a fashionable upcountry resort frequented by the likes of John C. Calhoun, several respected judges, and a host of other elected South Carolina officials; there slaves were used to maintain the hotel and the outlying cabins, prepare the meals, transport the guests from the railroad to the hotel, and serve the visitors who came from the lowcountry to escape the stifling summer heat.[6]

By 1825 the population of Spartanburg had increased to 13,665 while the number of slaves had increased almost 400 percent, from 866 to 3,308. The great increase in the number of slaves was in part a result of the increased number of acres planted in cotton, a labor-intensive crop.[7] Spartanburg was situated between the rich, red-clay soil south of town that permitted cotton agriculture (the only marketable crop for Spartanburg farmers) along with a variety of food crops. To the north, however, "gray soil scattered with small stones restricted farming to the principal provision crops of corn, wheat, and oats."[8] While most Spartanburg slaves worked on antebellum plantations where cotton was harvested, many rural slaves worked on small to mid-sized farms. In 1860 David Golightly Harris owned ten slaves and farmed one hundred acres in the Fair Forest area, about eight miles southeast of Spartanburg village, where he produced a small amount of cotton but raised mostly corn, wheat, and oats.[9] Grains and cereals dominated Spartanburg's agricultural production, and most local residents were white yeoman farmers.

Within Spartanburg village there was a growing professional class of lawyers, merchants, industrialists, and entrepreneurial farmers who purchased slaves to work primarily as house servants, such as Nina Scott, who was "owned" by Dr. Shipp, a professor at Wofford and future president of the college,[10] and fifty-six-year-old Nancy, a slave woman purchased in 1857 by another Wofford professor, James Carlisle.[11] Jimmy Johnson, his mother, and his sister were sold to Dr. Lionel Kennedy and made their home in the doctor's backyard. According to the *Spartanburg Herald* on the occasion of Johnson's death, "As soon as he was old enough, upon him was bestowed the proud distinction of driving his 'Master' to call on his patients."[12]

There were far fewer slaves in the South Carolina upcountry than in the low-country, but nonetheless white citizens felt the need to keep Spartanburg slaves under control. The legal codes governing the black population in Spartanburg developed as early as the late seventeenth and early eighteenth centuries. In 1690 all local white residents were required to supervise closely the daily activities of the slave population. The free movement of slaves was a concern to the community since white people believed that it afforded slaves opportunities to steal, gamble, drink alcohol, and worse, devise insurrectionary schemes against their masters. In 1712 regulations were passed restricting the movement of slaves, their religious worship, their work habits, and their relationships with white people. The Great Negro Law, which went into effect in 1740, stated that "no slave could assemble for any reason without approval; no slave could conceal the whereabouts of another slave; no slave could strike a white man other than in defense of his master; no slave could rent or own his own home or plantation and no slave could be taught to read or write or receive any mental stimulation."[13]

Police patrols were instituted throughout the South, and in 1831 every white male in Spartanburg was obligated by local laws to participate in a five-man patrol unit for one month out of the year. At approximately nine each evening a bell would ring ten times. Any slave found outside after the tenth chime would be rounded up and beaten by the white patrol.[14] The local magistrates and freeholders court handled all alleged crimes involving slaves and free black people. Magistrates were appointed by the governor of the state on advice from the local district, while freeholders (landowners) constituted a jury. Often juries were drawn from a local tax list, but in practice jury members were often selected among friends and associates of the magistrate.[15]

Despite the existence of police patrols, there was one incident of Spartanburg slaves openly resisting, and this was followed by a charge of insurrection. In October 1860 John Otts discovered a slave belonging to James Braddock in his father's barn. When confronted, the slave confessed that he had been hiding away since harvest season in the woods, which were "full of armed Negros [*sic*]." He also told of runaways who were living in a cave on the Otts' plantation as well as in the woods in Union County. According to the captured slave, a major slave uprising was being planned for Christmastime. The slaves' hiding place was raided, and five slaves were accused of insurrection. The magistrate's court sentenced the captured slaves to be blindfolded and given "fifty to eighty-five lashes well laid on the naked hide."[16] Most of the time, however, the magistrate's court meted out punishment to slaves for assault, stealing, poisoning, gambling, trespassing, and receiving stolen goods from free black people.[17]

By the time of the Civil War, slavery was important in every South Carolina county, and even in the upcountry every county except Anderson had at least one slaveholder who owned a hundred or more slaves. The impact of the Civil War on South Carolina was devastating and resulted in the loss of more than twenty-three thousand lives and the financial loss of four hundred thousand slaves, for whom the war's end meant freedom.[18] With the destruction of the slave system Spartanburg planters and former slaves struggled to come to terms with a new labor market. Most Spartanburg farms had become too large to be farmed by one family. Most landowners subdivided their land into thirty-five- to fifty-acre plots and rented them to sharecropper/tenant families.[19]

In Spartanburg newly emancipated black people, similar to freedmen throughout the South, desperately wanted to own their own land, and if they could not own their own land, they wanted at least to control the land they farmed. Landowner David Golightly Harris noted that freedmen were "anxious to rent land."[20] However, with no collateral to purchase land most African Americans became locked in a practice of working the land and dividing the crops with the landlords as wage and rent, with allowances for each party's contribution to seed, stock, tools, and shelter. Sharecroppers and tenants, whether black or white, often failed to earn enough to meet loans for living expenses and fell into perpetual debt and poverty."[21] A typical sharecropping contract filed with the Freedmen's Bureau in February 1866 states that Spartanburg landowner and former master David McDowell agreed to "Furnish Wiley McDowell (a freed man) and his family good quarters one lot of cleared land and an animal and all necessary farming implements to cultivate the said land in corn and give him (Wiley McDowell) one half of the corn raised on said land. Also I am to give Wiley one half bushel of wheat per day to accompany my portable thrasher in this neighborhood. And further Wiley is to assist me in clearing and cultivating a lot of land on my farm and supposed to contain eight acres for which I am to give him one half of the corn raised on the same." The second portion of the contract stipulates that Wiley McDowell "Promises and agrees to take good care of the animal and farming implements entrusted to my care and to cultivate the lot of land first named in the above contract to the best of my ability and to comply with the above contract in each and every particular until the expiration of the same or forfeit all my claims mentioned in the above. This contract is to commence with this date and close with the year." Wiley's mark and McDowell's signature, along with signatures of two witnesses, close the contract.[22]

David Golightly Harris transitioned from slave owner to landlord after the Civil War. After experiencing difficulties with his white sharecroppers, Harris thought that some freedmen would make good tenants, and he rented portions of his property to at least fifteen black people between 1865 and 1870. His contract with a freedman named Julius stated: "[Julius] promises to build two houses, clear one field, work five hands, board his family & give me half his crop." Harris was to furnish Julius with two mules, a harness, plows, and feed grain for the mules.[23] However, less than two months later Harris upped his portion of the crop to two-thirds, explaining that he could not afford his expenses with any less."[24]

According to the southern historian Lacy Ford, four major changes in the reconstruction of the region's economy would significantly affect the upcountry in the post–Civil War era: "the shift from slave to free labor; the rapid expansion of cotton production at the expense of subsistence crops; the rise of the town merchant as the principal figure in the financing and marketing of upcountry cotton[;] and the emergence of the towns themselves as important centers of economic activity, boosterism, and industrial promotion."[25] During the late nineteenth century Spartanburg's future began to change with its postwar emergence as a railroad hub and the realization by potential investors that Spartanburg County had a ready supply of its own cotton, abundant labor that resulted from depressed agriculture, and plentiful waterpower to drive the machinery of cotton.[26] Consequently the South Carolina upcountry began a period of rapid expansion in the textile industry. The efforts of local merchants and business leaders were visible in Spartanburg and its environs as the presence of cotton mills made Spartanburg the most industrialized county in the upcountry. African Americans, however, would be excluded from the largest-growing employer in Spartanburg County, first by custom and then by law. According to the historian Philip Racine, an unwritten agreement existed among workers and owners that African Americans could work only outside the mills, mostly in the yards unloading and loading trains.[27] In 1915 South Carolina legally recognized local customs when it passed an act that forbade white and black people from working together in the same rooms.[28]

The introduction of former slaves into the free labor market economy created significant postwar economic change in the upcountry as well as emotional trauma for those who had been slaveholders. In a diary entry of September 17, 1865, Harris wrote, "Family well, Horses well, Cattle well. Hogs well & everything else are well so far as I know, if it was not for the free negroes. On their account everything is turned upside down."[29] Negotiating new social and economic relationships—between newly freed black people and whites and between black sharecroppers and white landowners—would prove challenging for both freed people and white people for decades after the Civil War.

With the Civil War over, upcountry South Carolinians tried to get on with their lives. On a personal level the war had been a traumatic time for the people of Spartanburg who lost sons, husbands, and brothers. Approximately 25 percent of Spartanburg's men were killed or wounded in the Civil War, leaving many women to run farms and families by themselves. For Spartanburg County as a whole, the Civil War and emancipation produced a substantial economic loss. In 1860 Spartanburg's combined real and personal wealth was valued at over $16 million. By 1870 this combined wealth had plummeted to $4 million. The most dramatic change occurred in the loss of personal property with the emancipation of the district's 8,240 slaves.[30] Spartanburg's total property wealth declined from $10,375,887 in 1860 to just $1,365,021 in 1870.[31] According to the historian Bruce Eelman, investments in Confederate bonds and currency served to compound the economic crash. The strains of war combined with early postwar taxation left crops depleted and farmers with little money to restore their lands.[32]

In the immediate years following the war white southerners worried about the transition of former slaves to freed people. Elizabeth Turner has written that "whites moved to control and subordinate the former slaves while freed people—under the most tenuous of circumstances and with loosely defined political rights—sought economic and legal advancement under the protection of the Union."[33] The Thirteenth Amendment had emancipated slaves, but in 1865 and 1866 southerners instituted "Black Codes" to limit their freedom.[34] At a special session of the South Carolina state legislature in September 1865 the first Black Code was passed. The historian George Tindall maintains that "this code was the first effort by the whites of the state to redefine the relations of the races under the new conditions. The nature of the black code indicates that white South Carolinians could not conceive of blacks as truly free agents in their relationship to the economy of the state."[35] While they had been granted new legal rights, black people were limited by restrictions that relegated them to an inferior caste in southern society. According to Eelman, "black codes provided limited rights for blacks while restricting employment options, outlawing interracial relationships, and establishing apprenticeship laws that created a master-servant relationship and confirmed the continuation of a racial caste in South Carolina."[36]

Spartanburg court records from 1867 reveal that all those on criminal trial were black. The charges ranged from rape to burglary, grand larceny, and petty larceny. The high incidence of property crimes reflects the changed nature of southern labor relations: "before emancipation some slaves engaged in the practice of 'taking'; that is, they appropriated extra food or clothing from their master as part of their compensation. These cases of theft were often handled on the farm or plantation, and small incidents were not seriously investigated. Under the new postwar landlord-tenant arrangements, however, property crimes were more strictly prosecuted in large part to keep freedmen under their employer's control."[37] Sentences for convicted black men were unusually stiff. Following his conviction for burglary, the Spartanburg freedman William Dawkins was sentenced to be hanged. Two other black people were convicted of larceny and sentenced to fines and ten months in the new penitentiary.[38] Spartanburg white people made it clear that new black freedoms were subject to community standards. In November 1865 David Golightly Harris noted that several black men in the district had been severely whipped and a few had been hanged. Harris observed that this extralegal violence had the "tendency to keep them in their proper bounds & make them more humble."[39]

Discrimination in the courts, extralegal violence, and a general refusal on the part of white people throughout the South to accept the basic rights of black people eventually led to the Reconstruction Act of 1867.[40] This divided the South into five military districts and demanded that southern states ratify two more amendments: the Fourteenth, guaranteeing citizenship and protection under the law to freed people; and the Fifteenth, which claimed that the right to vote could not be denied anyone on account of race, color, or previous condition of servitude.[41]

Beginning in 1867 the Union army occupied the former Confederate states, oversaw elections, and supported the Freedmen's Bureau in its efforts to set up schools and mediate between white planters and black workers. Former Confederates were disfranchised, but voting rights were extended to black men as well as northerners (Carpetbaggers) and Union supporters (scalawags). Black voters and white Republicans had been elevated by the political changes in South Carolina, while ex-Confederates' power was diminished.[42]

The reality of Reconstruction with the presence of federal troops stationed in the South, the existence of a Freedman's Bureau to protect the rights of African Americans, and the creation of a militia made up of fourteen regiments of African Americans was more than most white southerners could tolerate. On November 24, 1870, the *Carolina Spartan* announced the Ku Klux Klan's first appearance in Spartanburg. "A party of mounted men variously estimated at from 20 to 50 visited our town about 2 am on Friday last."[43] The Klan had burst into violent action in South Carolina and centered its activities in Spartanburg, Union, and York Counties. There has been a great deal of speculation about why Klan violence seemed to be confined to the upcountry regions, where the black population was generally not as heavy as it was in the black belt or coastal regions. Several historians have argued that the recourse to violence as a method of political intimidation occurred only in areas where it had a reasonable chance of success, that is, in areas where the races were evenly balanced or where white people had a majority. Another generalization about the preponderance of Klan activity in the upcountry is that it was the poorer white classes vehicle of racial prejudice there and was based largely on the fear of the black man as a social and economic rival. Yet another interpretation argues that the order was created largely for political purposes; from this perspective the fundamental cause of the violence becomes the desire of the white people to reduce black people to political subordination by preventing them from voting.[44]

The historian Allen Trelease adds that Spartanburg was strongly Democratic in its political affiliation throughout the period. He also argues the importance of scalawags in producing Klan violence in the upcountry, and there is evidence to demonstrate the existence of scalawags in Greenville, Oconee, Pickens, and Spartanburg Counties. According to Trelease, "it is quite possible that the scalawags, combined with the black vote, could have acted as a swing group in an election. All of these arguments help explain the evolution of the Klan in the upcountry, but the historian J. C. A. Stagg emphasizes that the question of land and its control in the South Carolina upcountry was instrumental in deteriorating relations between the races to such a degree that violence was condoned by white society as a method for settling their grievances."[45] According to Stagg, the conflicts began in 1868 when the Freedmen's Bureau began issuing contract regulations that guaranteed black laborers a reasonable share of the crops. In mid-1868 the new state government assumed the function of the Freedmen's Bureau and attempted to ensure by legislation laborers' claims to the crops. This development quickly politicized the labor problem.[46] Under the new state constitution all land/labor disputes were to be solved by the trial justice, and planters and laborers soon realized that the control of local political institutions was the key to the solution to their agricultural problems. On the county level most planters recognized that such a policy would leave them in the hands of elected or appointed Republican officials who would be in control of all local institutions before the end of 1868. The planters thus focused on one goal: how to prevent the black man from casting his vote as a Republican. The *Carolina Spartan* reflected the view of most white Spartans, stating that it "was essential for white men to have a perfect control of all local questions."[47]

Economic coercion and discharge from employment were widely discussed as means of controlling black votes, but discharge from employment would leave the planters without a workforce. Thus violence became an easy solution for the planters' dilemma. Violence would intimidate the black man both as a voter and as a worker and would leave the planter in undisputed control on the farm and in the county courthouse.[48] In 1870 the South Carolina House of

Representatives strengthened the laborers' claim to the crop and his bargaining position with the landlord. This was done by giving the laborer a prior lien on the crop while making it impossible for landlords to prosecute as a misdemeanor unperformed work specified in a contract. Planters in the upcountry were generally unhappy with the situation, but Republican victory in the state election of 1870 denied them the prospect of any relief in the next two years.[49] In many upcountry counties the Klan terrorized black farm workers with whippings and worse. James Epping, South Carolina's congressman at large, stated plainly in the *Washington Chronicle* that the Ku Klux Klan disorder of 1870–71 "was mainly due to the difficulties that arose between the laborer and the hirer," and the majority of black victims who testified before the subcommittee in South Carolina appear to have been renters of land. In January 1871 the *Newberry Herald* denounced black people for stipulating contract provisions that farmers could not reasonably meet and run a successful farm at the same time. York County in 1870 reportedly had been suffering from an acute shortage of labor. This was believed to be due partly to the refusal of black women to work in the fields and partly to a drift of the laboring population to the west in search of higher returns.[50]

In addition to the labor disputes, there was a systematic campaign against the black militia that had been armed in the upcountry for the 1870 elections. The presence of armed black men in a community could not help but arouse fears among the white people. "For months armed bands of masked men patrolled the upcountry roads, breaking into black cabins in search of militia weapons. If weapons were found, they were broken in the presence of the militiaman, who was then whipped for being, or supporting a Republican."[51]

The course of political and economic development in the South Carolina upcountry had clearly created a situation in which the majority of white people believed that violence was a justifiable means of social control. The local professional and planter elites resented black people for exercising their political power and feared that they would attempt to influence the readjustment of the agricultural system. The majority of the poor white people also resented the new status of the emancipated slave. All the white population could agree that an armed black militia was a threat to the peace of southern society.

By 1871 the federal government took action against the rash of Klan violence that was taking place in Spartanburg, and the Seventh Cavalry under the command of Maj. Marcus Reno was ordered to lay down the law in the upcountry, where they assisted with a congressional subcommittee investigating southern outlaw groups. The congressional subcommittee heard testimonies on everything from election tampering to violence against African Americans. A black man named Clem Bowden testified to the committee that black people were scared but that "there is not so much uneasiness here in town since [the soldiers have] come to the place, but I don't know whether any change has come to the country or not."[52] The fear that African Americans felt was palpable. Many black people testified that they had been beaten and abused by the Klan. Between 1870 and the summer of 1871 nearly 227 people, both black and white, had been victimized by the KKK. According to the Reverend A. W. Cummings and P. Quinn Camp, who compiled the activities of the Klan in Spartanburg County from 1870 to 1871, "most of the Klan's victims had been whipped; but others had been whipped and driven from their homes." Calvin Petty, for example, was whipped and had his ears cut off; Mrs. Bird Jones was beaten with sticks and a shovel; Charity Blanton and her child were both shot; Reuben Phillips and his wife were beaten with sticks; Sallie Henderson was whipped and her house was burned; and Aaron Hughes, Robert Holcomb, and Anthony Johnson were all killed. Johnson was the first black trial justice appointed in Spartanburg as a result of the Reconstruction government. When Governor Scott appointed him as trial justice in October 1869, the *Carolina Spartan* announced that Johnson, "a colored individual who has a transient habitation . . . has recently been exalted from his stool in the chimney corner, to the magisterial bench." While the paper admitted no knowledge of Johnson's qualifications, it reminded its readers that the Republican governor tended to appoint radicals even if they were "unjust, partial, ignorant, and stupid."[53] Johnson's elevation from slave to lawman was clearly too much for some people in the white community to endure. Only months after his appointment, Johnson was brutally murdered by a band of white men while his mother watched in horror.[54]

The need to regain political and economic control in Spartanburg led the Klan to intimidate black people who supported the Republican government, referred to as the "radicals." In a testimony before the joint congressional committee in Spartanburg, Harriet Hernandez testified that the KKK came to her house twice and beat her and her child. The Klan warned her, "You can tell your husband that when we see him we are going to kill him." When committee members asked her why they wanted to kill him, Hernandez replied that "they said, 'He voted the radical ticket' . . . [and] men that voted radical tickets they took the spite out on the women."[55] Several outstanding white citizens of the community, weary of the Klan violence being perpetrated in Spartanburg, met at the courthouse in January 1871 and under the leadership of J. W. Carlisle and J. H. Evins passed the following resolution: "Resolved, That we as law-abiding citizens of Spartanburg County do look with abhorrence and condemnation upon the recent outrages against law and order perpetrated in our county; and we do feel it to be the duty of every citizen to use all efforts singly and unitedly in their power to arrest the perpetrators, and put an end to such a spirit of disregard of law and life."[56] Nonetheless the editor of the local newspaper reflected the mood of many white Spartans when he wrote, "While we live under

South Carolina Negro rule it is impossible to submit us to more tyranny or humiliation."[57]

Thus the first few years of independence for black people in the upcountry of South Carolina were not only marked with difficulties in transitioning to a free labor market but also were suffused with intimidation by white people who feared their own political and economic powers were being eclipsed. As the gulf separating poor white and black people narrowed, Spartanburg leaders responded by emphasizing white progress while working to restrict the mobility and opportunities for freed people. Despite all this, however, the African American community survived and continued to struggle against the odds as they attempted to stabilize their family lives and work the land, primarily as sharecroppers for white landowners who desperately needed their labor.

Black People in Agriculture

By 1880 cotton production in the upcountry had already reached levels that surpassed its pre–Civil War high of 6,671 bales in 1850. After producing a mere 2,851 bales of cotton in 1870, Spartanburg County rebounded with the production of 24,188 bales in 1880 and 35,383 bales in 1890.[58] The increasing specialization of upcountry farmers in cotton production can be seen also in the amount of acreage dedicated to the staple crop. Between 1880 and 1900 the number of acres planted in cotton in the upcountry increased by 30.3 percent, while the number of acres planted in corn increased by only 14.6 percent.[59] According to Lacy Ford, the shift away from subsistence crops and toward cotton production can be attributed to the introduction of guano, a cost-effective fertilizer. Use of guano made it possible to raise cotton profitably on lands previously unfit for the staple crop. In addition railroads lowered transportation costs and spurred the importation of food as well as fertilizer. The depletion of livestock herds as a result of war-time destruction was another factor leading to commercial agriculture. With imported feed grain available at competitive prices, upcountry farmers switched land and labor away from subsistence crops and to cotton.[60]

Many black people became entrapped in the sharecropper/tenant system on land used to cultivate cotton and other staple crops. David Golightly Harris divided one of his farms in Spartanburg among four former slaves. He charged fixed rent rather than a share of crops, but the tenants also were "to make considerable improvements beside paying the rent." In 1869 he noted in his journal that a former slave "had built a house, Stable & lot" and another tenant had "cleared and fenced ten acres of new ground."[61] For black agricultural laborers, sharecropping gave them control over their labor and families. According to the historian Vernon Burton, "with emancipation the black male's desire to control and provide for his family impelled him to elect a tenant arrangement as a compromise labor system."[62] Black sharecropping, writes the historian Jacqueline

Jones, allowed "husbands and wives [to] retain a minimal amount of control over their own productive energies. Sharecropping enabled mothers to divide their time between field and housework in a way that reflected a family's needs. Even more importantly, this system removed wives and daughters from the threatening reach of white supervisors."[63] The downside of sharecropping was that while the landlord furnished the land, shelter, rations, seed, tools, stock, and stock feed, he usually took one-half of the crop. According to Tindall, "this system prevailed widely in South Carolina, although in some sections of the Piedmont, notably Greenville, Fairfield, and Spartanburg counties, the landlord took two-thirds of the crop, leaving only one-third to the laborer."[64] According to Sam Lewis, who was born a slave on Major Hart's plantation in York County and came to work as a cook in Spartanburg in 1887, "When I got old enough to work (as a freedman) us jus' kinda rented from de Harts. They furnished us wid mules and groceries and clothes, and us work on de farm. When lay-by-time come, dey tuck out for de rent and what dey done give us. Sometimes, us raised 'nough cotton and corn to come out ahead wid some cash, and sometimes us come out in de hole if the crops is bad." Making a living was difficult for black sharecroppers, and bad weather meant that most local people, both black and white, were eating less in 1870 than they had been in 1860 because of the worst weather conditions the upcountry had experienced in decades.[65]

Sharecroppers' lives were filled with constant hard work. They generally lived in cabins and had few possessions. Their meager earnings were often invested in mules, oxen, plows, or wagons rather than domestic furnishings.[66] Jane Edna Hunter, born to black tenant farmers on an upcountry farm in the 1880s, recalled her home as a "two-room, frame dwelling which stood at the edge of a sloping field not far from the red clay road," with . . . "an old well, an apple orchard, and an abandoned sawmill." In a garden patch near the house her "mother tended the tomatoes, okra, onions, mustard and turnip plants"; she recalled that in the fields below, "father drove his plow through long rows of corn, cotton, and molasses cane."[67] The vegetables that her mother grew helped supplement a substandard, protein-poor diet of "meat, meal, and molasses," the standard fare of most sharecroppers in the late nineteenth century.[68]

While sharecropping and tenancy were the norm for most agricultural freedmen, some former slaves were able to accumulate enough money to purchase their own land. By 1880 a small minority of black farmers were reported as owning their homes or farms. In Spartanburg County the proportion was estimated at only 5 percent, while in Greenville County 16 percent owned either houses or land.[69] Barry Cunningham, for example, purchased thirty acres of land in Spartanburg for $360 in 1892 and owned almost ninety acres by the early 1900s.[70]

City Life

Not all African Americans were rural sharecroppers; in the upcountry black artisans and skilled workers generally settled in towns and cities. Black people who had developed skills in both free and slave occupations formed the basis of a merchant-artisan class. In Greenville, for example, the small black population showed a high ratio of skilled workers, with forty carpenters, fifty masons and plasterers, fifteen blacksmiths, fifteen shoemakers, and fourteen painters, in addition to an indefinite number of tinners, plumbers, harness makers, and other artisans.[71]

Since emancipation, small but steadily increasing numbers of former slaves had made their way to towns and cities. Black people often hopped trains and got off at hub stations, which Spartanburg was becoming. Women accompanied their husbands to town so that the family as a whole could benefit from the wider variety of jobs available to the men. Unmarried women, desperate to escape the drudgery of rural life, and widows trying to feed their children found more employment as well as educational opportunities in town.[72] In Spartanburg a small group of recently emancipated African Americans and their families created an enclave on Liberty Street, located just south of Main. Many of the males were artisans and tradesmen. One of the earliest residents of the black community was Joseph Miles Young, a fifty-two-year-old mattress maker and upholsterer, who resided in 1870 with his wife Priscilla, a thirty-eight-year-old homemaker, and their eight children. Several of Joseph and Priscilla's children and their spouses would become distinguished members of the community in the fields of education and business. One of their grandchildren, C. C. Woodson Jr., would serve as principal of Carver High School for thirty years. At the time of the 1870 census, Young already owned real estate valued at four hundred dollars and personal property valued at two hundred dollars, significant holdings for a black or white person at the time. Between 1873 and 1900 Joseph and Priscilla added to their landholdings on the south side, buying up what eventually became the business district of South Liberty Street.[73]

For southern black women, the physical demands of their domestic chores and fieldwork had not changed much since slavery.[74] Yet newly freed black men and women perceived domestic duties "to be a woman's major obligation, in contrast to the slave master's view that a female was first and foremost a field or house worker and only incidentally as the member of a family."[75] Most African American husbands preferred that their wives not work directly for white people and that if they had to, they labor in their own homes (as laundresses, for example) rather than in white women's kitchens. However, few African American families in the late nineteenth century could afford to emulate the model of white middle-class domestic life. Most African American wives and mothers found it necessary to contribute to the family economy by engaging in paid labor, and for the most part that meant working for white families.

Connections between work and family patterns in towns and cities differed from those in rural areas. In towns and cities black women found jobs in a limited number of occupations all clustered at the bottom of the wage scale. These jobs became associated with traditional black women's work in the South—domestic services performed for white families at nominal pay. In the first census taken after the Civil War, 218 African American women were listed as residents in Spartanburg in 1870 and 134 (or 63 percent) were gainfully employed. The 1870 census did not provide the marital status of individuals, so it is nearly impossible to estimate how many working women were married. However, it can be assumed that when later census data are examined, a large number of black married women did work outside the home. The largest number of African American working women in Spartanburg were employed as domestic servants (fifty-two or 39 percent); forty-three were employed as cooks (32 percent); twenty women worked as laundresses (15 percent); eight were farm laborers (6 percent); five women (4 percent) were employed as dry nurses (one who takes care of a baby but does not breastfeed); two women held jobs as pastry cooks (5 percent); two were seamstresses (1.5 percent); one woman worked as a day laborer, and one was a teacher (less than 1 percent each). Nearly all of the newly freed black families who resided in Spartanburg village lived in areas behind the large antebellum homes on both sides of North Church Street[76] (which provided black women easy access to the homes of their white employers). With the exception of farm laborers and teachers, the overwhelming majority of working black women labored for white families. Many white employers expected black women to work long hours for little pay. However, black women found ways to control certain aspects of their work. Most chose to live in their own neighborhoods and in their own homes. In that way they could avoid sexual harassment and could also limit their tasks to the time allotted rather than be on call all hours of the day or night. According to the historian Elizabeth Turner, "they concentrated on breaking down domestic service into specific tasks—such as cleaning one day and ironing the next—thus limiting energy spent on overall household chores and giving them the time to accommodate to their own families' needs. Freedwomen knew that boundaries were necessary if they were to remain laborers under the new system."[77]

As compared to white women, black women were employed outside the home in far greater numbers. During that same census year (1870), there were a total of 636 white women listed in Spartanburg and 181 were employed outside the home (28 percent). However, less than 1 percent of those working women were married. Even white, single women tended to remain at home: 24 percent (or 153). While some of these women were widows and elderly, the majority were young women who were unmarried.[78] During the next decade, an even larger number of black women in Spartanburg were gainfully employed.

According to the 1880 census, 404 women out of a total of 476 black women (85 percent) worked in Spartanburg. Married women accounted for 51 percent of all female workers (208), while single women made up 37 percent of the female workforce (148). Twelve percent (48) of all widows were also gainfully employed. Few black wives had the luxury of remaining at home; only 54 or 11 percent were listed as "keeping house," while 18 or 3.8 percent of single black females were "at home." Black women worked predominantly as washerwomen and domestic servants but were also employed as cooks, laborers, nurses, seamstresses, and teachers. Widows represented extreme hardship—for example, Charlotte Cleveland, who was still working as a washerwoman at the age of ninety-three, and eighty-year-old Lucy Brown, who served a white family as a domestic servant. The burden of work for black women commenced at a young age, as evidenced by girls as young as seven, ten, twelve, and fourteen who were employed as domestic servants, often working for white families whose daughters of the same age enjoyed the luxury of attending school.[79]

There were some advantages for black women who worked as laundresses or washerwomen. Washerwomen went from house to house picking up laundry and doing it in their own homes. Even the poorest southern white people employed black washerwomen because washing was such an arduous task.[80] Laundresses turned their yards into washing assembly lines: they hauled water to the kettles, stoked fires under steaming cauldrons of wash water, and scrubbed, rinsed, and wrung out the clothes and linens. They chopped wood and heated the heavy irons for the piles of ironing that followed. Turner asserts that "African American women chose this back-breaking labor over working in a white woman's kitchen for the independence it gave them."[81] Laundering became the nearly exclusive province of black women; thus washerwomen ranked highest on what Jacqueline Jones calls the "racial exclusion" scale, even higher than domestics by the late nineteenth century.[82]

Domestic servants, on the other hand, came in constant contact with white people since they worked in the homes of white families. Jones defines domestic service as the recapitulation of the mistress-slave relationship, noting that "domestic service made manifest all the tensions and uncertainties inherent in personal interaction between the female members of two different classes and races."[83] While a small number of white women worked as domestic servants in the South, black women constituted the vast majority of servants in southern towns and cities. In general the younger the black woman, the more likely it was that she worked in a white household, while slightly larger numbers of married women worked as laundresses (in their own homes). In many cases the length of the workday varied from day to day, with women expected to remain under their employers' roofs for twelve to fourteen hours at a time. The inexpensiveness of domestic labor meant that all but the poorest white families considered it an affordable necessity.[84] Servants were expected to arrive at their employers' houses quite early in the morning to prepare or serve breakfast to the white families. The responsibilities of domestic servants often varied, but most often they included housekeeping, cooking, and taking care of the children. Cooks were included in the job description of domestic servants, but not all domestic workers were cooks, and some black women worked exclusively as cooks. Cooks usually prepared breakfast, lunch, and dinner for the white families they served, and they were expected to leave their own families while they prepared Thanksgiving, Christmas, and Easter dinners for their employers.

Some black women were hired exclusively as "dry nurses" and took exclusive charge of the care of babies. The only skilled occupation in which black women worked included dressmaking and sewing. Black colleges offered courses in these skills, and some black women who had attended them returned home to establish small sewing schools, as did Ida Bozeman Gladden, the wife of a Greenville minister and a former student at Tuskegee.[85] Between 1870 and 1900 at least fourteen young black women in Spartanburg became teachers and taught students in the black community.

The majority of working black women resided in Spartanburg's African American community, which by the end of the nineteenth century had become more ethnically defined. By 1896 the black population of the south side had swelled to several hundred. At the same time, however, many black homes were built during this period in the backyards of the wealthy white homeowners along South Church Street. Hampton Alley was home to many black families who worked as gardeners and housekeepers at the white-owned mansions. The African American enclave in Spartanburg was the site of women and men engaged in a wide variety of occupations. Entrepreneurial activity started early in Spartanburg's black enclave, where African American males opened grocery stores and barbershops and operated their own blacksmith shops.[86]

A large number of black males held respectable positions within the community during the last quarter of the nineteenth century. They were grocers, shoemakers, butchers, and barbers. In Spartanburg more African American males held positions as skilled artisans than did white males; these included work as blacksmiths, masons, bricklayers, and carpenters. Black professional people, such as black businessmen, served chiefly their own race; they were occupied mainly as teachers, clergymen, lawyers, doctors, and newspapermen. Beginning in 1880 there was growth in the black medical community. Perhaps the best known in this early community was Phyllis Goins, the daughter of a slave from Ivory Coast, who was midwife to the babies of black families in Spartanburg.

There were also African American licensed doctors practicing in the Spartanburg area as early as 1895. The first physician was Dr. W. C. Rhodes. Born in North Carolina in March 1865, Rhodes graduated from medical school in Raleigh in 1892. In 1899 Rhodes and Dr. G. W. Harry, another Spartanburg-area doctor, organized the first statewide black physicians' organization.[87]

By 1890 resistance to African Americans holding political power in Spartanburg seems to have subsided. The *Charleston News and Courier* described Thomas Bomar, Spartanburg's first black city councilman, as being highly respected by those who knew him.[88] Beginning in the 1890s two "colored fire companies" and two "colored policemen" also served the city of Spartanburg.[89] However, there was one area of growing occupations in Spartanburg that largely excluded black people: textile mills. One mill superintendent in Spartanburg, who had no experience with black operatives, saw no reason why they were not "physically and morally competent to do the work if property trained," while another at Piedmont, who had worked with black slaves in a cotton mill, remembered that "they were very hard to manage even then" and believed that they could not be made into first-class workmen. The one experiment in hiring black mill hands occurred in 1899, when John Montgomery of Spartanburg purchased the Charleston Cotton Mill and renamed it the Vesta Cotton Mill. The management appealed to black ministers and other leaders of the black community in Charleston to encourage black laborers to work in the mill, which then operated through 1900 almost exclusively with black laborers.[90] However, by 1900 the mill, the only one in the state that had experimented with black labor, failed. Thus mill work, the premier growth industry in the upcountry, was quickly typecast as a white haven. The only positions open to black job seekers were floor sweeping and heavy lifting on loading platforms, which took place outside the mills.

As black people established themselves within the city, they bought their own land and established independent communities such as Little Africa, which was created in 1880 when the former slave Simpson Foster and the Cherokee Emanuel Waddell merged their lands.[91] As early as 1880 black people also owned shops on Church Street. Ptolemy C. White opened the first black pharmacy at 10 Kennedy Place, and Charles Bomar, who later became one of Spartanburg's wealthiest black citizens, ran a grocery store. In 1890 Edward McKissick, a traveling reporter for the *Charleston News and Courier,* reported that "Charles Bomar had one of the neatest stores in Spartanburg, black or white."[92] Bomar later became an undertaker in 1896, making his establishment the first funeral parlor in the African American community.

By the late 1890s African Americans in Spartanburg were represented in a wide variety of occupations in agricultural pursuits and business enterprise as well as skilled and unskilled professions. Black women, in particular, were gender segregated in jobs—such as laundresses and domestic servants—that were dependent on white employers. These jobs required long hours and arduous labor and included cooking and taking care of children as well as cleaning and serving white folks. Several African Americans, however, were able to attain higher education and came back to their community to teach, administer to the sick, or provide leadership to the newly emerging black churches.

Creating a Community

One of the most significant and permanent social changes that occurred during Reconstruction was the establishment of separate black churches. The center of social activity in the black community was the church, and it became one of the most highly organized of black institutions. Church services provided a form of worship that was unique to black Christians and provided an outlet for spiritual, emotional, and social expression. Special events such as singing conventions and camp meetings brought black people together, while church picnics attracted hundreds of black people during the summer months. Black churches created social settings and eventually provided political venues where black members could express their anger and frustrations with racial discrimination and segregation. They also offered avenues of upward mobility for African Americans. Black churches required an educated ministry, and by the end of the nineteenth century four institutions of higher learning existed to meet black educational aspirations in South Carolina.

In the late nineteenth century most African Americans in Spartanburg attended Methodist churches on the north side of town and at Silver Hill. Joseph Young was a founder of Mount Moriah Baptist Church. Construction of the first Mount Moriah church building began around 1877 at the corner of South Liberty and Young Streets on land owned by Young. By 1884 the church was also home to the first black public school in Spartanburg, Lincoln School, which operated in the basement. Silver Hill United Methodist Church was founded by James R. Rosemond, who was born to slave parents, Abraham and Peggy Thompson, in Greenville County. At a very young age he was separated from his parents and sent to live with a Methodist minister and his family, who provided him with his early religious training. As a young boy Rosemond expressed his desire to preach the gospel, but he needed the written permission of his master to enter the church. His master initially refused but eventually acquiesced, and Rosemond was given membership at a Methodist Episcopal church on a probationary status. Within five years Rosemond was appointed by the church to hold prayer meetings in Greenville County once a month. After passing stringent exams, he was granted a license to preach and to "perform all the duties and exercise all the privileges of a 'Colored preacher'" in 1854.[93] Rosemond entered Baker's Theological Institute in Charleston in 1867 and eventually established churches throughout the upcountry, including Silver Hill in Spartanburg in 1869.

Outside the churches the most common black social organizations were fraternal orders and benefit associations. According to the historian John Hope Franklin, "these were another manifestation of the struggle of African Americans to become socially self-sufficient."[94] They were formed largely during Reconstruction as means of providing cooperative insurance funds from which their members could draw in case of sickness or death. One of the most successful was the Future Progress Society, which had lodges scattered around the upcountry during the late 1880s. The organization was described as a benevolent society that aimed to "bury the dead and aid the sick, and encourage industry and schools."[95] Black lodges too developed throughout the state during this period. They included Masons, Odd Fellows, Good Templars, Pythians, and others. The Grand Lodge of the Independent Order of Good Templars had chapters throughout South Carolina, and in 1883 and 1884 officers were elected from Spartanburg as well as other parts of the state.

Another symbol of community development was the establishment of black newspapers. The first newspaper for African Americans was published in 1896 when Luther Gilliard began the *Spartanburg Advance*. A survey in 1899 revealed only six African American papers in South Carolina, and one of them was the *Spartanburg Piedmont Indicator*.[96] Unfortunately black newspapers in Spartanburg were generally short-lived publications, handicapped by a lack of advertisers, a lack of money, and a scarcity of literate readers to which they could address themselves.[97]

Spartanburg black people developed social relationships and organizations for religious, social, and emotional support. The development of these institutions was another demonstration that emancipation had brought them freedoms and rights, which they vigorously asserted. In 1899 members of the African American community rejoiced in their independence by celebrating "Freedom Day" and assembled at the courthouse steps to hear rousing speeches about Abraham Lincoln.[98] Over the years "Emancipation Day," as it was called in 1902, became more celebratory with parades, floats, carriages, and brass bands.[99] While rejoicing in their own freedom, they were also reaffirming to the community the rights and privileges they had won and were jealously defending.

Education for African Americans in Spartanburg

The historian Ron Butchart has written that "African Americans acted on the possibilities of freedom with an overwhelming surge toward the schoolhouse door."[100] Freedmen had a voracious thirst for education, but the educational advancement of black people in the upcountry was restricted by a white ideology that viewed access to learning as an important symbol of white superiority.[101]

While most white people acknowledged that the end of slavery would bring some system for black education, few were willing to pay the taxes necessary to support such a system,[102] and most feared that public schools "would contain both white and colored children."[103] Furthermore the problems of debt facing South Carolina in the immediate postwar period left little money for public education for white children as well as black ones. Aside from the limited operation of the Freedmen's Bureau in the upcountry, no provisions were made for schooling former slaves during Reconstruction. According to Bruce Eelman, "early Reconstruction attempts to organize schools, hire teachers, and develop curriculum were hampered by the failure of the general assembly to pass a permanent common school law for two years after the ratification of the Republican constitution."[104] As a result, much of the initiative for freedmen's education came from within the black community. In the summer of 1866 E. J. Snetter, a black educator in Spartanburg, obtained verbal support from the South Carolina Freedman's Bureau superintendent of schools to start a school for African Americans. However, four months after beginning classes, Snetter had no formal authorization for the school and he and an assistant had yet to receive any pay.[105]

For those who were organizing schools for black students in Spartanburg during Reconstruction, the difficulties were nearly insurmountable. In 1867 the teacher Eva Poole opened such an educational facility in Spartanburg. By spring 1869 there were over 100 students enrolled in the school, which was housed in a building owned by the estate of John Bomar, an industrialist. In addition to overcrowding, Poole also had to deal with poor material conditions and overdue pay. By September 1869 Poole and two black female assistants were teaching 150 students. At the end of the month the school had to close for repairs.[106] Although both races struggled to improve educational opportunities in the early postwar period, far fewer black children in the county were able to attend the handful of schools located in town. In 1870 just under 30 percent of the county's white student population of 4,709 actually attended school. By contrast, just 259, or less than 11 percent of Spartanburg's black student population of 2,414, attended school in 1870.[107]

However, Spartanburg freedmen continued to establish schools for their children, and increasingly improvements were made. In 1871 two more black schools opened, with enrollments at each of these schools averaging about forty pupils. African Americans' interest in education is significant when measured against that of white people. Between 1870 and 1875 the percentage of South Carolina white children more than doubled. Moreover, during the same period Spartanburg's black student attendance rate climbed from 10.7 to 49 percent.[108] Unfortunately, according to Eelman, "while Spartanburg's black student attendance outpaced white growth during Reconstruction, over half of the county's black children did not attend school when white Democrats regained control of the state government in 1877."[109] Democratic officials distributed a disproportionate share of funds to white schools, further impeding educational opportunities for black people. Each school for white people generally received about fifty-two dollars more than was given to each black school.[110]

With the adoption of the graded school system in 1884, Spartanburg officials took an important step in acknowledging the importance of preparing children educationally. That same year Tobe Hartwell and Charles Bomar, leaders in the African American community, were invited to a board of education meeting, where "plans for a graded school for colored children were discussed."[111] White residents were reassured by then governor James L. Orr that "mixing" in the schools would not happen. In a message to the South Carolina legislature he stated, "I deem the separation of the two races in the public schools a matter of the greatest importance to all classes of our people."[112] On August 27, 1884, Mr. R. M. Alexander was named principal of the "colored school" with a salary of thirty dollars per month, while Phyllis B. Bomar, Mary Hartwell, and Clara Farrow were hired to teach at a salary of "twenty-five dollars per month each."[113] The new facility, called the Lincoln School, opened in the basement of the original Mount Moriah Baptist Church on October 13, 1884. In October of the first school year, there were 186 white students attending their schools and 144 black students attending theirs. In February 336 attending were black, as compared to only 214 white students. This growth in the number of black students can be attributed to the generous support of the northern Presbyterian churches, which paid for the creation of the city's second black school, the Rendall Academy. This school was absorbed into the city's school system on February 9, 1885, only to be replaced by another school organized by Mrs. N. F. Young in the basement of Silver Hill Methodist Church. On February 9, 1885, the Rendall Academy was incorporated into the Spartanburg City School System.[114] During the 1885–86 school year five white women taught in the public schools and seven African Americans (including two ministers) taught in the black schools. With the exception of Reverends Baylor and Bethel, the teachers were black women. In 1886 the Grant School on Short Wofford Street opened for the education of black students, and in 1891 the Dean Street School was erected.

In later years Mary Honor Farrow established the Carrier Street School. Born in 1862 the daughter of Lot and Adeline Farrow, she was encouraged by her parents to pursue education. She attended Scotia Seminary in Concord, North Carolina, and graduated from Claflin College. In May 1879 the former slave accepted her first position as a teacher and established the Ben Bomar School in Inman. She often worked for no salary to insure that the children received quality education. She married William Wright in 1884 and eventually gave birth to ten children. Recognizing Spartanburg's need for a school on the south side, Wright started teaching out of her home at 388 South Liberty Street.[115] This institution eventually became the public Carrier Street School, and Wright became known as the leading black educator in Spartanburg. In 1952 the Carrier Street School was named the Mary H. Wright Elementary School, in honor of the woman who committed her life to educating black children.

In addition a Colored Industrial Training School was established in Spartanburg around 1891. The president of the school, Thomas A. J. Clemons, reported that the institution provided general education including the cultivation of taste and the acquirement of knowledge on the origin of beauty. Students were provided instruction in vocal music and in piano and instrumental music. The students paid no tuition and survived on public support. Modeled on the technical schools recommended by Booker T. Washington, the school, as reported by Clemons in May 1892, "has prospered educationally and industrially. With three teachers and a principal we have taught and trained 168 children—98 girls, 70 boys and 30 orphans in the several departments of the school. The boys, carpentry, making shuck collars, framing chairs, making willow baskets, bricklaying. The girls, cooking, sewing and general house keeping. We have made no charges for tuition this year and the school has been maintained through voluntary contributions."[116] However, Clemons desperately needed the continued goodwill and contributions of the white community, locally and nationally, to keep the school afloat. Contributions to the school came from local churches as well as local white businessmen and leaders such as Dexter Converse, J. H. Montgomery, A. H. Twitchell, Walter S. Montgomery, and Jas. G. Johnson. Clemons wrote that "the colored people of Spartanburg, SC banded together as they are in educating the Negroes of this section, both intellectually and educationally, and it is our intention to train step by step until we shall reach the high plain of civilization, right and Christianity."[117] Unfortunately the struggle to keep the school financially sound failed, and the institution eventually closed.

The increase in white resentment of black people and the perpetual dislike of paying taxes to send other people's children to school combined to cause both state and local governments to cut funding to schools, both white and black. All of the schools for African Americans except the Dean Street School, referred to on maps from 1891 as the "Colored Graded School," closed in 1891. This was largely because of the fact that the schools started to demand tuition and poor black people could not afford the "luxury of educating their children if they were to survive."[118] In 1892 the teachers at the two white schools received an average of thirty-nine dollars a month, while black teachers on average received twenty-six dollars.[119] Even with all the obstacles they faced, however, the first class of black students graduated from Dean Street School in 1898. They included Mamie Jeter, Lila Woodruff, Ella Montague, Catherine McNeil,

Drayton H. Nance, Gussie L. Gaither, Samuel Wiggins, Jos. H. Bomar, and Thomas Edwards.[120]

The basic problem of inadequate facilities and inadequate teachers plagued the black schools throughout the period. Slowly the number of professionally trained black teachers increased. An important innovation in the early 1880s was the establishment of state and county summer teachers' institutes. In 1880 the first statewide Normal Institute for white teachers was held in Spartanburg, and the first black county teachers' institute was held in Charleston that same year.[121] By the end of the century schools for African Americans were beginning to emerge from financial deprivation. The statewide decrease in black illiteracy from 78.5 percent in 1880 to 52.8 percent in 1900 indicated that progress had been made despite all the problems.[122] By the end of the century, black people also had four institutions of higher education to attend in South Carolina: Claflin College, South Carolina College of Agriculture and Mechanical Arts, Benedict College, and Allen University.

By the end of the twentieth century African Americans in Spartanburg had successfully transitioned from slavery to freedom, despite the violence, limited job opportunities, and unequal educational facilities. African American men in particular were engaged in education, business, skilled jobs, and professions. Many of these included providing services to the growing black community. African American women, with the exception of teachers, were occupationally segregated largely as a result of being confined to domestic service and laundering, work that was dependent on white employers. Socially and culturally, however, African Americans maintained a separate existence from white society.

In the late nineteenth century segregation rapidly became an established and unquestioned fact in all the institutions and relationships of the two races. The historian George Tindall summarized it this way: "by the end of the century a new social arrangement had been established by statute, by custom, by direction of the dominant white people, and by the institutional segregation of schools, churches, and private organizations. Slavery was replaced as an instrument of maintaining the subordination of the black by a caste system based on race under which white and black seldom came into personal contact except in the relationship of employer and laborer."[123]

Throughout the late nineteenth century it became evident that white factions were competing with one another for the black vote and thus frequently giving black people the balance of power. With this realization, most white people believed that it was time for black disfranchisement. Gradually one state after another wrote laws that guaranteed white supremacy by disfranchising black voters. In 1895 South Carolina followed the lead of Mississippi to end black political power by requiring of black voters two years' residency, a poll tax of one dollar, the ability to read and write any section of the constitution or to understand it when read aloud, or the owning of property worth three hundred dollars, along with the disqualification of convicts.[124] In 1896 the Supreme Court upheld segregation in its "separate but equal" doctrine set forth in *Plessy v. Ferguson.* For advocates of white supremacy who kept the races apart in order to maintain things as they were during the antebellum period, there was reinforcement at the close of the nineteenth century that the law, the courts, the schools, and almost every other institution in the South favored white people. For African Americans in Spartanburg, as in the entire South, the turn of the twentieth century ushered in a new era that black people would struggle against for the next six decades. But even in the grip of segregation, Spartanburg African Americans would build a "colored hospital" and extend the business center of the black community with hotels, funeral parlors, lunchrooms, cabstands, and pharmacies. Black educators and ministers would continue to inspire members of the African American community, and the institutions and communal life they established in the post–Civil War era would guide them through the years of segregation and a second reconstruction.

Notes

The author would like to thank her former Furman University Advantage student Andrew Cuadrado for his research assistance on this project. A special thanks as well to the staff at the Kennedy Room of the Spartanburg County Public Library for their help.

1. Bruce W. Eelman, *Entrepreneurs in the Southern Upcountry: Commercial Culture in Spartanburg, South Carolina, 1845–1880* (Athens: University of Georgia Press, 2008), 8.

2. Ibid.

3. See http://wwwnationalregister.scgov/spartanburg (accessed July 28, 2011). See also http://wwwrootsweb.ancestry.com (accessed July 28, 2011), on Nicholls-Crook Plantation.

4. Historic Walnut Grove Plantation, 1765, Spartanburg County Historical Association, Kennedy Room, Spartanburg County Public Library, Spartanburg, S.C. See also Tom Moore Craig, ed., *Upcountry South Carolina Goes to War: Letters of the Anderson, Brockman, and Moore Families 1853–1865* (Columbia: University of South Carolina Press, 2009), xv.

5. See http://www.spartanburghistory.org/pricehouse (accessed August 15, 2011).

6. William Cinque Henderson, "Spartan Slaves: A Documentary Account of Blacks on Trial in Spartanburg, South Carolina, 1830–1845" (Ph.D. diss., Northwestern University, 1978), 45. See also Lawrence Fay Brewster, *Summer Migrations and Resorts of South Carolina Planters* (Durham, N.C.: Duke University Press, 1947); Mrs. T. Sumter Means, *Glenn Springs, So. Ca: Its Location, Discovery, History, Personal Sketches of Its Habitues, What It Will Cure, &c.* (Spartanburg, S.C.: Trimmier's Printing Office and Bookstore, 1888), 30, copy in Kennedy Genealogical and Local History Room, Spartanburg County Public Library, Headquarters Branch, Spartanburg, S.C.

7. Henderson, "Spartan Slaves," 109.

8. Eelman, *Entrepreneurs in the Southern Upcountry,* 8.

9. Philip Racine, *Piedmont Farmer: The Journals of David Golightly Harris, 1855–1870* (Knoxville: University of Tennessee Press, 1990), 1.

10. Nina Scott, WPA interview by F. S. DuPre, Spartanburg, S.C., May 17, 1937, Kennedy Room, Spartanburg County Public Library, Spartanburg, S.C.

11. "The African American Experience in Slavery and Freedom," Black History Month exhibit at Sandor Teszler Library Gallery, Wofford College, Spartanburg, S.C., February–March 2011.

12. *Spartanburg Herald,* February 13, 1925.

13. Henderson, "Spartan Slaves," 18.

14. Dwain Pruitt, *Things Hidden: An Introduction to the History of Blacks in Spartanburg* (Spartanburg, S.C.: City of Spartanburg Community Relations Department, 1995), 30.

15. Henderson, "Spartan Slaves," 157.

16. Ibid., 30.

17. Spartanburg District Court of Magistrates and Freeholders, Trial Papers ("Slaves and Free Blacks"), 1825–65.

18. Ibid., 52.

19. Jeffrey Willis, "Textile Town Pioneers 1816 to 1879," in *Textile Town: Spartanburg County, South Carolina,* ed. Betsy Wakefield Teter (Spartanburg, S.C.: Hub City Writers Project, 2002), 27.

20. Racine, *Piedmont Farmer,* 396.

21. Jack Bass and W. Scott Poole, *The Palmetto State: The Making of Modern South Carolina* (Columbia: University of South Carolina Press, 2009), 66.

22. Freedmen's Bureau contract, February 10, 1866, on freed people in Spartanburg and Atlanta, Georgia; quoted in Emily Neely, "Paper Dolls: Four Southern Women Share Stories of Friendship, Family, and the Color Line," unpub. ms. in Neely's possession, 53–54.

23. Racine, *Piedmont Farmer,* 396.

24. Eelman, *Entrepreneurs in the Southern Upcountry,* 147.

25. Lacy Ford, "Rednecks and Merchants: Economic Development and Social Tensions in the South Carolina Upcountry, 1865–1900," *Journal of American History* 71, no. 2 (September 1984): 294–318.

26. Philip Racine, "Boom Time in Textile Town 1880 to 1909," in *Textile Town,* ed. Wakefield Teter, 37.

27. Ibid., 55.

28. Allen Stokes, "Vesta Mills: An Experiment with Black Labor," in *Textile Town,* ed. Wakefield Teter, 83.

29. Racine, "Boom Time in Textile Town 1880 to 1909," 392.

30. Bruce Eelman, "Progress and Community from Old South to New South: Spartanburg County, South Carolina, 1845–1880" (Ph.D. diss., University of Maryland, 2000), 259.

31. U.S. Bureau of Census, Statistics of the United States in 1860, Washington, D.C.

32. Eelman, *Entrepreneurs in the Southern Upcountry,* 135.

33. Elizabeth Turner, *Woman and Gender in the New South, 1865–1945* (Wheeling, Ill.: Harlan Davidson, 2009), 18.

34. Ibid., 18.

35. George Tindall, *South Carolina Negroes, 1877–1900* (Columbia: University of South Carolina Press, 1952), 7.

36. Eelman, *Entrepreneurs in the Southern Upcountry,* 215.

37. Ibid., 216.

38. Ibid.

39. Ibid.

40. Ibid., 217.

41. Turner, *Women and Gender,* 19–20.

42. Ibid.

43. "Ku Klux," *Carolina Spartan,* November 24, 1870, p. 2.

44. J. C. A. Stagg, "The Problem of Klan Violence: The South Carolina Up-County, 1858–1871," *American Studies* 8 (Fall 1967): 303–18.

45. Ibid., 309.

46. Ibid., 309–11.

47. Ibid., 313.

48. Ibid., 312.

49. Ibid., 314.

50. Ibid., 315.

51. Ibid.

52. Susan Thomas, "Spartanburg's Civil War," Reconstruction Folder, Kennedy Room, Spartanburg County Public Library, Spartanburg, S.C.

53. *Carolina Spartan,* October 14, 1882, p. 2.

54. Eelman, *Entrepreneurs in the Southern Upcountry,* 221.

55. Gerda Lerner, *Black Women in White America: A Documentary History* (New York: Vintage Books, 1972), 182–83.

56. *Carolina Spartan,* February 2, 1871, p. 2.

57. *Carolina Spartan,* April 4, 1872.

58. Ford, "Rednecks and Merchants," 301.

59. Ibid., 306.

60. Ibid., 307.

61. Racine, *Piedmont Farmer,* 487.

62. Orville Vernon Burton, *In My Father's House Are Many Mansions: Family and Community in Edgefield, South Carolina* (Chapel Hill: University of North Carolina Press, 1985), 8.

63. Jacqueline Jones, *Labor of Love, Labor of Sorrow: Black Women, Work and the Family, from Slavery to the Present* (New York: Basic Books, 1985), 460.

64. Tindall, *South Carolina Negroes,* 97.

65. W. J. Megginson, *African American Life in South Carolina's Upper Piedmont* (Columbia: University of South Carolina Press, 2006), 233.

66. Jones, *Labor of Love, Labor of Sorrow*, 86.

67. Jane Edna Hunter, *A Nickel and a Prayer* (Cleveland: Elli Kani, 1940), 13.

68. Jones, *Labor of Love, Labor of Sorrow*, 88.

69. Tindall, *South Carolina Negroes*, 103–4.

70. "Grandson of Former Slave Takes Pride in His Family's Home and the Deep Roots," *Spartanburg Herald*, January 30, 2011, pp. A1, A9.

71. Tindall, *South Carolina Negroes*, 130, quoting *Columbia Daily Register*, January 23, 1886.

72. Jones, *Labor of Love, Labor of Sorrow*, 98–99.

73. Beatrice Hill and Brenda Lee, *South of Main* (Spartanburg, S.C.: Hub City Writers Project, 2005), 2–3.

74. Ibid., 91.

75. Ibid., 93.

76. Ibid., 1.

77. Turner, *Women and Gender*, 32.

78. Population Schedules of the Ninth Census of the United States, 1870 South Carolina, vol. 14, Spartanburg County.

79. 10th Census of Population 1900, S.C., 1880.

80. Susan Tucker, *Telling Memories among Southern Women: Domestic Workers and Their Employers in the Segregated South* (Baton Rouge: Louisiana State University Press, 1988), 272.

81. Turner, *Women and Gender*, 33.

82. Jones, *Labor of Love, Labor of Sorrow*, 125.

83. Ibid., 127.

84. Ibid., 128.

85. Tindall, *South Carolina Negroes*, 130.

86. 12th Census of Population 1900, S.C., vol. 46, Spartanburg County.

87. Pruitt, *Things Hidden*, 52.

88. *Charleston News and Courier*, July 28, 1890, p 5.

89. Damon Fordham, *True Stories of Black South Carolina* (Charleston, S.C.: History Press, 2008), 75–76.

90. Ibid., 13.

91. Pruitt, *Things Hidden*, 42.

92. *Charleston News and Courier*, July 28, 1890, p. 5.

93. MacArthur Goodwin, Editor, *Silver Hill United Methodist Church, 1869–1898* (Spartanburg, S.C.: Kennedy Room, Spartanburg Public Library), 8–9.

94. John Hope Franklin, *From Slavery to Freedom: A History of African Americans* (New York: McGraw Hill, 1994), 286.

95. Tindall, *South Carolina Negroes*, 283.

96. Ibid., 150.

97. Ibid., 149.

98. "Freedom Day," (Spartanburg) *Evening Star,* January 2, 1899, p. 1.

99. *Spartanburg Journal,* December 31, 1902.

100. Ronald Butchart, *Schooling the Freed People: Teaching, Learning, and the Struggle for Black Freedom, 1861–1876* (Chapel Hill: University of North Carolina Press, 2010), 2.

101. Eelman, *Entrepreneurs in the Southern Upcountry,* 194.

102. Eelman, "Progress and Community," 434.

103. Jessie Eleanor Rushton, "The Development of Education in Spartanburg County prior to 1876" (master's thesis, Columbia College, 1928), 66.

104. Eelman, *Entrepreneurs in the Southern Upcountry,* 193.

105. Ibid., 428.

106. Report of the Free Schools in Spartanburg County, September 1869, Department of Education Files, Kennedy Room, Spartanburg County Public Library, Spartanburg, S.C.

107. Eelman, *Entrepreneurs in the Southern Upcountry,* 194–95.

108. *Reports and Resolution of the General Assembly of the State of South Carolina for the Year 1870* (Columbia, S.C.: Calvo and Patton, State Printers, 1871), 370–73; *Reports and Resolutions of the General Assembly of the State of South Carolina for the Year 1875* (Columbia, S.C.: Calvo and Patton, State Printers, 1876), 454–57; Eelman, *Entrepreneurs in the Southern Upcountry,* 194–95.

109. Eelman, *Entrepreneurs in the Southern Upcountry,* 201–2.

110. Ibid., 205.

111. Board of Education Minutes, August 8, 1884, Kennedy Room, Spartanburg County Public Library, Spartanburg, S.C.

112. Rushton, "Development of Education in Spartanburg County," 67.

113. Minutes of the Board of Trustees of the School District of the City of Spartanburg, August 27, 1884, Kennedy Room, Spartanburg County Public Library, Spartanburg, S.C.

114. Pruitt, *Things Hidden,* 56.

115. Hill and Lee, *South of Main,* 5.

116. Annual Report of the Colored Industrial Training School of Spartanburg, South Carolina, ending May 20, 1892, Spartanburg Schools—Early File, Pamphlet Collection, Kennedy Room, Spartanburg County Public Library, Spartanburg, S.C.

117. Ibid.

118. Pruitt, *Things Hidden,* 56.

119. Ibid.

120. Minutes, Board of Trustees of the School District of the City of Spartanburg, Kennedy Room, Spartanburg County Public Library, Spartanburg, S.C. (1898).

121. Tindall, *South Carolina Negroes,* 219.

122. Ibid., 223.

123. Ibid., 302.

124. Franklin, *From Slavery to Freedom,* 260.

African Americans and the Presbyterian Church

The Clinton Presbyterian Church and Sloan's Chapel

Nancy Snell Griffith

Like other Christian denominations, Presbyterians struggled for decades over the issues of slavery and race. Before the Civil War, they had lengthy discussions on whether slaves should join the church, under what circumstances their children should be baptized, and whether it was sinful to hold slaves or worship beside slaveholders. Members in the North advocated for the abolition of slavery, while many members in the South advocated vigorously for its justification on biblical grounds. These divisions would ultimately result in a split between the northern and southern churches in 1861. Following the Civil War, there was continuing discussion about how to treat the freedmen, many of whom had been church members. The southern branch of the Presbyterian Church (the Presbyterian Church in the United States, or PCUS) was unsure of whether to admit freed slaves as members of existing white churches or to set up separate black congregations. The general assembly of the northern church (the Presbyterian Church in the United States of America, or PCUSA) was working hard with the freedmen and quickly established black congregations and educational institutions in the South.[1]

The southern church's lengthy deliberations and its continued resistance against setting up churches under the control of black ministers and elders ultimately doomed the efforts of the PCUS to failure. Historians who have examined the history of evangelical churches and race in the South have focused on the tendency of southern theologians to view slavery as an individual moral issue rather than a societal one. This resulted in the church losing its moral authority to speak out on one of the pressing social issues of the day. Historians have also consistently noted the slowness of the PCUS to respond to the needs of its former black members, especially as compared with the efforts of the northern church.[2]

Original building of the Clinton Presbyterian Church, built c1855.
Courtesy of Presbyterian College Archives.

The situation in Clinton, South Carolina, reflected the situation of the Presbyterian Church as a whole and provides an illuminating case study of the Presbyterian debates about race and the status of African American members. Before the war the black membership of the Clinton Presbyterian Church far exceeded the white membership. After the war numerous attempts were made to set up Sunday schools, worship services, a mission, and even a separate congregation—ultimately named Sloan's Chapel—for the freedmen. But because of the rules established by the PCUS, all of these efforts hinged on the new congregation being under the control of the session of the Clinton Presbyterian Church, and the newly freed slaves were not content with this arrangement. They wanted their own self-governing church, served by ministers of their own race. Thus the effort of the Clinton Presbyterian Church to accommodate its former black members ultimately failed, and the fledgling Sloan's Chapel eventually came under the control of the PCUSA.

Slavery and the Presbyterian Church

Many members of the Presbyterian Church owned slaves, and in many South Carolina churches, especially in the lowcountry, the number of black members far exceeded that of white ones. Most Presbyterian congregations in the South made provisions for the slaves of their members to attend Sunday school and church and to be received as members. The southern church, however, faced a dilemma: "how to treat the slave as a human being, capable of repentance and salvation yet to find him recognized only as property in the law of the State."[3]

This dilemma had faced churchgoing South Carolinians for over a century. In 1712, to counter the notion that being baptized was not consistent with a state of slavery, the South Carolina legislature passed an act declaring it lawful for any Negro to profess the Christian faith and to be baptized. Even after this, however, churches did little to minister to their slave populations until after the American Revolution. They increased their focus on the slaves even more after the Great Revival of the early 1800s.

As early as 1787 debates about the morality of slavery had occurred in the Presbyterian Church. That year members of the church's general assembly recommended that every church and family under their care strive for the abolition of slavery and the education of black people, both slave and free.[4] In 1799 an overture was presented to the Synod of South Carolina asking the organization to appoint a committee to encourage members of other denominations in the state to petition the state legislature to begin planning for gradual emancipation. Robert Walker brought this overture to the Presbytery of South Carolina at its meeting in February 1800, and the presbytery advised that "any attempt at the present to bring about a legislative reform in this case, in this State, would not only be attended with want of success, but would be attended with evil consequences to the peace and happiness of our country." The following year the synod agreed to lay the overture aside, although it did urge the churches to educate the slaves in preparation for any future emancipation.[5]

In 1818 the members of the church's general assembly spoke out even more strongly on the matter. While they expressed sympathy with southern slave owners who had had slavery thrust upon them and recognized the problems inherent in the sudden emancipation of slaves, they declared "the voluntary enslaving of one portion of the human race by another, as a gross violation of the most precious and sacred rights of human nature, and as utterly inconsistent with the law of God . . . and . . . the spirit and principals of the gospel of Christ." The measure was approved unanimously by northern and southern representatives alike, partly because, as indicated by the South Carolina resolution discussed earlier, opposition to emancipation in the South had not yet hardened as it would later. In addition the motion was raised late in the meeting, when many members had left, and it contained no language constraining its members to do anything. There was apparently some resentment among South Carolina ministers, however, because at the meeting of the Synod of Georgia and the Carolinas in 1837 there were repeated attempts, all of which ultimately failed, to pass a resolution declaring that the 1818 action of the general assembly was unconstitutional and that "the relation of master and slave is a civil and domestic institution, and one on which no judicatory of the church has the right or the power to legislate."[6]

During the 1830s abolitionist sentiment began to grow in the country as a whole and among ecclesiastical bodies. Southern churches felt increasing pressure to endorse emancipation, and in consequence they hardened their position against it. They resented the North pressuring them on abolition, especially since New York did not actually abolish slavery until 1827 and Pennsylvania's law did not take total effect until 1847. Even free black people in the North, like slaves in the South, were not admitted into white churches on an equal footing and so organized their own congregations. In addition there was no doubt that the North profited from the slave trade it so abhorred and that New England's textile industries relied on the cotton produced by southern slave labor.[7]

According to the church historian James H. Moorhead, church governing bodies "could move neither too far ahead nor lag too far behind their constituencies, lest disaffected minorities secede. . . . In an era of contradictory commitments, unity could be purchased only by moral platitudes and purity by schism." The religious historian C. C. Goen concluded that this resulted in a moral vacuum on the part of church leaders, a vacuum that some scholars see as one of the root causes of the Civil War. These conclusions are based on statements such as that made in 1867 by Albert Barnes, a theologian and New School Presbyterian, who noted, "There are those in the ministry, and those who are private members of the churches, who, whatever may be their real sentiments, are, from their position, their silence, or their avowed conservatism, classed in public estimation with the apologists for slavery, and whose aid can never be relied on in any efforts for the emancipation of those who are in bondage." This moral vacuum was worsened by the fact that Presbyterian pastors who favored abolition were leaving the South in large numbers and becoming vocal advocates for emancipation.[8]

Even as late as 1833 few Presbyterian pastors belonging to the Presbytery of South Carolina were ministering to the slave population. In addition slave members were not allowed to participate in church governance. According to the historian Donald Mathews, "the message was filtered through the gauze of whites' moral perceptions . . . since whites were, as they understood such matters, the very personification of Christian civilization." Presbyterians in South Carolina certainly would have agreed with this assertion. In 1847, in reference to the attempt to establish a special mission to the slaves in Charleston, a committee appointed by Charleston Presbytery noted that the slaves "must be supplied with God's word as they are supplied with their daily bread—by the hands of their masters."[9]

In 1844 the Presbytery of South Carolina first made note of significant efforts to provide slaves with religious education, pointing out that this work was "commanding serious and awakened consideration" and that not only were slaves included in regular church services but also "there are many opportunities afforded them, when they are addressed exclusively, and instructed catechistically in the fundamental doctrines of the gospel." By 1846 there were two domestic missionaries working among the slaves in upstate South Carolina, one in Newberry District and one in the Savannah River area of Abbeville District. This arrangement, however, was to last only two years, after which the ministers of individual churches were expected to take over this responsibility. This made the effort less effective since most pastors were already greatly overworked, serving several churches at one time, and it often proved difficult to gather the slaves together to receive special instruction.[10]

In 1838 the Presbyterian Church split into two separate bodies, mostly on doctrinal grounds. It is clear, however, from the minutes of the Synod of Georgia and the Carolinas that slavery played a big role in this decision. Almost the entire session of the synod in 1837 was devoted to the conflict between the two warring parts of the denomination. Repeated attempts were made to pass resolutions declaring the general assembly's 1818 opinion on slavery unconstitutional and asking the synod to "look upon whatever acts heretofore passed by the Assembly which have been of the nature of legislative acts on the subject of Slavery, as without authority and void." In 1838 the synod threatened to leave the denomination altogether and become independent, but eventually, like most southern churches, it chose to go with the more conservative group in the denomination, which became the Old School church, while the more liberal churches joined the New School.[11]

By 1840 many churches in the Synod of Georgia and the Carolinas were beginning to offer special services for black people because the slaves' total ignorance of the Bible rendered the regular services attended by both black and white people ineffective. In the synod as a whole that year, around 5,000 slaves were receiving special religious instruction and there were 863 black church members. This was not yet the case in most of the Presbytery of South Carolina, however, where only "where we have large congregations of the coloured population" were "special sermons . . . preached for them."[12]

In 1845 the Old School Presbyterian Church addressed the biblical stance on slavery, refusing to denounce it because slavery existed in the early days of the church and early slaveholders were admitted as members. However, the general assembly cautioned that masters were also constrained by the Bible and should treat their slaves humanely. Morality, in the case of slavery, was to be considered an individual rather than a societal matter. In a rare reaction to a general assembly action, the Presbytery of South Carolina responded affirmatively to this decision: "The decision on the Slavery question we regard as scriptural, and as a distinct recognition of the principles, not only of the religious but also of the civil compact among the States of this Union. And we fervently hope, that the question may ever rest upon this decision." James Henley Thornwell, a prominent South Carolina theologian, was one of those most vocal on this issue. In 1847 he argued that the church, a spiritual body, "has no right to interfere directly with the civil relations of society." Questions of abolition were thus the purview of statesmen, not ministers—for men as citizens but not in their role as church members.[13]

In 1849 the synod's "Narrative of the State of Religion" noted a general increase in religious instruction among the slaves, calling such instruction "both politically and morally the great question with us—it is one which involves alike our domestic and religious peace—it is as delicate in its nature as it is important in its results—it is a subject which we feel pressed upon us, at this particular crisis, claims equal to any other." This idea of domestic peace played a large part in the church's desire to provide the slaves with religious education. In an 1832 sermon Rev. Charles Colcock Jones of Savannah emphasized that "obedience is inculcated as a *Christian duty,* binding on the Servants, and thus the authority of Masters is supported by considerations drawn from eternity . . . the simple presence of a white man at stated times amongst the Negroes, will tend greatly to the promotion of great order."[14]

During the deepening national crisis over race in the 1850s, the Synod of South Carolina and some individual Presbyterian ministers began to be more vocal on the subjects of religion, slavery, and states' rights. In reality South Carolina had a secession crisis ten years before finally seceding from the Union in 1860. The state's secessionists, upset by southern acceptance of the Compromise of 1850, which decided the issue of slavery in the new territories won by the United States in the war with Mexico, demanded that the state secede. At its meeting in November 1850, the Synod of South Carolina noted the "cheering fact," not known by abolitionists, that nearly all of its ministers provided separate preaching and instruction to African Americans in addition to the regular services provided for both races. "We deeply deprecate the crusade against the institution of slavery, and the hindrance thrown in our way . . . by fanatical and ignorant intermeddlers. Our slaves are contented, nay happy, in their position, and rejoice in the religious instruction they receive."[15]

Secessionists had control of the South Carolina General Assembly when it met in December 1850. In a sermon delivered at the Second Presbyterian Church in Charleston by Rev. Ferdinand Jacobs (father of William Plumer Jacobs, future pastor of the Clinton Presbyterian Church) during this legislative session, he declared: "Our rights have been invaded; ourselves, our institutions, our manner of life most flagrantly defamed; we are contemned, despised,

scorned;—and even in our most sacred relations,—our relations in the Church
. . . we have, in some of its branches, been told to stand aside. . . . Let us plant
ourselves upon the justice of our cause. And, *if we cannot agree; if we must separate; -* then, LET THE SEPARATION COME!"[16]

During all of this discussion, however, the southern church was diligent in
bringing the gospel to its black members. The first mention of black church
members in the Presbytery of South Carolina appeared in October 1850, when
presbytery rolls indicate that 146 black members had been added. The minutes for November of that year indicate that of 2,706 total communicants in
the presbytery, 309 were black. These numbers continued to rise, and by April
1854, 531 of the church's 2,664 members were black. Indeed in the Presbytery of
South Carolina that year, the "Narrative of the State of Religion" noted that "in
some churches there is more interest among, and more additions from this [the
instruction of black people by local ministers] than from the white part of the
congregation." It is important to note, however, that religious instruction was
often used as a means of advocating hard work and obedience on the part of the
church's slave members.[17]

African Americans and the Clinton Presbyterian Church

During the antebellum period, the picture at the Clinton Presbyterian Church
(now First Presbyterian Church, Clinton) was reflective of the situation throughout the South. Slaves were admitted to membership but had no standing in
church governance. They attended regular church services, sitting in the galler-
ies that surrounded the sanctuary on three sides. The church session established
a Sunday school for them after the war and even made repeated efforts to build
them a chapel governed by the session of the Clinton Presbyterian Church. This
resulted in the formation of Sloan's Chapel, but because of the inability of the
PCUS to decide how to treat black congregations, by 1875 the fledgling church,
like many others in the South, had been ceded to the PCUSA.

Clinton was founded in 1852 at an intersection called Five Points, where the
Greenville–Columbia and Spartanburg–Augusta roads intersected with another
road that came in from the northwest. Five Points featured a racetrack and was
also a traditional gathering place for chicken fighting, drinking, hunting, and
gambling. This spot was one mile west of Holland's Store, which in 1809 was the
only post office in the eastern part of Laurens County. There were several early
homes located near Five Points. There were also a few commercial buildings,
including a railroad depot and a barroom. Streets were laid out, and the lots for
the new town were sold in September 1852.[18]

According to William Plumer Jacobs, who first saw the town in 1862 and returned in 1864 as the first pastor of the Clinton Presbyterian Church, Clinton was
definitely a country town. Every family had a large garden and kept chickens,

turkeys, cows, pigs, and horses. There were no regular Presbyterian services in Clinton until 1853, when Rev. Zelotes Lee Holmes, a resident of Laurens, began to preach in a grove on Musgrove Street. By this time the town was growing. The prospect of the new Laurens Railroad, which was chartered in 1847 and completed in 1854, caused a land boom in Five Points, and additional homes and stores were built between the depot and Holland's Store. Once the railroad opened, large quantities of cotton were shipped through town.[19]

Two years after Reverend Holmes began preaching in Clinton, the Presbytery of South Carolina authorized him to organize a church. Reverend Holmes was also serving the churches at Duncan's Creek and Rocky Spring at the time and so could devote only part of his attention to Clinton. The Clinton Presbyterian Church was formally organized on July 28, 1855. With Reverend Holmes presiding, twenty-three women and eight men united to form the new congregation. The church had already purchased a lot on Irby Street (now Carolina Avenue) and erected a forty-by-fifty-foot frame building with a gallery on three sides of the sanctuary. The first slaves were admitted to membership only two months later: Crecy, who belonged to Dr. Bell; and Huldah and Vincent, who were owned by Robert Bell. Apparently, according to later records, a slave who was to receive membership required a certificate of character and a permit from his or her owner. A comparison between those slaves baptized and their owners and the number of slaves possessed by each owner in the 1860 slave schedules shows that most owners who belonged to the Presbyterian church had presented only a small number of their slaves for membership.[20]

The new church grew slowly but steadily. In 1856 Reverend Holmes reported to the presbytery a total of forty-five communicants, six of whom were African American. By April 1858 the number of communicants had increased to fifty-seven, ten of whom were African American. By 1860 there were fifty-eight communicants, fifteen of whom were African American. There was a storm on the horizon, however, and Presbyterian pastors were breaking their long silence to express their opinions. In December 1860, with Lincoln having been elected and secession fever sweeping the South, Rev. B. M. Palmer, a South Carolina native and former professor at Columbia Theological Seminary, preached an impassioned sermon at the First Presbyterian Church in New Orleans that shows just how far southern ministers had progressed in commenting on what they used to call "civil matters." He noted that he had steadfastly avoided preaching on political subjects, but "at a juncture so solemn as the present, with the destiny of a great people waiting upon the decision of an hour, it is not lawful to be still. Whoever may have influence to shape public opinion, at such a time must lend it, or prove faithless." He spoke of the individuality of character that defines a people, calling it "providential" and "the pledge of the divine protection," and he concluded: "If then the South is such a people, what, at this juncture, is their providential trust? I answer, that it is *to conserve and perpetuate the institution of domestic slavery as now existing* . . . we should at once . . . proclaim to all the world that we hold this trust from God, and in its occupancy we are prepared to stand or fall as God may appoint. If the critical moment has arrived at which the great issue is joined, let us say that, in the sight of all perils, we will stand by our trust." He urged the southern states to consider seceding from the Union; within two weeks South Carolina had done so, and Louisiana would follow a month later.[21]

The next year, with the outbreak of the Civil War, the Presbyterian Church split into two branches, the southern church (PCUS) and the northern (PCUSA). The minutes from the inaugural meeting of the PCUS, held in Augusta, Georgia, in December 1861, contain a long report on the reasons for the separation, addressed to all of the churches in the world. According to this report, the root cause for secession was the antagonism between the North and the South on the subject of slavery. Though the Presbyterian Church as a whole had refused to make slaveholding a sin, "the North exercises a deep and settled antipathy to slavery itself, while the South is equally zealous in its defense." As they had earlier, the founders of the PCUS insisted that the issue of abolition was a political one: "in our ecclesiastical capacity, we are neither the friends nor the foes of slavery . . . we have no commission either to propagate or abolish it. The policy of its existence or non-existence is a question which exclusively belongs to the State."[22]

Following the formation of the PCUS, the new denomination assigned missionary operations among the black people to its Committee on Domestic Missions. A committee was also appointed to write a pastoral letter on the religious instruction of the slaves to be submitted to the general assembly in 1862. The matter was continually referred to different committees until 1865, when the last committee was discharged without ever having reported.

Religious instruction of the slaves was consistently provided during the war, however, to the point that in 1863 the general assembly of the PCUS was able to say that more was being done than at any previous time. This was the case in Clinton, where there were twenty-three black people among the sixty-one total members of the church. When William Plumer Jacobs preached his first sermon at the church in 1862, he noted that "the negroes were very earnest and attentive." Meanwhile the Civil War temporarily stopped development in the fledgling town. Most of the men were serving in the Confederate army, the stores and post office were closed, and the railroad was running only one train per week. No federal troops ever came into Clinton, although they came as far inland as Pomaria, only thirty-five miles from town, and Clinton experienced a flood of refugees from Fairfield, Lexington, and Richland Counties.[23]

After the Clinton church was founded in 1853, Reverend Holmes declined to serve as its permanent pastor, and in 1864 Reverend William Plumer Jacobs, a graduate of the College of Charleston and Columbia Theological Seminary, was called as the first pastor. When he was hired, his charge also included the nearby Shady Grove and Duncan's Creek churches. By September of that year Reverend Jacobs had received many more members of both races into the congregation, and there were 135 communicants, a majority of whom, 72, were black. It is interesting that there were almost three times as many female African American members as male African Americans. The situation was similar at the Johns Island Presbyterian Church, where between 1856 and 1861, 95 African American females and 56 African American males joined the congregation. Although in the case of both Clinton and Johns Island it was higher than average, this plurality of women members was typical of evangelical churches as a whole and applied to both black and white members. The historian Stephanie McCurry, in *Masters of Small Worlds*, notes that the average percentage of female members among both black and white congregations in Presbyterian churches in the lowcountry during the antebellum period was 61 percent.[24]

Early in Reverend Jacobs's ministry, he began to hold separate services for the black members twice a month. Because the slaves could not read, their services had to be conducted on a plan different from that for white members. Reverend Jacobs, in handwritten notes dated 1864, described his method of instruction:

> On entering the Church, I take my stand before the pulpit, open with a short prayer, then sing two verses of a familiar hymn & after that review last Sunday's catechismal lesson in about five minutes. Then I raise my hand—the class rises & we sing two or more verses of a hymn. They then resume their seats & I go over the next lesson with them. Then I teach them the text I am to preach from, & ask for last Sunday's text. After that we study a hymn together; try to sing the hymn. During this singing I go into the pulpit. After the singing, I take my text, the congregation repeating it & all the heads of my discourse &c &c after me. I conclude with a prayer, in which all unite in repeating the Lord's Prayer, a hymn and the benediction.[25]

In December 1864, only months before the end of the war, the session of the Clinton Church suggested that several black members "of strict integrity and morality" be selected to report all misdemeanors among "their colored brethren" to the session. Several more were to be selected to "maintain order and quiet in the congregation when assembled or assembling, and to see that none remain standing about the doors." Those appointed were to appear before the session to learn their duties and "to be warned against being puffed up in their own conceit." These individuals' names as well as the names of their owners were recorded in the minutes: Spencer (J. H. Bell) and Wash (R. S. Vance) were appointed watchmen, and Jim (R. S. Phinney) and Neally (W. H. Henry) were appointed to keep order. This plan was to be followed for six months on a trial basis, and if it failed to produce the desired effect, it would be annulled. Apparently Wash (Vance) never served as a watchman, since by December 23 Spencer (Bell), Jim (Phinney), and Neally (Henry) had received their instruction as watchmen.[26]

Church records reveal little about these men. Spencer Bell joined the church on September 2, 1860, and his daughter Dora was baptized there on October 30, 1865. At the time of the 1870 census, he was still living in Jacks Township and was sixty years old. Wash Vance joined the church on May 5, 1860, and died on June 7, 1865.[27]

When the war ended, the northern branch of the church (PCUSA) began actively working in the South to set up black churches and educational institutions. When the PCUSA's general assembly met in Pittsburgh in 1865, it appointed a special committee on freedmen. There were already 36 teachers and missionaries in the South supported by local missionary societies. By the following year, with the centralization of the work, there were 55 missionaries educating over 3,000 students and training an additional 2,000 in Sunday schools. By 1869 there were 179 missionaries serving 72 churches and 5,600 communicants in the South; 126 of these missionaries were black, and 26 of those were ordained ministers. The institutions established by the northern church were instrumental in providing an educated group of clergy for African American churches. Along with Lincoln University in Pennsylvania and Princeton Seminary, they provided almost all of the ordained ministers for black Presbyterian churches in the South, including those for the eventual offshoot of the Clinton church, Sloan's Chapel. Among the significant institutions in the Carolinas were Wallingford Academy, established in Charleston in 1865; Biddle Memorial Institute and Biddle Seminary (now Johnson C. Smith University) in Charlotte, established in 1867; and Fairfield Institute in Winnsboro, established in 1869.[28]

In contrast to the northern church, "The Presbyterian Church in the United States was so slow in establishing a postwar racial policy that it lost most of its black communicants, who may have numbered as many as ten thousand in 1861." In addition Presbyterian divines such as Robert Dabney were warning that admitting black people on an equal footing would lead to the social mixing and ultimate "amalgamation" of the races.[29]

In 1865 the general assembly of the PCUS asked "what course should be pursued toward the colored people within our bounds" and declared that "the abolition of slavery by the civil and military powers has not altered the relations . . . in which our Church stands to the colored people, nor in any degree lessened the debt of love and service which we owe to them, nor the interest with which we would still desire to be associated with them in all the privileges of our common Christianity." According to the general assembly, black Presbyterians would be allowed to organize their own churches, but these bodies were not to be considered wholly independent. They were to be supervised by white pastors and elders until African Americans could be sufficiently trained to hold those offices. The African American congregations, however, were permitted to elect their own superintendents or watchmen to oversee their operations and report to their sponsoring sessions. Noting the shortage of black men qualified for ordination, the assembly suggested that presbyteries could license qualified African Americans as "exhorters" under their supervision.[30] .

While there was continued interest in religious and educational improvement of the freedmen, the purpose of this education was often to maintain the old tradition of white superiority. Black people were seen as simple, educable only to a certain degree. They were also seen as immoral. Many seemed to have lost all interest in church, and those who were still interested declined to worship with white people. This did not seem to be the case in Clinton, however. In April 1865 the congregation consisted of 68 white and 93 black communicants. By September of that year there was only 1 additional white member, but the total of black members had risen to 109. Reverend Jacobs began to perform marriages for the freedmen and to baptize their children. Between 1865 and 1873 he performed 59 such marriages and baptized 39 black children.[31]

By 1866 the church had 125 black members and 83 white ones. That year the session began to consider organizing the Clinton Colored Presbyterian Church under the control of First Presbyterian. The feeling was that, despite limited funds, it would be wise to erect a separate building for this purpose. Reverend Jacobs was to present this idea to a meeting of the black members; if they expressed interest in the idea, a collection would be taken up each second Sunday for the purpose of acquiring land and putting up a building. By 1867 black membership had increased to 143 while white membership stood at 94. The efforts of the church to provide religious opportunities for the newly freed slaves would continue for almost a decade, taking disparate forms and reflecting the confusion in the PCUS. This confusion and the increasing political turmoil of the Reconstruction era ultimately doomed their efforts to failure.[32]

Clinton's plans for an all-black church were changed somewhat when, in April 1867, the Presbytery of South Carolina decided that no church could be organized on the basis of race. At the April 23 meeting of the church's session a committee to obtain land for a Presbyterian church for black people was appointed; at the meeting on May 16, 1867, it was resolved that the black members should be organized into the Second Presbyterian Church, Clinton. The session minutes explicitly state that, in accordance with the recent presbytery decision, the new church would be required to admit white members as well as African Americans. The church would elect its own deacons, but the elders of First Presbyterian would serve as their elders. The members of this new congregation would meet at First Presbyterian until a suitable building could be erected for their use. Each elder and deacon at First Presbyterian was expected to aid in the construction of the new church and was to solicit funds from other sources.[33]

By May 18 a meeting had been held with the African American members of the church. They approved the plan for the new church, and 143 members were dismissed from the Clinton Presbyterian Church to form the Second Presbyterian Church, Clinton. Governance of the new church was to be vested in its own session. This plan was never executed, however, and the names of black members were restored to the roll. A note in the session minutes indicates that some "difficulty having subsequently arisen among the colored members, it was resolved, at a meeting of the congregation to stay proceedings for the present that the white people might build a church for the colored people, the title of the same to be vested in the white bd. of Trustees."[34]

In 1868 the Presbytery of South Carolina requested that member churches remove from their rolls all members who had either moved outside the bounds of the presbytery or were currently unknown to the church. As a result, one hundred black members were removed from the rolls of the Clinton church. This resulted in a decrease in black membership to fifty-two, the first time in a number of years that it was less than the white membership of seventy-three. This situation was apparently reflective of the situation in the presbytery as a whole. According to the minutes of the Presbytery of South Carolina for April 1868, "The disposition of our colored members generally is very much the same as reported to the last Assembly; the majority holding aloof; some attending occasionally upon the preaching of the gospel and the sacrament of the Lord's Supper, and a few worshipping with us as of old."[35]

In June 1868 the session returned to the plan of building a separate black church and decided to use the unexpended funds raised for the freedmen's church to purchase a lot. R. W. Phinney and E. T. Copeland were appointed as a committee of two to oversee this process. Apparently nothing had happened by the following February, when Reverend Jacobs was authorized to preach to the black members in the church's lecture room once a month and to ask the presbytery's Committee on Sustentation if there were funds available to help them build a church. By March, Reverend Jacobs was preaching to the freedmen twice a month, and the session records noted, "They are very much interested in their privileges, tho' many who were once with us, stand aloof."[36]

In 1869 the session of the Clinton church decided that a mission for African American members rather than a separate church would be organized. Called the Mission of the Presbyterian Church, Clinton, S.C., this new organization was to be governed by the session of the Clinton Presbyterian Church, and Reverend Jacobs was to serve as its pastor. The mission members were to elect their own deacons, subject to approval by the session. They were to raise money to underwrite their own expenses. Members of "approved character" were to conduct the Sunday school. The session appointed a committee of five to consider providing a building for the mission.[37]

By May the decision had been made to put an addition on the church's session house to serve as the freedmen's mission. The Committee on Sustentation of the PCUS provided two hundred dollars toward the cause. Plans were turned over to the building committee to be executed. In September 1869 these plans were laid out in the church's narrative to the Presbytery of South Carolina, which was reproduced in the session minutes:

> In April last, the Session determined to organize a mission to the blacks. For this purpose we have with their consent separated their roll from ours—they having no other connection with us than that they are under our control as a Session. This mission occupies a small building on our Church premises, which we are enlarging to suit their congregation. They have organized a Sabbath school conducted & taught by colored men. They have a small library and a regular weekly prayer-meeting. Rev. Wm. Jacobs is pastor of the Church, by virtue of his relation to us. We ask, if it is proper to have this mission, entered upon the roll of Presbytery, as the "Clinton Colored Mission," & that as such it be assessed. By way of making the way clear, we wd. State that the constitution of the Church requires the session to be white men.

By November, however, the session, following its pattern of constant vacillation, ruled that "all former actions of this body in regard to altering the Session House be hereby repealed."[38]

The following month the session once again decided to buy a lot for a freedmen's church and appointed Robert Phinney, W. H. Henry, and Joel Foster to find something suitable. In May 1870 the group purchased a 1.5-acre lot from T. E. Sloan for $87.50 and began to raise funds and find a contractor to erect a building. Mr. Sloan donated an additional .25 acre, to make the whole plot 1.75 acres. By July the members of the mission had been removed from the roll of the church.[39]

Just as the Clinton church was struggling with its black members, the PCUS was searching for a plan to accommodate black members around the South. In 1869 the general assembly decided that black Presbyterian churches, while deemed "independent," were initially to be led by white pastors from nearby churches and would be represented at meetings of presbyteries by these white pastors and their white elders. This arrangement was to continue until "they are sufficiently educated to warrant their becoming independent." Once African Americans could pass the ordination exam, presbyteries were permitted to license them. Once black ministers were licensed, "Presbyteries may either ordain and install them over such churches still holding their connection with us, or ordain and install them" over separately governed churches. This action of the general assembly was permissive rather than mandatory, however, and still left churches and their black members in a kind of limbo.[40]

Meanwhile the political situation in South Carolina was beginning to erode the amicable relationship between black and white in the local church. In September 1869 the Presbytery of South Carolina bemoaned the "unhallowed and inimical partisan spirit which is abroad in our land, and which is brought to bear so directly on that portion of our population as to produce in many places bitterness, alienation, and every evil work." Times were increasingly hard in Clinton. The railroad was no longer running, and there was a local black militia, organized by Joe Crews, patrolling and generally terrorizing the area. In August 1870 two hundred armed black men threatened the town, but conflict was avoided. Dr. Jacobs proclaimed that "the races are in a highly excited state and I fear that evil will yet result from it." Two days later groups of black and white men met near Clinton, and the black group reportedly fired on the white one. The fire was returned, and four were wounded. The black crowd assembled at Crews's mill, but over a thousand white locals streamed into town in response. This event too ended peacefully.[41]

In his "Personal Recollections of Clinton," William Plumer Jacobs described the effect this strife had on the local church:

> Hoping to be still able to retain our hold upon this people, notwith-
> standing the fierce political contests of the hour, the session organized
> this membership into a colored mission. . . . Presbytery however de-
> clined to organize them on the Assembly's or any other plan. This
> and the rapidly increasing political excitements destroyed our hopes.
> Through political preaching, in one case enforced by outside influences,
> the negroes were incited to violent thoughts against their former mas-
> ters, and they being then in control of the State Government, common
> danger threw the whites into an attitude of trembling self-defense. The
> colored membership deserted our church by scores. . . . It was a dreadful
> time, past forever, thank God. Still our church continued through all
> this its regular services for the instruction of the negroes.[42]

The racial violence caused the plans for the new mission to founder. In December 1870 Mr. Bell from the freedmen's chapel committee reported to the session that although the frame of the building was up and the shingles bought, "the freedmen had entirely deserted the church." On motion of R. S. Phinney, work was suspended on the project. The matter was brought up again in February 1871, and in April, R. H. Williams agreed to put up a building sometime during the summer. Apparently this did not happen, because by August 1872 the freedmen were still attending a mission Sunday school in the session house and the session was once again planning to renovate it. By September the session had decided to sell the lot purchased for the freedmen's chapel and to use the resulting funds to finance the renovations to the session house. The land was ultimately sold in February 1873.[43]

African Americans continued to attend Sunday night services in fairly large numbers, however. On April 22, 1871, Dr. Jacobs reported preaching to thirty white and sixty black people. In March 1872 the session reported that "our colored people attend our church very well. They are generally out in good numbers at night and we think they [would] attend anywhere, where proper efforts were made to bring them in." By August 1872 the church had founded a mission Sunday school for its black members. It was operating under the management of the church session, and fifty students attended the first meeting. By the second meeting this number had increased to ninety-five. By the following August there were still forty-two members, and the black members had a thriving prayer meeting with thirty attendees each Tuesday night.[44]

The area, however, was in turmoil. This was the time of the famous Ku Klux Klan trials in South Carolina, and President Ulysses S. Grant had called in federal troops to restore order. A number of Clinton residents, including several members of the church, were arrested, and the railroad, the backbone of the village, went bankrupt. During the early months of 1873, the mission Sunday school was suspended. By September it had resumed, with forty-seven members led by the deacons Henry Todd, James Johnson, William Young, and Tom Ferguson.[45] Dr. Jacobs was holding services for the mission every Sunday afternoon, and according to the session's report to the Presbytery of South Carolina, "Latterly the congregation has considerably increased and they manifest much interest in their church." The freedmen were still holding prayer meetings in the chapel on Tuesday nights, although the session asked that the deacons "see that order and propriety . . . be maintained."[46]

By 1874 some white Presbyterians were beginning to decry the PCUS's lack of focus on the freedmen, observing that "no plan has been adopted which has elicited the approval and active support of the church . . . as an organized church, we are doing almost nothing." Of the estimated 13,837 black people who had been affiliated with the Presbyterian Church in the South in 1860, only a few could still be found. The church formulated a new plan to establish and develop separate, self-sustaining African American churches to be led by trained black preachers. Synods and presbyteries were asked to encourage the formation of such churches, and congregations were asked to contribute to a Colored Evangelistic Fund to support them. In order to educate ministers to serve in these churches, the PCUS established Stillman Institute in Tuscaloosa, Alabama, in 1876.[47]

This feeble effort came too late for the Presbyterian congregation in Clinton, however. In January 1874 the freedmen asked that Reverend Daniel Gibbes, a minister in the PCUSA, or "northern" church, be allowed to preach one sermon to them. Reverend Gibbes was at the time serving the 2nd Presbyterian Church of Laurensville, which became Mt. Pisgah Presbyterian Church in 1876. He was also serving the Pitts Church in Mountville (which still exists and was renamed Piedmont Presbyterian Church in 1979). This would be the first step in the complete transference of the mission Sunday school from the PCUS to the PCUSA. Reverend Gibbes was an interesting man. Born into slavery in Charleston in 1827, he received an education at Wallingford Academy in Charleston and was ordained around 1871. At the time of his death he was described as "an effective preacher, an earnest worker, and devoted to the welfare of his race."[48]

By May 1874 Reverend Jacobs was lamenting the failure of his efforts among the black community: "All my efforts to build up a colored church have come to a dead failure. I intend giving up the attempt finally and leave the field clear to the northern church. My members have all gone over to the Northern Presbyterian Church. I have been laboring faithfully but unsuccessfully. The labor, preaching three times a day is greater than I can bear and I shall encourage the new organization to my utmost." By May 1875 the Clinton church's black members had received permission to have Reverend Gibbes preach to them once a month. This marked the organization of Sloan's Chapel Presbyterian Church, part of the northern church, and ended the Clinton Presbyterian Church's efforts to establish a separate African American Presbyterian church.[49]

Sloan's Chapel Presbyterian Church (PCUSA)

The new church seemed to flourish. It soon boasted a school, which by 1878 had an enrollment of fifty. By 1879 the church was sharing a lot with the public school on Academy Street. Daniel Wallace Culp had succeeded Reverend Gibbes as the church's pastor and was also serving Pitts in Mountville and Mt. Pisgah in Laurens. He was working under the sponsorship of the Freedman's Board of the northern Presbyterian Church. Culp had been born a slave in neighboring Union County, South Carolina. He entered Biddle Memorial Institute in 1869 and was among its first graduates. He graduated from Princeton Theological Seminary in 1879. He later attended the University of Michigan Medical School and the Ohio Medical School, from which he graduated in 1891. He practiced medicine in Florida and Georgia until his health began to fail. He also edited a book entitled *Twentieth Century Negro Literature.*[50]

In 1880 the congregation began raising funds to put up a building. In April 1880 Dr. Jacobs noted in *Our Monthly:* "We suppose nearly every citizen of this village has had a call from the indefatigable deaconess of this Colored Presbyterian Church (Sloan's Chapel), now being erected in this village. This is a small

Rev. Daniel Wallace Culp, who was the pastor at Sloan's Chapel around 1879. He later became a doctor. Courtesy of Johnson C. Smith University.

organization, and they are struggling earnestly to put up a building . . . we are glad to know that many of our citizens have subscribed liberally to their aid." Members of Clinton Presbyterian Church answered this call, dedicating their collection on the fifth Sunday in May for this cause. Their statistical report to Enoree Presbytery indicates that they managed to raise thirty-five dollars.[51]

By 1881 the congregation was being led by Rev. George Dillard, and Miss Emma Galloway was playing the organ. Reverend Dillard was a native of Winnsboro and a graduate of Fairfield Institute. He later graduated from Biddle University. He was to serve Sloan's Chapel and Mt. Pisgah for nine years. Reverend Jacobs described the church's progress in *Our Monthly:*

> The Colored Presbyterian Church of this village, which is in connection with the Northern Assembly[,] shows signs of vitality. Rev. Geo. Dillard (colored) who is their pastor is laboring hard to make the church

a success. It is now quite probable that their house will be put in neat order and complete repair. The membership is small, but the Sabbath-school under charge of an efficient superintendant, is large and prosperous. It is also proposed by the colored people of the community to put up a commodious school building. We rejoice at these evident signs of progress and trust that they will result in good.

The Clinton church continued to support them, donating fifteen dollars in 1883. By August 1883 Sloan's Chapel had a new twenty-six-inch bell, ordered from the Blymer Manufacturing Company.[52]

By 1887 Sloan's Chapel listed 77 members, with 125 enrolled in the Sunday school. Joseph Schofield Williams served both Sloan's Chapel and the Pitts church from 1889 to 1892. Williams was born in Laurens and was a graduate of both Biddle University and Biddle Seminary. This was to prove the high point in the church's history, both in enrollment and church development. The chapel building must have been deteriorating during this time, however, because in *Our Monthly* Dr. Jacobs announced that the members were preparing to build a new church.[53]

During the remainder of the nineteenth century, Sloan's Chapel was served by a number of pastors, most of them remaining for only one or two years. It is interesting that all of these men were well educated, which seemed to belie the PCUS's idea that there would be a shortage of educated ministers to take over the Presbyterian field in the South. Samuel John Onque (1895) was a graduate of Lincoln University in Pennsylvania and Princeton Theological Seminary. Peter Moone (1896–99) graduated from Biddle Institute and Biddle Seminary in Charlotte. John Tillotson Wright (1899) was a graduate of Lincoln University and also Lincoln Seminary.[54]

By the beginning of the twentieth century, the church was declining. Between 1901 and 1907 it was served by seven stated supplies, only one of whom, Alfred A. Wright, stayed for more than one year. He remained from 1904 to 1908. Josiah Woolridge and John E. G. Small supplied the church in 1908 and 1909–10. In 1909 the membership stood at around twenty-five. Homer Y. Kennedy was the stated supply in 1911, and in 1912 the pulpit was vacant. A. H. Reasoner, a teacher at the Harbison Institute in Irmo, began to work as the stated supply at Sloan's Chapel in 1914. By 1922 the membership had declined to twelve, with thirty-one attending the Sunday school. None of these early twentieth-century pastors was an ordained minister.[55]

There was renewed hope for Sloan's Chapel in 1924, when the Clinton barber Sam Patterson bought a lot for the church with hopes of building a small chapel. The Clinton community was contributing to the effort, and well-known local banker and businessman W. J. Bailey was serving as the fund's treasurer. It is not known if this effort ever met with any success. The church staggered on under Reasoner until 1936. By that time membership stood at ten, with thirty-five enrolled in the Sunday school. Its last known pastor was Robert C. Johnson, who was presiding over a flock of only ten members in 1937. The church was removed from the rolls of the PCUSA in 1940.[56]

Thus ended the noble experiment begun seventy years earlier by Reverend Jacobs and the Clinton Presbyterian Church. Its varied history was reflective of the African American Presbyterian Church in South Carolina and the South. The slowness and inconsistency of the PCUS's response to the needs of its newly freed black members doomed its efforts to failure. The earlier and much more cohesive efforts of the PCUSA and other Protestant denominations ensured that they would ultimately win the day. To this day there is no church for African American Presbyterians in Clinton; the closest such church is Piedmont Church in nearby Mountville.

Notes

1. For an interesting perspective on how various churches, both northern and southern, dealt with the religious education of African Americans during the eighteenth and early nineteenth centuries, see Charles Colcock Jones's lengthy examination in *The Religious Instruction of the Negroes in the United States* (Savannah: Thomas Purse, 1842).

2. See especially Donald G. Mathews, *Religion in the Old South* (Chicago: University of Chicago Press, 1977); James H. Moorhead, *American Apocalypse: Yankee Protestants and the Civil War, 1860–1869* (New Haven, Conn.: Yale University Press, 1978); C. C. Goen, *Broken Churches, Broken Nation* (Macon, Ga.: Mercer University Press, 1985); Janet Duitsman Cornelius, *Slave Missions and the Black Church in the Antebellum South* (Columbia, S.C.: University of South Carolina Press, 1999); Erskine Clarke, *Wrestlin Jacob: A Portrait of Religion in the Old South* (Tuscaloosa: University of Alabama Press, 1979); Daniel L. Fountain, *Slavery, Civil War and Salvation* (Baton Rouge: Louisiana State University Press, 2010); and H. Shelton Smith, *In His Image, but . . . Racism in Southern Religion, 1780–1910* (Durham, N.C.: Duke University Press, 1972). An older but still useful study is Carter Woodson, *The History of the Negro Church* (Washington, D.C.: Associated Publishers, 1921). For information more specific to the Presbyterian Church, see Ernest Trice Thompson's seminal three-volume series *Presbyterians in the South* (Richmond, Va.: John Knox Press, 1963–73); Albert Barnes, *The Church and Slavery* (1857; reprinted, New York: Negro Universities Press, 1969; Andrew Murray, *Presbyterians and the Negro* (Philadelphia: Presbyterian Historical Society, 1966); F. D. Jones and W. H. Mills, *History of the Presbyterian Church in South Carolina since 1850* (Columbia, S.C.: R. L. Bryan, 1926); and Erskine Clarke, *Our Southern Zion: A History of Calvinism in the South Carolina Low Country, 1690–1990* (Tuscaloosa: University of Alabama Press, 1996).

3. Jones and Mills, *History of the Presbyterian Church in South Carolina,* 73.

4. To understand the discussions on slavery in the Presbyterian Church, it is necessary to understand the denomination's governance structure. Presbyterian congregations are governed by sessions, made up of elders elected by the congregation. Ministers and representatives of the sessions of different churches meet periodically at presbytery meetings. Presbyteries are the most local form of organization among congregations. They are empowered by the church to license, ordain, call, and dismiss ministers; send overtures to the general assembly on various issues; and to vote on substantive rulings or changes in the book of order made by the general assembly. They also keep records on the churches within their bounds. During most of the period under discussion, the Clinton church was part of the Presbytery of South Carolina; in the late 1870s it became a part of Enoree Presbytery. Several presbyteries are combined into a synod, which is a regional group of presbyteries drawn from one or more states. Synods are also able to comment on various issues in the church by way of submitting bills and overtures to the general assembly. The ultimate governing body of the church is the general assembly, which usually met yearly during this time. Discussions about slavery and the status of African American members took place at all of these various governmental levels.

5. Samuel J. Baird, ed., *A Collection of the Acts, Deliverances and Testimonies of the Supreme Judicatory of the Presbyterian Church, from Its Origin in America to the Present Time* (Philadelphia: Presbyterian Board of Publication, 1855), 817–18; George Howe, *History of the Presbyterian Church in South Carolina*, vol. 2 (Columbia: W. J. Duffie, 1883), 172–73.

6. Baird, *Collection of the Acts, Deliverances and Testimonies*, 820; Thompson, *Presbyterians in the South*, 1:331; Minutes of the Synod of Georgia and the Carolinas, 1837. Available in the Department of Archives and Special Collections, Thomason Library, Presbyterian College, Clinton, South Carolina, 10.

7. For more information, see Murray, *Presbyterians and the Negro*, 30ff.

8. Moorhead, *American Apocalypse*, 16; Goen, *Broken Churches*, 169; Barnes, *Church and Slavery*, 17; Thompson, *Presbyterians in the South*, vol. 1, 336–38.

9. Mathews, *Religion in the Old South*, 145; Howe, *History of the Presbyterian Church*, 607.

10. Minutes of the Presbytery of South Carolina, April 1844, 8; April 1846, 4; April 1847, 8; September 1848, 14. The church printed a limited number of copies of synod and presbytery minutes for attendees. Copies may be found in the Department of Archives and Special Collections, Thomason Library, Presbyterian College, Clinton, South Carolina.

11. Minutes of the Synod of Georgia and the Carolinas, 1837, 23; 1838, 17.

12. Minutes of the Synod of Georgia and the Carolinas, 1840, 23, 28.

13. Baird, *Collection of the Acts, Deliverances and Testimonies*, 824; Presbytery of South Carolina, October 1845, 5; James Henley Thornwell, "Article III: The General Assembly," *Southern Presbyterian Review* 1 (September 1847): 102.

14. Minutes of the Synod of South Carolina, 1847, 21; 1849, 25; Charles Colcock Jones, *The Religious Instruction of the Negroes: A Sermon Delivered before Associations of Planters in Liberty and M'Intosh Counties, Georgia* (Princeton, N.J.: D'Hart & Connolly, 1832).

15. Walter Edgar, ed., "The Secession Crisis of 1850–51," in *The South Carolina Encyclopedia*, ed. Edgar (Columbia: University of South Carolina Press, 2006); Synod, 1850: 18.

16. Ferdinand Jacobs, *The Committing of Our Cause to God, a Sermon Preached . . . on Friday, the 6th of December, a Day of Fasting, Humiliation and Prayer Appointed by the Legislature of South Carolina, in View of the State of Our Federal Relations* (Charleston, S.C.: A. J. Burke, 1850), 22.

17. Minutes of the Presbytery of South Carolina, November 1854, appendix D; April 1854, Annual Report, appendix A.

18. Nancy Snell Griffith, *Clinton: A Brief History* (Charleston, S.C.: History Press, 2010); *Laurensville Herald*, September 17, 1852, 2.

19. Thornwell Jacobs, ed., *William Plumer Jacobs: Literary and Biographical* (Oglethorpe, Ga.: Oglethorpe University Press, 1942), 42.

20. Comparison of 1860 U.S. Census and William P. Jacobs, "Pastoral Record of the Ministerial Work of Wm. P. Jacobs," Clinton, South Carolina, 1867. Available in the archives of the First Presbyterian Church, Clinton, South Carolina.

21. Presbytery, April 1856, appendix C; April 1858, appendix; April 1860, appendix; B. M. Palmer, *The South, Her Peril and Her Duty* (New Orleans: Office of the True Witness and Sentinel, 1860), 5–10.

22. G. F. Nicolassen, ed., *A Digest of the Acts and Proceedings of the General Assembly of the Presbyterian Church in the United States, Revised Down to and Including Acts of the General Assembly of 1922* (Richmond, Va.: Presbyterian Committee of Publication, 1923), 891–92.

23. Jacobs, *William Plumer Jacobs*, 19.

24. "Records of Session, Presbyterian Church, Clinton So. Ca." (1855[–72]): 25. Available in the archives of the First Presbyterian Church, Clinton, South Carolina; Thornwell Jacobs, ed., *The Diary of William Plumer Jacobs* (Oglethorpe, Ga.: Oglethorpe University Press, 1937), 97; Jacobs, *William Plumer Jacobs*, 19; "Records of Session, Presbyterian Church, Clinton So. Ca." (1855): 35; figures from the session minutes of the Johns Island Presbyterian Church, provided by Dr. Charles E. Raynal Jr.; Stephanie McCurry, *Masters of Small Worlds: Yeoman Households, Gender Relations and the Political Culture of the Antebellum South Carolina Lowcountry* (New York: Oxford University Press, 1997), 160.

25. William P. Jacobs, "Hymn-Book for the Use of Our Coloured Congregation," Clinton, S.C., 1864, which can be found in the archives of the First Presbyterian Church, Clinton, South Carolina. Jacobs's method of instruction was similar to that suggested in Rev. Charles Colcock Jones, *Religious Instruction of the Negroes* (1842) and in Rev. William S. Plumer, "Thoughts on the Religious Instruction of the Negroes of This Country" (Princeton, N.J.: John T. Robinson, 1848). According to Jones (264), there were numerous manuals, published by different denominations, that laid out methods for instructing African Americans. Caroline Gilmore, in a note added to her *Recollections of a Southern Matron* (New York: Harper and Brothers, 1838), describes similar services conducted by black "class leaders" in churches in Charleston.

26. "Records of Session," 1855, 55–56.

27. Population Schedules of the Ninth Census of the United States, 1870, South Carolina. Washington, D.C.: United States Census Office, 1870. Jacobs, "Pastoral Record of the Ministerial Work of Wm. P. Jacobs" (1867).

28. Smith, *In His Image,* 222–23.

29. Ibid., 237; Robert L. Dabney, *A Defence of Virginia, and through Her, of the South* (New York: E. J. Hale and Son, 1867), 352–53.

30. Nicolassen, *Digest of the Acts,* 302–3.

31. "Records of Session," 1855, 62, 69; Nancy Snell Griffith, *All Beautiful the March of Days: First Presbyterian Church, Clinton, South Carolina, 1855–2005* (Columbia, S.C.: Professional Printing, 2005), 15.

32. "Records of Session," 1855, 80, 89.

33. Ibid., 92.

34. Ibid., 94–95.

35. Ibid., 98; Minutes of the Presbytery of South Carolina, April 1868, 15.

36. "Records of Session," 1855, 116.

37. Ibid., 119–21.

38. Ibid., 134–35, 141.

39. Ibid., 142, 158, 166.

40. Nicolassen, *Digest of the Acts,* 306.

41. Jacobs, *Diary of William Plumer Jacobs,* 133.

42. Minutes of the Presbytery of South Carolina, September 1869, 15; Jacobs, *Diary of William Plumer Jacobs,* 132–33; Jacobs, *William Plumer Jacobs,* 64.

43. "Records of Session," 1855, 181, 192; "Sessional Meetings" (Clinton Presbyterian Church), 1872[–76], 42–43, 77.

44. Jacobs, *Diary of William Plumer Jacobs,* 137; *Our Monthly* 9 (September 1872): 55; 10 (August 1873): 36. (Copies of *Our Monthly* are available in the Department of Archives and Special Collections, Thomason Library, Presbyterian College, Clinton, South Carolina.)

45. Church and census records reveal little about these deacons. Henry Todd joined the church on July 23, 1865, and married Sylvia Hipp on August 20, 1870. At the time of the 1870 census, he was a farmer, forty-two years of age, and living in Scuffletown Township with his son, Perry. James Johnson had his children Miranda, Louise, and Elizabeth baptized on November 11, 1866. Tom Ferguson and his wife, Sallie, had their daughter Florence baptized on September 13, 1869, and children Mary and Amelia baptized on August 1, 1873. See *Population Schedules of the Ninth Census of the United States, 1870, South Carolina.* Washington, D.C.: United States Census Office, 1870. Jacobs, "Pastoral Record of the Ministerial Work of Wm. P. Jacobs" (1867).

46. "Sessional Meetings" (1872): 108, 110.

47. "Evangelization of the Colored People," *Southern Presbyterian Review* 25 (April 1874): 228–29, 238.

48. [Daniel A. Gibbes obituary], *Presbyterian Banner,* May 27, 1891.

49. Jacobs, *Diary of William Plumer Jacobs,* 171.

50. Information on Dr. Culp came from the Inez Moore Parker Archives and Research Center at Johnson C. Smith University, Charlotte, N.C.

51. *Our Monthly* 17 (April 1880): 80; Clinton Presbyterian Church, "Sessional Records III," 1877–78, 68.

52. Edgar Sutton Robinson, *The Ministerial Directory: Of the Ministers in the Presbyterian Church in the United States (Southern), and in the Presbyterian Church in the United States of America (Northern), Together with a Statement of the Work of the Executive Committees and Boards of the Two Churches, with the Names and Location of Their Educational Institutions and Church Papers,* vol. 1 (Oxford, Ohio: Ministerial Directory Company, 1898), 239; *Our Monthly* 18 (January 1881): 44; "Sessional Records III," 144; *Our Monthly* 20 (August 1883): 179.

53. *Our Monthly* 28 (April 1891): 153.

54. Robinson, *Ministerial Directory,* 425, 551.

55. *Minutes of the General Assembly of the Presbyterian Church in the United States of America.* (Philadelphia: Presbyterian Board of Publication, 1901–1922); Jacobs, *Diary of William Plumer Jacobs,* 400.

56. *Minutes of the General Assembly of the Presbyterian Church in the United States of America.* (Philadelphia: Presbyterian Board of Publication, 1937).

"Murder takes the angel shape of justice"

Rape, Reputation, and Retribution in Nineteenth-Century Spartanburg

Carol Loar

On June 12, 1879, the *New York Times* reported that "threats of lynching are openly made" in Spartanburg and "intense feeling exists against" John J. Moore, then in jail on suspicion of having raped and murdered a "young white girl named Woodward" a week earlier.[1] Those threats came to fruition several days later when Moore was seized from the custody of sheriff's deputies, taken to the spot where the girl's body had been found, and lynched. The *Times* continued to follow the case for over a month, as did other national, regional, and local papers. The original crime and subsequent lynching generated such widespread attention for three reasons: a sympathetic victim, a locally notorious suspect, and an element of novelty. John J. Moore was white.

In the antebellum South, most victims of lynching were white; generally speaking, slaves were too valuable to be subject to such acts of "justice," and other forms of punishment—both on the plantation and through the courts—were readily available to slave owners or victims of crime.[2] In the postwar era, however, the tables were turned. Lynching became an act overwhelmingly associated with the extralegal punishment of black people, although, as in Moore's case, white men and women were occasionally treated to the same kind of popular justice. According to John Hammond Moore (no relation to John J.), between 1880 and 1900 only six of eighty-six documented cases of lynching in South Carolina involved white victims.[3]

The vast majority of scholarship on lynching has focused on those incidents involving black men and white women.[4] Such cases were not only far more prevalent but also crucial to understanding issues of race and gender in the postwar South. Lynchings of white people, such as Moore, however, anomalous as they may have been, are worth exploring for what they reveal about values and ideas in the nineteenth-century upcountry. While lynchings in general can be seen as a form of popular justice (however misconceived and brutally expressed), the decision to lynch a white person was less reflexive and more thoroughly considered than it would have been for an African American victim.

In nearly all cases of white lynchings in late nineteenth-century South Carolina, the perpetrators were also white; they were lynching "their own." In the more common scenario, that of a predominantly white crowd lynching a black man, the victim was more easily characterized as "the other," a person to whom it took little effort to attach all the negative stereotypes associated with black men. In other words, he was less likely to be known and perceived as an individual than someone such as Moore, who came from within the group. Moore was a lifelong resident of the community; many in the crowd that attended his death would have known him, or at least known of him. It was John J. Moore who was being lynched, not a semianonymous black man. Moore was surprised by his lynching; newspaper accounts suggested that even when the noose was around his neck and the manner of his death was being discussed, he apparently doubted that the crowd would actually carry out the deed.[5] What was it about Moore that led hundreds of people, some of them well-respected members of the community, to subject him to the same kind of public humiliation and execution more commonly reserved for African Americans? Why were they unwilling to wait just one week for the regularly scheduled meeting of the circuit court to indict and try Moore? Why did the grand jury that convened the week after the lynching refuse the directions of the circuit court judge to indict those responsible for carrying out the lynching? The answers to these questions lie in the reputations—real or constructed—of the murdered woman and her accused killer, in the nature of the crime, and in one additional element: the literal demonization of John Moore. Only by stripping him of his humanity could his lynching be justified. Only then could the use of extralegal punishment be reconciled with the belief that those who carried it out were moral, upstanding citizens saving the community from an insidious influence.

"Grafted on a Tree"

The execution of Moore was provoked by the discovery on June 8, 1879, of the decomposing body of a young woman in the woods near his house.[6] Two local men, T. McElrath and G. W. Duncan, "attracted by the stench and vultures," found the body, which was later identified as Frances Heaton and/or Frances Woodward.[7] The *Charleston News and Courier,* then the most influential and widely read paper in the state, spared its readers few of the gruesome details, including a full description of her body: "Buzzards had picked out her eyes, her body was much swollen and discolored, the clothes were thrown up about her waist, her throat was cut from ear to ear, and into the backbone, a bullet hole was in her right breast, [and] worms [were] crawling in countless multitudes in every cavity—her hair was kept in motion by them." The horrified

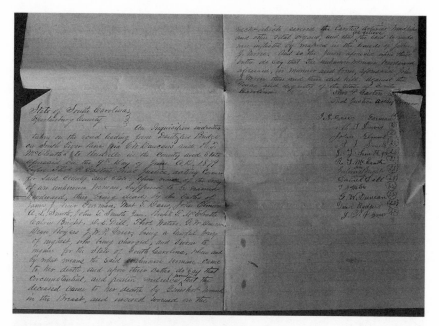

Verdict of coroner's inquest into Woodward's death, 1879. Courtesy of South Carolina Department of Archives and History.

correspondent concluded by praying, "God grant I may never again see such a sight!"[8] The *Carolina Spartan*'s account was no less explicit, but the *Spartanburg Herald* and the *Weekly Union Times* showed more restraint; the latter paper "omit[ted] some of the details of the crime as being too revolting and . . . unfit to appear in the column of a journal that reaches the homes of virtuous and refined people." While the more horrific particulars were only hinted at, both papers made clear what the more graphic versions merely implied; "it was plain to see that Woodward had been outraged."[9]

A coroner's jury was sworn in that night, and suspicion quickly fell on Moore.[10] When the inquest reconvened the following day, witnesses testified that the young woman had come to Spartanburg County from Pickens in search of an uncle she believed to live in the area. They had pointed her toward Reidville; her route had taken her past Moore's house, where she stopped to ask for directions. Moore's wife invited her to join them for dinner (which Woodward may have "paid for"),[11] after which Moore offered to show Woodward the way through the woods toward Reidville. She was not seen alive again. Several witnesses described the earrings and brooch Woodward had been wearing; those items, along with her purse, were missing. Dr. L. H. Peebles swore that he examined Moore the morning after Woodward's visit and "found him

*Warrant for the arrest of John J. Moore, June 1879. Courtesy of
South Carolina Department of Archives and History.*

suffering apparently from some mental aberration. . . . Moore seemed restless
and troubled about his financial affairs." Furthermore, Peebles testified that he
not only saw Moore drinking whiskey that morning but also "considered him
to some extent under its influence."[12] The acting coroner, the trial justice T. P.
Gaston, immediately issued a warrant for Moore's arrest. By the following day
Moore was in jail and rumors that he would be lynched, reported by the *New
York Times,* had begun to circulate.

Moore remained in custody for a week, by which time newspaper stories,
new information about the victim, and local gossip had combined to inflame
public opinion against him. On the night the body was found, most of the coroner's jury "stayed to help watch the corpse, which could not be moved" until
the inquest reconvened and a verdict was delivered.[13] The author of this report
commended the jurors for their steadfastness in the face of such a gruesome
sight. Within days of Moore's arrest, rumors of further incriminating evidence
had begun to circulate. Several papers reported that he had "assaulted [Wood-
ward] twice within sight of his own house."[14] According to other sources, on
the night of the crime Moore "occupied the bed with his wife, an unusual oc-
currence," and a witness staying in the house reported that she overheard him

warn his wife, "For God's sake Sally, never tell it."[15] Stories also placed Moore, "hatless and shoeless," near the scene of the crime; the examination of footprints found near the body "corresponded with the size of [Moore's], and showed that they had been made by shoes run down at the heels and on the side. His footgear was all in that condition." Even more damning was the report that he "had blood on his pantaloons when he returned to the house."[16] The contents of the autopsy report also likely became public and further inflamed public opinion; after relating the necessary physical and medical details, the physician concluded the report by claiming that "the murder of this poor defenseless woman has had but few equals in either savage or civilized life."[17]

At the same time, more information about the victim was becoming available. She was described as "a poor but good girl,"[18] "well clad for a poor girl, as she claimed, and appeared to be, and every person who saw her at Vernonsville agree to her respectable appearance."[19] Because Woodward was "one of three orphan sisters," the readers would have been reminded that she lacked a father who could both protect her in life and avenge her in death.[20] The fact that she died, as multiple sources recorded, defending her virtue only increased sympathy for her and outrage against her murderer.

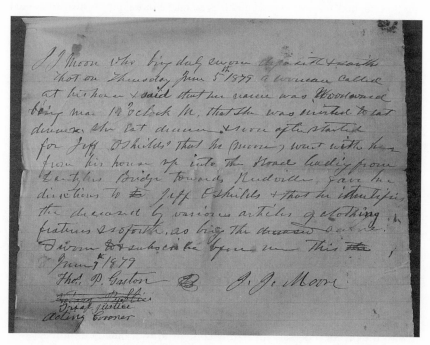

Moore's affidavit concerning Woodward's death. Courtesy of South Carolina Department of Archives and History.

On Saturday, June 14, a group of roughly one hundred men met at Dant-zler's Bridge on the South Tyger River, near the scene of the crime. The stated purpose of the meeting was to search for those items presumably stolen from Woodward, dragging the river if necessary. One account of the events has the men dividing into teams or groups for the search. According to the *Greenville News*, "what was found is not known, but enough was learned to fully satisfy them that Moore was the guilty man."[21] What seems to have transpired next was a plan to lynch Moore; those who opposed the plan were asked to leave. The plotters were motivated not only by a desire to avenge the crime but also by a rumor that Moore "would obtain a change of venue from this county and be defended by able counsel."[22] The possibility that Moore would somehow escape punishment was not to be countenanced. Plans for the lynching were carefully prepared. A "jury was drawn and with 'Judge Lynch' presiding, a trial was held: Moore was returned 'guilty.'"[23]

The fear that Moore would elude justice, combined with the arrival of Frances Woodward's sisters from Pickens County on June 16, dictated the tim-ing of the lynching. That night a crowd of armed men, variously estimated at between 150 and 600 members, stormed the jail. Anticipating such an event, Sheriff Thompson had first tried to raise a *posse comitatus* to protect the jail; fail-ing that, he had assigned several deputies to take Moore out of town and asked railway authorities to make an unscheduled stop so that Moore could be gotten safely out of the county. The mob searched the jail and, upon discovering that Moore was no longer there, "broke into squads, each one of which was under the command of a leader, to whom all yielded implicit obedience, orders being issued in military style and promptly executed."[24] The squads rode off to search the area, and just before midnight one of them, reportedly led by a former Spar-tanburg police officer or detective, found Moore and his guards hiding under the Chinquapin trestle on the Air-Line railroad awaiting the arrival of a train to Charlotte.[25]

The squad took Moore back to town "amid silence and order," and there the mob reassembled and began the roughly fifteen-mile journey back to the site where Woodward's body had been found, arriving around dawn.[26] According to all accounts, the crowd was orderly and sober; "there was not a drop of whiskey carried along," and the size of the crowd continued to grow as it drew nearer to the destination.[27] By the time of the lynching, the audience was estimated at between six hundred and one thousand people, who chose what the *News and Courier* called a "committee of arrangements" and the *New York Times* referred to as a "judge and jury."[28] Regardless of this group's title, the crowd entrusted it with the practical details, apparently content to wait quietly until the action started. Members of the mob came not only from Spartanburg County but Pick-ens and Greenville Counties as well. Woodward's two sisters were in attendance;

one of her uncles may also have been there. Moore's family was present too—his wife and children, mother, and mother-in-law "were weeping and imploring mercy"—although they were persuaded to leave before Moore was hanged.[29]

The lynchers were in no hurry to finish the job. They set the time of Moore's "execution" for 10:00 A.M. and discussed exactly how he should be killed—by gunshot, hanging, or burning—taking care to consult Woodward's sisters on this point.[30] They drafted a reporter to take Moore's statement; before Moore would speak, however, he wanted the "committee" to confirm that he had been granted the right to choose the manner of his death in exchange for his statement. The "committee" put the proposition before members of the crowd, and it was only after they assented that Moore began to speak. Everyone but him seems to have understood the agreement to mean that in order to choose the manner of this death, he would have to confess to Woodward's rape and murder; he believed that as long as he told all he knew of the circumstances, he could still maintain his innocence. For most in the crowd, who had no doubt about his guilt, Moore's continued claims of innocence merely confirmed that he was unrepentant and undeserving of the mercy for which his family was begging. The pleas of his family had no effect on him; despite the "terrible wailing," praying, and weeping, so moving that "many of the crowd turned away, unable to bear the distressing sights and sounds," Moore said nothing to them, and as his family departed, his "eyes were hardly dampened."[31]

After his family left, the sisters of the murdered woman then approached. Once again Moore refused to confess. At that point the sisters reportedly decided that Moore should be hanged. According to the *News and Courier*'s correspondent, the crowd, which had been so quiet that the "tapping of a woodpecker and the chirping of some small bird" could be heard, became incensed and began calling for Moore's immediate execution. Anxious to preserve the impression that this was an orderly, reasoned process and not the actions of a frenzied mob, the "committee" brought in a minister to speak and pray with Moore. As before, he refused to give way, and his "demeanor was so stolid and indifferent, that the minister in apparent despair stepped out."[32] Nothing remained to be done but to find a suitable tree from which to hang Moore.

That task accomplished, a rope was placed around his neck and tied to a sturdy tree branch. Before he was hanged, he was given the opportunity to address the crowd. He asked that his body be spared any postmortem mutilation and then, one more time, maintained his innocence, saying that "he didn't blame them, thinking as they did, for what they were about to do, but hoped that after he was dead the right man would be found and they would say that John Moore, for once, spoke the truth."[33]

One outsider made a last-minute attempt to dissuade the crowd from its purpose. Maj. T. W. Woodward, who was passing through Spartanburg on his way from Fairfield County to Furman University, "pleaded eloquently and well" for Moore's return to official custody.[34] Woodward (no relation to the victim) arrived on the scene as Moore was being prepared for hanging. His description of the scene confirms the newspaper accounts of the lynching. "A large crowd, in which there were many women, was silently watching the preparations. Seeing many old men present, I attempted to awake their sense of right by a direct appeal to their patriotism, and by picturing the evil effects of mob law. They seemed astounded at my temerity, and demanded to know my name, which I gave, supplemented with a recital of my Confederate Army record. Further remarks were cut short by the venerable, white-haired leader who said: 'Colonel [*sic*], we have had enough of this; postpone further talk until after the hanging.'"[35] The *Carolina Spartan* confirmed that Woodward's words "made no more impression on the calm, determined multitude than a light rain on a mass of granite."[36] Woodward's efforts on behalf of the prisoner at an end, Moore was placed in a buggy, which at a signal from one of the dead woman's sisters was then pulled out from under him at about 8:00 A.M., two hours ahead of the appointed time. His body was left hanging for at least half an hour before Dr. Hugh Toland (the same physician who had performed the autopsy on Frances Woodward) declared Moore dead. As promised, his body was returned unscathed to his family, and the rope used to hang him was cut into small pieces and distributed as souvenirs. The crowd dispersed even as people continued to make their way to the area, some reportedly coming from "Spartanburg, in an omnibus," hoping to see the action.[37]

In the days following Moore's death, the governor issued a proclamation "calling on the civil officers of the law to use all means at their command to arrest and bring to trial all persons concerned in the hanging of Moore."[38] The following Monday, June 23, the court of general sessions convened in Spartanburg. In his charge to the grand jury, Judge Pressley referred to the return of the Democrats to power in South Carolina and stated that "whatever [Moore's] crimes may have been, there was no possible excuse for this unlawful act. The Courts are now in our own hands; not like they were a few years ago, when juries could be packed and public officials induced to compromise cases or pardon the convicted. There is no danger from these causes now. The term of Court was at hand, when a fair and speedy trial might have been secured, and there was no excuse for the people taking the law in their own hands and executing the prisoner, who was awaiting trial." The judge continued, arguing that the example this case provided threatened to set a precedent that would lead to further lynchings, perhaps even of innocent men. "No man is safe. Good men may be executed. Our only safety is in good government, when the laws are fairly administered." He closed by reminding the jury that they were "the custodians of the peace and good order of the county"; it was their "duty to inquire into this affair."[39] The *Spartanburg Herald* commended the judge for having "discharged the delicate business faithfully and wisely under all the circumstances."[40] All that remained was for the grand jury to summon witnesses and hand down an indictment for Moore's death.

The jury had no intention of cooperating, however. In a lengthy presentment, they justified both the crowd's actions and their own inaction. The response began by claiming that the coroner's inquest had sufficiently established Moore's guilt in what they referred to as "the greatest of all possible crimes." It went on to argue that the purpose of the law is "the administration of simple and exact justice." As Moore was so obviously guilty, the crowd that lynched him had "done nothing more than a simple act of justice." Furthermore the death penalty in murder cases was "the law of God written on the heart"; thus the crowd was guilty of nothing more than "act[ing] in obedience to the dictates of justice." To the judge's claim that justice could be preserved only through the proper administration of the law, the jury replied that "public opinion . . . is the source and fountain of all human law." A clearer example of public opinion in action could not be found.

The response continued on less philosophical grounds. While the jury denounced the *routine* resort to lynching and emphasized the importance of trial by jury, it blamed a number of specific factors for the actions of the crowd. First, the penitentiary system was not, in the jurors' minds, "calculated to repress the disorders of society." Just the opposite, in fact had occurred: "crime has increased, wherever penitentiaries have been established." The fear of "the too great leniency of juries in capital felonies" was also a concern. Lest the judge (or the community) think that the jury was completely abdicating its role, however, the jurors expressed their willingness to indict "persons living together in our county in open violation of the law" in order to "maintain the high standards of morals which the people of Spartanburg have always upheld."[41] As far as the court was concerned, this was the end of the matter.

The repercussions from the case continued, however. A week after the local papers reported on the court, an alarmed citizen contacted the *Spartanburg Herald*. A. H. Dean wrote to the paper, hoping to clear his name of what he referred to as "base charges alleged against" him over Moore's death. He denied having warned the sheriff of the impending lynching and having advised Moore to maintain his silence rather than to confess. He claimed to agree that "Moore received a merited punishment," and he concluded by writing that whoever was "so base as to circulate such charges coupled with threats of violence against an innocent law-abiding citizen, deserves to be called as he is, a coward and a liar." Despite the grand jury's refusal to indict the lynchers, Dean clearly deemed it necessary to distance himself from any potential future legal action directed against his accusers—or vigilante justice aimed at him.[42]

Though Dean's letter effectively ended the case as far as the people of Spartanburg were concerned, the lynching of John Moore resonated for decades. In 1911 the *Spartanburg Herald* reprinted an article that had recently appeared in the *Roanoke Times.* The account of a recent brawl and gun battle in Spartanburg prompted the *Times* to retell Moore's story, casting the locals as "mountain men" and Frances Woodward as a "sturdy, honest mountain girl to whom a 30 mile walk [from Pickens] was no great matter." Aside from some colorful new details (a lean "mountaineer [who] leaned forward and spat accurately into an ant hole he had been watching" while waiting for Moore to confess, and a mule-riding black man who swore not to inform on the lynchers, adding, "to tolle you the truf, I think myself Mr. Mo' got off mighty light"), the paper's version of the story was essentially accurate.[43]

The *Roanoke Times* article was not the last on the Moore case to appear in the records. In 1938, nearly sixty years after the lynching, James Coan related his recollections of the lynching to a WPA worker recording stories of life in the nineteenth-century South. Coan had been a fourteen-year-old resident of Spartanburg County at the time and remembered having witnessed the lynching. According to his account, the "cavalcade came by [his] home," and while his brother went "in for a sandwich," James joined the crowd. He told the interviewer that "over five hundred people attended [Woodward's] funeral, and, very likely, it was there and then that indignation reached the height wherein the purpose to lynch was formed." Moore, on the other hand, was buried with "few attendants" and no ceremony.[44]

"Well It Was Not a Negro!"

Reaction to the lynching varied along geographical lines. Local, state, and regional papers generally condemned lynching in the abstract while approving of it in Moore's case. The *Charleston News and Courier* argued that extralegal punishment was "a procedure which, in grave emergencies, is almost a necessity" but could only too easily be "perverted into a means of gratifying passion or satisfying vengeance." The proper functioning of the legal system in South Carolina meant that "every criminal, high or low, is sure to be brought to justice quickly." Nevertheless, the paper declared, the lynching of John Moore was "a deed that we cannot condemn, whatever its abstract impropriety and manifest unlawfulness." The editorial made it clear that Moore's guilt and conviction at trial "by any fair and impartial jury" would have been inevitable. What was in doubt, however, was the availability of an unbiased jury; "in a State where there is a large population of ignorant and passionate persons, it [rape and murder] cannot with safety be treated like an ordinary offense against person or property." Given these circumstances, Moore's lynching was almost laudable; "when it is found that outrages like that for which Moore died are punished instantly by the people, without reference to other judge or jury, we shall hear no more of atrocities that make the blood run cold."[45] The *Carolina Spartan* reprinted the *News and Courier's* editorial in its entirety, presumably signaling its agreement with the Charleston paper's sentiments.[46]

The *Weekly Union Times* took an even more favorable position with respect to the lynchers. As had the other papers, it condemned the practice of lynching, but the editor then stated that "we are impelled to believe, from the many outrages committed of late upon defenceless women, and little girls, that the law is too tardy and uncertain in dealing with the devils who commit them . . . . we are inclined to wink at the decision of Judge Lynch."[47] "Winking" hardly constitutes a forceful denunciation.

The *Spartanburg Herald* took a less conciliatory position. Agreeing that Moore's guilt was never in doubt, the editor still decried the lynching and claimed that "we made an honest effort to prevent it, not for his sake, but that the law might be vindicated." Given the prevailing public opinion, this was a brave admission. Nonetheless the editorial was unwilling to denounce the lynchers completely. It noted that they "were prompted, we know, by the best of motives" and that the crowd was "no excited mob of men, under the influence of liquor, but was composed of some of the best men in the county who were determined to rid the county of a villian [*sic*] of the deepest dye." It then reiterated the paper's preference that the legal system should have been allowed to deal with this case—but concluded that "if Lynch law ever was justifiable in any case, it was in this case."[48]

The *Charlotte Observer's* reaction was more equivocal than the *Herald's*. Like the South Carolina papers, it deprecated lynching in general but then expressed sympathy for the state, arguing that "its enemies have been given a peg upon which to hang a charge of insubordination to lawful authority." Remarkably the editorial goes on to express relief that Moore was white, not black; "otherwise the cry of race prejudice and persecution would have been raised against our sister State, and would have been heralded, no matter how unjustly, from one end of the country to another, for the purpose of exciting sectional and partisan bitterness against a portion of the country than which there is none more law-abiding."[49] Major Woodward's appeal to the crowd's patriotism can also be seen as concern for the state's image. This reaction—the question of how outsiders would perceive the lynching—was not an isolated one. The *Carolina Spartan* noted that "there has been considerable anxiety to know how the lynching of Moore would be received by the press of the State and the North."[50] It was a worry that would prove warranted.

All of the South Carolina editorials discussed above agreed on one other point. The behavior of the crowd was an important element in the papers' qualified approval of the lynching. Not only was the crowd well behaved and sober, but as several papers noted, "there was no concealment in Spartanburg. To their honor the people went about their work with fearful dignity, their faces exposed to the bright light of day. They were not ashamed of their purpose, and have no reason to blush for their act."[51] Even the *Spartanburg Herald,* which was slightly less sympathetic to the lynching, praised the fact that "the hanging was done publicly by unmasked men in open day-light, in the presence of a thousand spectators."[52] By avoiding disguise and waiting until morning, the lynchers had acted with honor and were to be commended for that, if nothing else. The emphasis on the lack of disguises and the time of day is significant; the papers were anxious to avoid any intimation of KKK involvement. By 1879 community leaders in Spartanburg had distanced themselves from the Klan and its activities and were anxious that public memory of those activities fade as quickly as possible.[53] In other words, these papers, along with the *Charlotte Observer,* were as much concerned with the effect of the lynching on South Carolina's image and economy as with the lynching itself.

The *Anderson Intelligencer* took a firmer line when it came to condemning lynching in general. Like the other South Carolina papers, it agreed that Moore deserved to die; when "guilt is clearly established, as the offense is unparalleled in gravity and infamy, a speedy and unusual punishment may be justified— not as the act of an excited and wild mob, but as the exhibition of the burning indignation and fearful wrath of the peaceful and law-abiding citizens of the land." Moore's case met these criteria; it was the grand jury's rationale for refusing to indict the lynchers that drew the paper's ire. The dangers inherent in recourse to lynching included not only the "large amount of prejudice and passion" that accompanies mob law, but also the more troubling likelihood that innocent lives would eventually be lost. To the charge that the courts were broken, the paper responded by reminding its readers that citizens had the power to see that the flaws in the legal system be fixed. Among the papers in South Carolina, these were the harshest words directed at Spartanburg over Moore's death; significantly, however, those words were aimed not at the lynchers but at the grand jury—and then only for the argument in their presentment, not for their failure to indict anyone.[54]

In late July support for the lynchers came from a completely unexpected source. Judge Aldrich, the circuit court judge who had presided at the March session of court in Spartanburg, discussed the Moore case at length in his charge to the grand jury in neighboring Greenville County.[55] He argued that "sometimes human nature will and must assert its dignity and defend the virtue and chastity of woman." In such cases, "'when dishonor stalks to our hearths, law ceases, and murder takes the angel shape of justice.' And so it was when Moore paid the penalty of his double crime." Even more remarkably for a judge, he blamed the legal system for having driven the lynchers to their task, claiming that "outraged humanity will not and cannot wait for the slow and uncertain process of the law's delay. It too often happens that by ingenious use of the instrumentalities that hedge around the accused, he escapes the just punishment of his crimes." The judge agreed with the editorials that emphasized the lack of disguises and the fact that the lynching took place in the daylight. The opposite circumstance—masked men operating under cover of darkness—was too reminiscent of the KKK and "condemned by good men everywhere." The conduct of the crowd in Moore's case thus became a sign, not of the lawlessness of South Carolinians but of the progress the state had made since the days of the "KuKlux [*sic*] reign."[56]

Northern papers were not so sympathetic either to the lynchers or to those who defended the lynchers. The *New York Herald* remarked sarcastically that "South Carolina is at last reconstructed; they have lynched a white man down there."[57] The *National Republican* was outraged by a *Washington Post* article that referred to Moore's death as "the first case of lynching that has occurred in this state for many years."[58] The *National Republican* responded sarcastically, writing that "we infer from this claim that 'stringing up a nigger' for voting the Republican ticket is not a case of lynching."[59] The *Albany Law Journal* expressed its horror at Judge Aldrich's defense of the lynching and its effects on the people of South Carolina, saying, "When officers of justice, grave judges, utter such sentiments as these, what can be expected of the community, except a continuance of such wild and irresponsible 'justice'?" Nor would the effects be limited to the legal system; the editorial warned that Judge Aldrich himself might become a victim along the lines of the "Kentucky tragedy."[60]

The *New York Times,* which covered this story for more than a month starting with the discovery of Woodward's body, commented at length. The paper referred to the lynchers as "Regulators" and blamed state and county officials for allowing the crowd to seize Moore.[61] Its editorial in response to the grand jury's refusal to indict any lynchers was absolutely scathing, an undoubted example of the reaction that the *Carolina Spartan* had feared. The grand jury, in the opinion of the *Times,* "proceeded to justify and extol the proceeding, as is quite proper and natural. No reasonable community should constitute itself Judge, jury, and hangman without giving excellent grounds for its somewhat unusual course." The editorial characterized the community's attitude toward the legal system as something "which an effete civilization has provided for this alleged purpose [the administration of justice]. Justice is justice, and it really makes no difference, according to Spartanburg opinion, whether the courts or the citizens administer it." The editorial then proceeded to demolish each of the grand jury's arguments systematically, concluding with the statement that in Spartanburg, public opinion and law were fully synonymous. Since that was the case, "why bother the courts? Or, what is better, why be bothered by the courts?" The

contempt fairly oozed from the page.[62] The sentiments of Judge Aldrich in his
charge to the Greenville County grand jury later that month seem to have rendered the *Times* speechless; it settled for repeating the judge's words without further comment.[63] Such outrageous statements would have confirmed northern
views of the South, especially the upcountry, as beyond redemption and thus
worthy of the paper's derision and scorn.[64]

Why?

The question remains: why was there so much support, at least in South Carolina, for Moore's lynching? On the surface of it, the crimes of rape and murder
would seem to be sufficient; it was those crimes that were most closely associated in people's minds with the lynchings of black men. The link between
honor and a woman's virtue is well known, and concern for honor was at least
implicit in local reaction to the lynching. Yet Moore was not the only person
in Spartanburg County charged with rape in the spring of 1879; the index of
Spartanburg County indictments shows that one Yorke Berry was indicted for
the rape of Pauline Gist. Furthermore there does not seem to be any mention
of the case in the local newspapers.[65] Clearly not all rapes generated the same
level of public anger; nor was honor equally at stake in all cases. The description of Woodward—the innocent, virtuous orphan, the poor-but-good girl—
disappeared quickly from the newspapers; the focus was overwhelmingly on
Moore, not his alleged victim.[66] Even her funeral, which would have provided
plenty of opportunity for pathos over a defenseless orphan so cruelly slain, seems
to have gone unreported. While Woodward's status may have played a part, it
was not the primary motive that led the crowd to lynch Moore.

Part of the answer to the question of "why Moore" lies in his reputation.
According to the *Spartanburg Herald,* Moore was "perhaps the worst man that
ever lived in Spartanburg County." So bad was he that "it is a monument to the
peace and law-abiding character of our people that he has been permitted to
live in this County" as long as he had. By Moore's own alleged admission, "he
had committed every crime known to the law except suicide."[67] According to
the *News and Courier,* Moore had "escaped, through legal loopholes, from the
consequences of half a dozen ugly charges."[68] If half of the allegations about
him are to be believed, the fact that he escaped popular justice for so long sup-
ports the argument that the bar to lynching a white man was higher than for an
African American. Moore's crimes were tolerated for decades before anyone took
extralegal action against him.

Moore's poor reputation dated back to the early 1860s, when he was implicated in the poisoning of "Wiley Wood."[69] Letters written to the governor
in the mid-1870s claimed that Moore had had to flee the area to avoid being
charged in that case, a charge that newspapers repeated at the time of Moore's

death. Around the same time, in 1861 or 1862, Moore, who was then a private in the Confederate army, was reportedly "drummed and marched out of camp at the point of Bayonets—having had the buttons cut off his coat for stealing."[70] Despite these offenses, in May 1874, at the urging of the Seventh Circuit solicitor W. Magill Flemming, Republican governor Franklin J. Moses appointed Moore to the position of trial justice in the county. Flemming assured the governor that Moore was "more competent to perform the duties than nine tenths of our Trial Justices." Even more valuable than his work as a trial justice would be Moore's ability to help procure Moses's reelection.[71] The following month, however, Moore was indicted on charges of malicious injury and trespass for having damaged a chimney and removed trees from the property of a neighbor over a period of several years.[72] Later in June another trial justice, W. J. Parker, wrote to the governor urging that Moore be fired from office. Parker's letter described what he saw not only as significant corruption on the part of Moore, among others, but also a personal vendetta against Parker himself.

According to Parker, Moore had been arrested and brought before him in early June 1874, accused of trespass and malicious damage. Because several witnesses were present to testify against Moore, he was bound over to appear before the grand jury, which indicted Moore on the charges; the solicitor—the same one who had asked for Moore's appointment to office—declined to prosecute the case, the official reason being because Moore had alleged that Parker was guilty of official misconduct in his handling of the case. Unofficially it seems clear that Flemming was protecting his ally and protégé, Moore. Parker was, in fact, indicted on what seem to be charges of bribery or extortion; his letter to the governor was prompted in part by a desire to clear his name in the matter. Parker's determination to fight the charges against him may have led to an escalation of hostility on Moore's part. On June 22 Parker and Moore met at or near the Air-Line depot while waiting to take the "cars" back to the Duncan area. Upon hearing that Parker was planning his legal defense, Moore allegedly "got mad and struck [Parker] a very severe blow on the side of [his] face and head, seizing [his] throat at the same time." Moore then "threatened to whip [Parker] before [he] got home or throw [him] off the train." Parker offered the governor the names of numerous witnesses who would corroborate his version of the events. He went on to itemize a list of other offenses that Moore had allegedly committed. In addition to repeating the claim that Moore had been drummed out of the Confederate army, Parker wrote that Moore had had to flee the county "under suspicion for poisoning one of our staunch citizens. . . . [He also h]arbored a squad of Ku Klux Klan 3 days and nights in his garret tops— loaned them his double Barrell [*sic*] shotgun one month (these facts I have from his own lips)." Furthermore, Parker cast serious doubt on Moore's Republican ties, saying that he had always voted Democratic and was even then "an officer

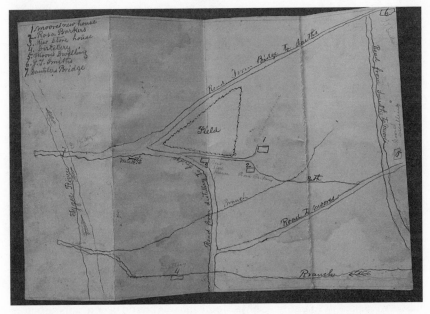

Moore's house and vicinity in 1879. This map was drawn for use in Albert Ralph's trial, but Frances Woodward was found in the same area, near the river. Courtesy of South Carolina Department of Archives and History.

in the grange department" and a "viscous [*sic*] man." Only in passing did he complain about Moore's lack of education and qualifications for office.[73]

Parker's allegations about Moore and his own claim to be able to deliver some "3 to 5 thousand votes" for Moses were confirmed by a letter signed by nine men urging the governor to retain Parker in office. The letter described Parker as the "Presiding Elder of the Methodist Episcopal Church" in the county and said that Moore had instigated the fight on the train and Parker had acted only in self-defense. All the other allegations against Parker were baseless in the authors' estimation. One signatory added that "from personal observation, I think Mr. John Moore utterly incompetent to fill the office of Trial Justice, both morally and intellectually." There is no indication in the letter that Governor Moses acted to remove Moore from office. As Moore was the appointee of a Republican governor in a heavily Democratic county and possessed an already dubious reputation, his tenure as trial justice would have further contributed to his status as a pariah, even if, as it seems, he was an opportunist rather than a real Republican; it was, after all, Republicans who petitioned the governor to recall Moore from office on the grounds of incompetence and Klan ties.[74]

Moore seems to have led a quieter life for the next several years; his name does not appear in trial records or in newspapers from that time. All that changed, however, in February 1879. Moore owned and operated a licensed distillery in Vernonsville. On Sunday, February 16, a young man named Albert Ralph visited the distillery to purchase whiskey for his ailing mother. He began drinking with the men already present; some time later, after he had become drunk, Ralph and James DeYoung began an argument, which ended when Ralph drew his pistol and shot DeYoung. The grand jury indicted Ralph for murder; however, testimony at the trial not only cast doubt on the element of premeditation but also seemed to implicate Moore in the killing. According to John Dempsey, Moore had urged the victim to pursue Ralph, even after the defendant had said, "Don't follow me or I will shoot you." In addition John Dempsey, Pete Dempsey, and other witnesses questioned Moore's statements regarding the positions of Ralph and DeYoung on the road; the issue was important enough that a map was drawn to be shown to the jury.[75] In his summation to the trial jury, the judge acknowledged the unreliability of Moore's evidence but reminded the jury that "the witnesses produced that contradict Moore will only affect his reliability. . . . It may induce you to throw out Moore's testimony and can have no other effect; and you will have to decide the case on the testimony of other witnesses, who are not impeached." Ralph was convicted of manslaughter and sentenced to two years of hard labor in the penitentiary.

Newspaper accounts of the homicide placed Moore's distillery in Wellford. One resident of that community sought to clarify the matter, saying, "J. J. Moore's distillery is at least four miles from Wellford. Even between it and us are the Middle Tyger and South Tyger Rivers. Wellford is not J. J. Moore's Post Office."[76] Moore and his distillery could apparently taint a community's reputation simply through proximity.

Questions about Moore's involvement in the case continued. At his lynching he was asked about his role in DeYoung's death; he adamantly denied having any responsibility in the matter. Skeptics were not convinced. The *Greenville Enterprise and Mountaineer* reported in its account of the lynching that Moore had been "guilty of poisoning a number of years ago a man named Wood, and of being instrumental in the shooting of another one," presumably James DeYoung.[77] Moore's denial, like Major Woodward's pleas on his behalf, fell on deaf ears.

At Ralph's trial the judge—the same judge who later applauded the lynching of Moore—condemned both the practice of "carrying deadly weapons and the maddening effects of mean whiskey! The holy Sabbath day, dedicated to rest and the worship of the good god was desecrated." The grand jury took the opportunity to inveigh against the sale of "spiritous [*sic*] liquors, [which] unless governed by strict police regulations, such as exists in towns and cities" are "dangerous and demoralizing to any community." The jury linked the sale of alcohol at establishments such as Moore's with "a large per cent of the business which crowds the Serious Docket of this Court."[78] Even if Moore had not been implicated in the killing, his status as the landlord of a such a disreputable enterprise would have been yet another black mark against his reputation. It is important to note that this grand jury was the same group that would refuse to indict anyone for Moore's lynching several months later. His already poor reputation in the community and the events of earlier that year help shed some light on the jury's unwillingness to act against his lynchers in June.

Moore's reputation alone was not enough to prompt his lynching, however. The depiction of Moore is essential both to understanding how the community perceived him and to justifying his lynching when it finally occurred. Moore was cast as a devil in disguise; from the physician who conducted Woodward's autopsy, to the grand jury that refused to convict him, to the various newspaper accounts of the murder and lynching, he was routinely described in terms that served to portray him as so evil that only by eliminating him could the community protect itself. The kindest things any of the regional papers said about him were that he was a "thief, sharper, and desperado" and a "terror for years,"[79] as well as a "lawless putrid pest" who was "black with crimes" he had committed.[80] Dr. Toland, who performed the autopsy on Woodward, wrote that her murder "has never since Adam or Eve were driven from the Garden of Eden had a superior in diabolical crime."[81] The grand jury charged with investigating the lynching referred to Moore as "the demon in human form."[82] The *Spartanburg Herald* described the rape and murder as a "diabolical act" and a "Fiendish Murder."[83] The *Weekly Union Times* carried the *Herald*'s report nearly verbatim but referred instead to Moore's "Fiendish Act."[84] "Fiendish" and "diabolical" appear in several other articles and editorials.[85] Furthermore, Moore was a "cruel monster" who had "desecrated" Woodward;[86] in committing rape and murder, "the devil had accomplished his hellish deed."[87] These descriptions were not mere rhetorical flourishes, however. They were an essential part of both explaining and excusing the lynching, creating in the public mind the idea that Moore was too dangerous for his fate to be entrusted to the whims and vagaries of the judicial system.

The site where the crime occurred is an important part of the process of justifying the lynching. Multiple accounts said that Moore raped Woodward "twice within sight of his own house."[88] The idealization and sanctification of hearth and home in the nineteenth century meant that only the most callous, brutal, and diabolical of men could have even contemplated committing such a heinous crime so close to home.

The repeated references in the newspapers to the charge that Moore had poisoned Wiley Wood are also significant in this context. Poison was traditionally linked with witches, whose powers came from the devil. Because of its association with witchcraft, poison was also typically understood to be a "woman's" weapon. Therefore, Moore was "guilty" on two counts: an association with the devil and an unmanly act. The poisoning allegation was thus part and parcel of the effort to stigmatize him further and to suggest that his death at the hands of a crowd was necessary.

Descriptions of the events of June 17 were rife with symbolism. Moore was taken back to the area where the crime had been committed. The buggy that carried him remained on the road, but when Moore refused to confess, he was led by the rope around his neck to the exact spot where the body had been found. "Here, more fiercely, more bitterly than ever, the crowd gathered around, and listened as he was begged for God's sake not to die with a lie on his conscience."[89] Only the most hard-hearted villain—or demon—could have withstood such entreaties on the very spot where Woodward had been murdered. Refusing to confess, he was led back to the buggy. Moore's obstinate rejection of the minister's overtures, especially his refusal to pray, fit with his "demonization," whether in print or in the minds of the crowd. Furthermore, "at the junction of two dim country roads . . . a good-sized post oak was selected" to serve as a gibbet.[90] The area was heavily wooded; located some fifty yards from the scene of the crime, the tree was chosen not because of its proximity to the crime but because of its location at the crossroads. Historically crossroads were used as burial sites for criminals and suicides, who could not be interred in consecrated ground; crossroads were also associated with witchcraft and magic, which belonged to the realm of the devil. Once again the symbolism, whether conscious or not, contributed to the process by which Moore became not (just) a career criminal but a malevolent force who needed to be exorcised from the community. The lynchers were not simply practicing vigilante justice; they were purging the community of the evil that had befallen it. Tellingly, they acted with "God's sun shining in their eyes."[91]

Moore still posed a threat to the community, however. According to the *Greenville Enterprise and Mountaineer,* the family tried to have his body buried at "Mt. Zion Church yard, but they refused it interment there." The family was forced to look elsewhere, and at press time the paper could report only that "it is thought he will be buried at Cedar Hill Graveyard."[92] Significantly this burial ground was located near the Greenville county line, away from the community that had lynched him. Having tolerated his presence for so long, the citizens were no longer willing to allow him to remain among them, even in death.

The attempted lynchings of two black men and the successful lynching of a third in the mid-1880s provide a useful contrast to Moore's case and support the idea that his situation required the community to recast him as a demon before his lynching could be fully justified. In 1885 Ed Bundy was arrested for the murder of a white woman, Annie Heckman, a "common prostitute." Bundy, a waiter at Merchant's Hotel in Spartanburg, killed Heckman in a fit of jealousy, shortly after purchasing a gun from a local store. Bundy was described as "almost white" and "polite . . . and very attentive to all his duties." In contrast, Heckman's life provided a cautionary tale. She had lived in Spartanburg for eight or nine years, having been deserted by the "revenue officer" who had brought her to town. She seems to have been working as a prostitute since that time, if not before. According to the *Carolina Spartan,* "public sentiment . . . has no sort of sympathy for the shameless and vicious course she resolutely pursued even to her death." In many ways these two were the opposites of Moore and Woodward; the killer, Bundy, was a poor but respected waiter, while the victim, Heckman, was a sad example of a "miserably guided and mispent [*sic*] life."[93] Bundy was convicted of murder on June 25, 1885, but appealed his sentence on the grounds of mental illness; he was in the Spartanburg jail awaiting the outcome of the appeal when the mob came for him in September.

Also in the Spartanburg jail at that time was Charles Hawkins, who had been arrested for "criminally assaulting an insane white woman" on or about August 15, 1885. A witness claimed to have seen Hawkins "choking" and attempting to rape the woman. He fled, was arrested in Greenville about a month later, and was returned to Spartanburg. At that point a crowd of men from Reidville, where the alleged assault had occurred, organized a lynch mob. They were joined by a group from Spartanburg, and the two converged on the jail; the "country boys" were to grab Hawkins, and the "town boys" were supposed to seize Bundy.[94] The sheriff was not anticipating trouble. In fact he claimed to be unaware of the planned lynching until September 14, when "he was shown a letter from Greenville asking when the lynching was to take place as the writer wanted to be present at it."[95] Sheriff Gentry immediately wired Gov. Hugh S. Thompson, saying, "I fear an attack on the jail tonight to lynch prisoners. . . . I will do what I can but fear the result." The governor responded by telling the sheriff to "summon a *posse* and defend the prisoners."[96]

Gentry did as he was advised, but "members of the posse spoke in favor of the lynching," and he was able to raise "only a corporal's guard of defenders . . . because the victim of Hawkins's crime was a member of a much respected family and the people did not care to risk shooting good men in his defence." The sheriff was thus forced to try to smuggle the prisoners out of the jail and hide them until they could be put on the train to Columbia. The prisoners and four guards left the jail at 10:00 P.M. and remained in hiding for two nights until it was safe for them to board the train in Cedar Springs, en route to Columbia.[97] Hawkins remained in Columbia until March 1886, when he was smuggled back to Greenville under an alias; the original plan called for him to be brought, unannounced, to Spartanburg for trial, but authorities, fearing that Hawkins would be lynched, obtained a last-minute change of venue. He pleaded guilty to his crime, was sentenced to fifteen years in the penitentiary, and was quietly hustled out of town again.[98] The state supreme court denied Bundy's appeal, and he was sentenced to be hanged on August 6, 1886.[99]

Before either Hawkins's or Bundy's case had been fully resolved, however, Spartanburg citizens witnessed a successful lynching. Obe Thompson, an African American, was arrested on Sunday, February 28, 1886, and charged with having raped a pregnant white woman near Glenn Springs, in the southern part of the county. This assault reportedly followed Thompson's attempted rapes of two other women, one black and one white. In those cases, each victim managed to fight off her attacker. The day following his arrest was a "sale day" in town, and the area around Main Street was crowded; as many as two thousand people may have been present. Thompson was seized from the jail in midafternoon and taken to a nearby grove, where the mob "found a convenient limb" to serve as a gallows. He then asked to speak. Unlike Moore, Thompson followed the conventions that crowds expected in such cases by both confessing and asking to pray. According to the local paper, he said, "I did the deed. I am guilty and ought to suffer. I don't know what got into me. . . . Let me have a little time to pray." When he finished speaking, he was hanged. The coroner was summoned, and the inquest jury returned a verdict of "death by strangulation at the hands of a mob (unknown to the jury)."[100]

The newspapers' descriptions of these three men stand in stark contrast to the depictions of Moore. Bundy was portrayed as a respectable waiter with a family history of mental illness and who was led astray by hopeless love for a depraved woman. Little was written of Hawkins at the time of his arrest, beyond the fact of his race. The account of his disguised return to the upcountry the following year provided a physical description of him but emphasized the fact that he was thoroughly cowed by the situation. "The perspiration poured from him from the time he left Columbia until his arrival" in Greenville; "the pallor of confinement [brought] out the pits on his face," and he had an "anxious expression."[101] Thompson was described as a "wretch"[102] who "deserved the ignominious death which he suffered."[103] The story of Annie Heckman's life received more attention than the three men's stories combined. In addition, while Moore was thoroughly demonized in newspapers and in the courts, the only reference to anything "diabolical" or "fiendish" in reference to Bundy, Hawkins, or Thompson came in the comments at the opening of the court session following the lynching of the latter man; Judge Kershaw referred to rapists as "demons [to be] put out of the way."[104]

Judge Kershaw's words were not directed specifically at Thompson or even at black men in general; in using the word "demons," he was speaking collectively of rapists. No demonization was necessary when it came to Bundy, Hawkins, and Thompson. In the minds of the lynch mobs, they already possessed the necessary characteristics that qualified them for lynching: they were black men who had attacked white women. As the historian Joel Williamson has pointed out, according to the racial stereotypes of the time, "African Americans, free from the civilizing restraints of slavery, were 'retrogressing' to the savage state that was their true nature."[105] Whereas the lynching of Moore could be justified only by repeatedly linking him with the devil, no such rationalization was necessary for black defendants; tendencies to violent acts such as rape and murder were assumed to be inherent in the race.

The differences with Moore's lynching do not stop there, however; attitudes toward vigilante justice seemed to be shifting as well. Despite his mention of demons, the larger import of Judge Kershaw's speech was that lynching was not to be tolerated: "A man in custody of the law should be protected. The honor and credit of the State are pledged to give this class a fair trial. . . . it is well known that the shield of the law cannot be broken in one instance without impairing it all together."[106] Only two state papers defended Thompson's lynching; the *News and Courier* took the stance that "there is one offense in South Carolina with which the courts cannot be expected to deal."[107] The *Greenville News* agreed but made it clear that all rape victims, regardless of race, deserved to be avenged; all rapists, also regardless of race, deserved to be lynched.[108]

In general, though, the region's papers were less tolerant of the actions of the mob than they had been in 1879. Reporting just after Hawkins's arrest in September 1885, the *Carolina Spartan* noted that rumors of a lynching circulated, but the paper argued that "for the sake of law and order and the safety of human life, it will be infinitely better to let the law take its course. In this county there is no excuse of lynching, for our courts do not spare vicious criminals, whether white or black."[109] The *Augusta Chronicle* contended that "lynch law can find little to commend it anywhere and under any circumstances. . . . The law can work its best reform by promptly punishing criminals and relieving armed bands of all responsibility, and public opinion can best prevent them by condemning all those, who in the perverted name of the law, distrust her power and anticipate her success."[110] Though the *News and Courier* supported the lynching of Thompson, it was even stronger in its support for Sheriff Gentry's foiling of the attempt to do the same to Hawkins and Bundy. After making the now-expected comment about the lack of disguises used by the lynchers, the paper commented that the "still better feature was that the Sheriff, by his dutiful and timely action, prevented the proposed crime, and thereby saved his county and state from the reproach of a double murder by a mob." In a surprising move, given its reaction to the successful lynching of Thompson, the paper argued that "the self-appointed executioners deserve no less condemnation because they failed in their cruel and criminal purpose."[111]

The public sentiment to which the *Augusta Chronicle* referred seems also to have begun to shift. This change seems to have been motivated in part by economic concerns—the fear that extralegal violence would frighten potential investors—and the not unrelated desire of white townspeople to disassociate themselves from what they argued was a phenomenon of "rednecks."[112] The *News and Courier* reported that many in Spartanburg were not only "relieved now that the prisoners are away" but also hoped that the failed lynching would "deter parties in the future from making similar attempts."[113] The grand juries that met after the two incidents also condemned the mobs. The jury responding to the attempts to lynch Bundy and Hawkins claimed that it was "a matter of serious and general regret that any of our people should have unwisely deemed it necessary to try to take the law into their own hands . . . no matter how great the provocation, or how intense the indignation for or against the commission of a crime may be, it is still the duty of every good citizen to await the action of and assist and sustain the decisions of those tribunals which they have themselves created."[114] The grand jury charged with investigating the lynching of Obe Thompson likewise criticized the actions of the mob that "executed [him] without judicial process of any kind or character." Referring to the lynching as "the late disturbance in our community," the jury suggested that the crowd was motivated by "distrust" of the law produced by repeated delays in trials of those accused and punishment of those convicted of crimes.[115] Despite their repudiation of lynching, it is important to note that neither grand jury chose to indict anyone for having participated in these cases. Censure was one thing; legal action was another. The confrontational approach of the grand jury in Moore's case may have disappeared, but the unwillingness to see friends and neighbors punished for what many still saw as a form of popular justice still remained.

Conclusion

The lynching of John J. Moore provides a window into the process by which a late nineteenth-century community dealt with threats to order, stability, and morality. By the time of his death, Moore's reputation had earned him the disapprobation of his neighbors; to them, he was a reprobate whose continued presence among them was a source of more than just a little irritation. Yet when the opportunity came to remove him permanently from the community, Moore's character and crimes, both past and present, were not a sufficient pretext to justify the use of extralegal justice. He had to be dehumanized before his hanging could be countenanced. The descriptions of him in the newspapers, the details of the crime, and the symbolism of the events surrounding his death all contributed to the construction—real or imagined—of John J. Moore as a fiend whose continued presence posed a threat to sober men and innocent girls alike. His actual culpability for the crimes alleged against him and the accuracy of the details of the lynching are not important; what matters is how they were used. They were crucial parts of the process of demonizing Moore and absolving those who killed him of the charge of mob rule. Without those allegations, without those "facts," and without the public's acceptance of both, the lynching of John J. Moore would have been received differently, if it had happened at all.

Notes

1. "Criminals and Their Offenses," *New York Times,* June 12, 1879.

2. John Hammond Moore, *Carnival of Blood: Dueling, Lynching, and Murder in South Carolina, 1880–1920* (Columbia: University of South Carolina Press, 2006), 45.

3. Ibid., 205–8. Across the South murder was the most common accusation leveled against white lynching victims who were lynched by white mobs. See Stewart Tolnay and E. M. Beck, *A Festival of Violence: An Analysis of Southern Lynchings, 1882–1930* (Urbana and Chicago: University of Illinois Press, 1995), 94.

4. The South, especially the upcountry areas, had a long tradition of extralegal violence and vigilantism, starting in 1767 with the Regulators in what is now Fairfield County, South Carolina. According to several historians, extralegal violence in the South grew, at least in part, from a distrust of state institutions and a belief that individuals or local communities should deal with problems without outside—i.e., state—assistance. See Bertram Wyatt-Brown, *Southern Honor: Ethics and Behavior in the Old South*, 25th anniversary ed. (Oxford: Oxford University Press, 2007), esp. 48, 365–66, 402; Edward L. Ayers, *Vengeance and Justice: Crime and Punishment in the Nineteenth-Century South* (New York and Oxford: Oxford University Press, 1984); Michael Hindus, *Prison and Plantation: Crime, Justice, and Authority in Massachusetts and South Carolina, 1767–1878* (Chapel Hill: University of North Carolina Press, 1980), 59, 122, 235. W. Fitzhugh Brundage, ed., *Under Sentence of Death: Lynching in the South* (Chapel Hill: University of North Carolina Press, 1997), 3, argues that, while extralegal violence had been common across the nation before the Civil War, in the late nineteenth century northern states developed institutions and mechanisms that "worked to preserve social order by actively suppressing violent crowds. In the South no comparable institutional opposition developed to discourage collective violence." Richard Maxwell Brown, *Strain of Violence: Historical Studies of American Violence and Vigilantism* (Oxford: Oxford University Press, 1975), 73, locates both the origin and the persistence of extralegal violence in the South Carolina upcountry in the "vindictive and brutal" violence with which the Regulators "punished" their victims, violence that ended only when the colonial government responded to the demands for "district courts and sheriffs." Brown argues that "the clear distinction between the regular system of courts and law enforcement on the one hand and vigilantes and lynch mobs on the other dissolves when the behavior of all elements is observed. Most striking is the wide extent of collusive practices and shared values that have united vigilantes and

legal authorities" (146–47). The behavior of the grand jury in Moore's case clearly fits that paradigm.

5. *Charleston News and Courier,* June 23, 1879.

6. "Grafted on a Tree," *Washington Post,* June 18, 1879.

7. *Carolina Spartan,* June 18, 1879. Heaton was her stepfather's name, and Woodward was her birth father's. She introduced herself as Woodward when she came to Spartanburg, but the newspapers used both names. "Woodward" will be used throughout this essay.

8. *Charleston News and Courier,* June 16, 1879. The *News and Courier's* account was taken, with acknowledgment, from a description of the body in the June 11, 1879, edition of the *Greenville Enterprise and Mountaineer.* The details were provided by a Mr. F. A. Perry, who was so eager to get the news to Greenville that he accompanied the story with a hurried note that read, "No more paper—stores closed. I wrote you notice before day this morning. The only chance to mail was to stick it under strap of mail pouch, which was hung in usual place. Had no stamp to put on it."

9. "Fiendish Act Summarily Avenged by an Indignant People," *Weekly Union Times,* June 20, 1879; "A Fiendish Criminal Summarily Executed by Indignant Citizens," *Spartanburg Herald,* June 18, 1879.

10. The coroner's inquest, which includes the testimony of witnesses as well as the postmortem report of Dr. Hugh Toland, who conducted the autopsy, can be found in Spartanburg County Court of General Sessions, Coroner's Inquisition, South Carolina Department of Archives and History, Columbia (the latter is hereafter cited as SCDAH).

11. *Atlanta Daily Constitution,* June 18, 1879. None of the other papers mentions that Woodward paid for her meal.

12. Spartanburg County Inquisitions, June 9, 1879, SCDAH.

13. *Greenville Enterprise and Mountaineer,* June 11, 1879; *Charleston News and Courier,* June 16, 1879.

14. *Charleston News and Courier,* June 18, 1879; *Anderson Intelligencer,* June 26, 1879. The *Shenandoah Times* in Woodstock, Virginia, reported the same thing, but it would be difficult to see how this affected public opinion in South Carolina. *Shenandoah Herald,* June 25, 1879. http://chroniclingamerica.loc.gov/lccn/sn85026941/1879–06–25/ed-1/seq-2/ (accessed February 19, 2011).

15. *Greenville Enterprise and Mountaineer,* June 18, 1879. This statement is not among the testimony from the inquest; if it was given under oath, it no longer survives.

16. *Charleston News and Courier,* June 18, 1879. It should be noted that none of this information is included in the file of the coroner's inquest. By June 18 the *News and Courier* seems to have had its own reporter in Spartanburg and was no longer relying on the *Greenville Enterprise and Mountaineer's* stories.

17. Spartanburg County Inquisitions, June 9, 1879, SCDAH.

18. *Greenville Enterprise and Mountaineer,* June 18, 1879.

19. *Carolina Spartan,* June 18, 1879.

20. *New York Times,* June 18, 1879. In 1881 the name Vernonsville was changed to Duncan.

21. *Greenville News,* printed in the *Anderson Intelligencer,* June 26, 1879.

22. *Charleston News and Courier,* June 18, 1879.

23. *Anderson Intelligencer,* June 26, 1879.

24. *Charleston News and Courier,* June 18, 1879.

25. *New York Times,* June 18, 1879. The sheriff's plan seems to have been to put Moore on the first train through town—in this case to Charlotte—and from there on another train to Columbia, where he could be safely held until trial. According to the *Greenville News* (as quoted in the *Anderson Intelligencer*), an engine sans cars was on its way to rendezvous with the deputies. The same paper described the leader of the squad that found Moore as "a detective of some repute in our State" (*Anderson Intelligencer,* June 26, 1879).

26. *Charleston News and Courier,* June 18, 1879.

27. *Carolina Spartan,* June 18, 1879. The June 25, 1879, *Shenandoah Herald* of Woodstock, Virginia, claimed that "invitations were sent out to the neighbors to witness the execution," http://chroniclingamerica.loc.gov/lccn/sn85026941/1879–06–25/ed-1/seq-2 (accessed February 19, 2011).

28. *New York Times,* June 18, 1879.

29. *Charlotte Observer,* quoted in *Charleston News and Courier,* June 19, 1879.

30. Ibid.; *Chicago Daily Tribune,* June 20, 1879.

31. *Charleston News and Courier,* June 23, 1879.

32. Ibid.

33. *Spartanburg Herald,* June 18, 1879.

34. *Charleston News and Courier,* June 23, 1879. Woodward had been invited to speak to a joint meeting of the Adelphian Literary Society and the Philosophian Literary Society at Furman. See Adelphian Literary Society, box 5, record book, January 4, 1874–April 30, 1880, and Philosophian Literary Society, box 2, minutes, November 2, 1860–June 7, 1888, Furman University Archives, Greenville, S.C. See also *Carolina Spartan,* June 4, 1879. Woodward had served in the South Carolina State House from 1860 to 1862, was a state senator from 1884 to 1892, and supported Wade Hampton's election to the governorship in 1876. Woodward had served as a major in the Sixth South Carolina Volunteers (SCV) during the war. See FitzHugh McMaster, *History of Fairfield County* (1946; repr., Spartanburg, S.C.: Reprint Co., 1980), 115, 118, 125. Ironically, only months after intervening in Moore's lynching, Woodward served as the foreman of the Fairfield County grand jury that called for an overhaul of the jury system, as "one villain is equal to eleven honest men, and may in all cases even of the most flagrant nature, defeat the ends of justice. . . . without some change we fear that trial by jury, although the boasted bulwark of civilization, will be brought into ridicule" (Fairfield County Criminal Journals, September 1879, SCDAH). It is probably not surprising that the only person to intervene in the lynching was an outsider. As such, he was more able to view the situation objectively; it was not *his* community that Moore was threatening.

35. *New York Times,* June 19, 1879.

36. *Carolina Spartan,* June 18, 1879. The *Atlanta Daily Constitution* (18 June 1879) claimed that Woodward's speech prompted the mob's leaders to move the lynching ahead several hours in case Woodward had "excite[d] sympathy in the hearts of the majority," who might then withdraw their support for the execution.

37. *Chicago Daily Tribune,* June 20, 1879. Moore's widow and children left Spartanburg within months after his death. They appear in the 1880 census listings as living in Highland Township, Greenville County.

38. *Anderson Intelligencer,* June 26, 1879. Neither of the Spartanburg papers nor the *News and Courier* seems to have printed a copy of the proclamation, though Judge Pressley made reference to it in his charge to the jury.

39. *Carolina Spartan,* June 25, 1879.

40. *Spartanburg Herald,* June 25, 1879.

41. Ibid. Much of the grand jury's presentment is taken verbatim from "An Essay on the Ground and Reason of Punishment," *United States Magazine and Democratic Review* 19, no. 98 (1846): 100–102. Ironically this article argues against the use of lynch law; the antilynching passages were, understandably, edited out before inclusion in the presentment. The grand jury's comments regarding illegal cohabitation and sexual crimes reflect a postwar fear that the social order was in danger from newly freed, and therefore "uncontrolled," black people. Between 1877 and 1895 the Spartanburg grand jury produced roughly seventy-five indictments for crimes such as rape, fornication, bigamy, and bastardy, but only one of those indictments—a rape charge—predates Moore's death. See Spartanburg County Sessions Journals, 1877–95, SCDAH.

42. *Spartanburg Herald,* July 2, 1879.

43. *Roanoke Times,* February 4, 1911, reprinted in *Spartanburg Herald,* February 8, 1911.

44. James E. Coan, American Memory Project no. 3613, www://lcweb2.loc.gov/ wpa/30080410.html (accessed June 20, 2010). Coan attributed the antilynching provisions of the 1896 South Carolina Constitution to Moore's death; there is no evidence to support such a belief, nor is it likely. It is evidence, however, of the importance some witnesses attributed to this case.

45. *Charleston News and Courier,* June 19, 1879.

46. *Carolina Spartan,* June 25, 1879.

47. *Weekly Union Times,* June 20, 1879.

48. *Spartanburg Herald,* June 18, 1879. An article in the *Charleston News and Courier* bearing the dateline "Spartanburg, June 17, 1 A.M." reported that Moore had been captured and that the "mayor and other prominent citizens are now organizing a committee to follow the lynchers and endeavor to induce them to respect the majesty of the law" (June 19, 1879). It seems likely that the editor of the paper had been among those "prominent citizens." No account of the events of the morning of June 17 mentions any attempt to stop the lynching other than that of Major Woodward.

49. Quoted in *Charleston News and Courier,* June 19, 1879. The section of the paper in which this passage was quoted was titled "Well It Was Not a Negro!"

50. *Carolina Spartan,* June 25, 1879.

51. *Charleston News and Courier,* June 19, 1879, quoted in *Carolina Spartan,* June 25, 1879.

52. *Spartanburg Herald,* June 18, 1879.

53. See, for example, Bruce W. Eelman, *Entrepreneurs in the Southern Upcountry: Commercial Culture in Spartanburg, South Carolina, 1845–1880* (Athens: University of Georgia Press, 2008), 224–26.

54. *Anderson Intelligencer,* July 3, 1879.

55. The *Spartanburg Herald* hailed Aldrich's appearance, saying, "it is a real pleasure to see Judge Aldrich once more on the Bench—the Judge who doffed his gown and stepped down rather than obey the orders of a military satrap when the Radical hordes took possession of the State under reconstruction laws" (*Spartanburg Herald,* March 19, 1879).

56. "The Spartanburg Lynching: A South Carolina Circuit Judge Also Justifies It," *New York Times,* July 21, 1879. The same article appeared in the *Chicago Daily Tribune,* July 25, 1879. Aldrich was quoting Sir Edward Bulwer-Lytton's play *Richelieu.*

57. Quoted in the *Carolina Spartan,* June 25, 1879.

58. *Washington Post,* June 18, 1879. The following month the *Post* ran an editorial suggesting that "Judge Lynch should set up shop in Anderson county, Tennessee" in order to bring an end to "brutally barbarous incidents" there (*Washington Post,* July 14, 1879).

59. *National Republican* (Washington City [D.C.]), June 20, 1879, http://chroniclingamerica.loc.gov/lccn/sn86053573/1879–06–20/ed-1/seq-2 (accessed February 19, 2011).

60. *Albany Law Journal* 20 (August 1879): 102. The "Kentucky tragedy" probably refers to the killing of Solomon P. Sharp by Jereboam O. Beauchamp in 1824.

61. *New York Times,* June 18, 1879. "Regulators" referred to a group of vigilantes formed in South Carolina in 1767.

62. "Spartan Law," *New York Times,* July 2, 1879.

63. "The Spartanburg Lynching: A South Carolina Circuit Judge Also Justifies It," *New York Times,* July 21, 1879.

64. According to Christopher Waldrep, *The Many Faces of Judge Lynch: Extralegal Violence and Punishment in America* (New York: Palgrave Macmillan, 2002), 114, in the 1870s the *New York Times* argued that lynching "was too likely to kill innocent persons, especially African-Americans." Over the next decade the concern shifted to the lack of due process in such cases.

65. Court of General Sessions, Spartanburg County Indictments, May 19, 1879, SCDAH. The trial justice listed for this case is George H. W. Legge. It is unclear why the case did not receive any press coverage, though it is possible that the index in which the case was listed was wrong about the date. No disposition for the case is listed in the index either.

66. The *Chicago Daily Tribune* (June 20, 1879) noted that Woodward "had left her home on account of unpleasantness in the family." If this was true, and depending on

the nature of the "unpleasantness," it might account for the failure of the local papers to devote more attention to the victim and her character.

67. *Spartanburg Herald,* June 18, 1879.

68. *Charleston News and Courier,* June 18, 1879.

69. *Greenville News,* cited in *Anderson Intelligencer,* June 18, 1879; originals of the Greenville paper do not survive from this year. The *Spartanburg Express* issue from October 16, 1862, includes the announcement of a lawsuit, possibly involving Wood's estate, but does not provide a date or cause of death.

70. Governor Franklin J. Moses Papers, box 8, folder 2, and affidavit of George A. Sebster, June 24, 1874, SCDAH.

71. Governor Franklin J. Moses Papers, box 7, folder 22, letter dated May 4, 1874, SCDAH. Flemming's career was not without controversy of its own. The *Carolina Spartan* accused him of "prostituting the high office to which he has been elected," more concerned with financial gain than true justice. He was accused of "hunting up men who have been guilty, of a violation of what is known as the 'TUPPER LAW'" so that he could extort money from them. On May 22, 1873, the *Spartan* reported that Flemming appeared in court too intoxicated to "attend to the prosecution of his case." The court was adjourned, Flemming was severely chastised the next day, and the paper called for the solicitor to be given "the severest penalty of the law" (*Carolina Spartan,* June 25, 1874). Moses likely was one of the most corrupt governors in South Carolina history.

72. Court of General Sessions, Spartanburg County, sessions rolls, State v. John J. Moore, June 1874, SCDAH.

73. Governor Franklin J. Moses Papers, box 7, folder 39, letter dated June 23, 1874, SCDAH.

74. Governor Franklin J. Moses Papers, box 8, folder 19, letter dated July 1874, SCDAH.

75. Court of General Sessions, Spartanburg County, Indictment of Albert Ralph, March 1879, SCDAH.

76. *Carolina Spartan,* February 26, 1879.

77. *Greenville Enterprise and Mountaineer,* June 18, 1879.

78. *Carolina Spartan,* March 26, 1879. Like the judge, the grand jury also urged the state legislature to enact "such legislation as will effectively suppress" the carrying of concealed weapons, which was "the cause of so much mischief, expense, and sorrow to the people." Moore's distillery was licensed.

79. *Charleston News and Courier,* June 18, 1879.

80. *Charleston News and Courier,* June 19, 1879.

81. Court of General Sessions, Spartanburg County, Coroner's Inquisition, June 9, 1879, SCDAH.

82. *New York Times,* July 2, 1879; *Charleston News and Courier,* June 27, 1879.

83. *Spartanburg Herald,* June 18, 1879.

84. *Weekly Union Times,* June 20, 1879.

85. *Carolina Spartan,* June 15, 1879; *Anderson Intelligencer,* July 3, 1879; *Spartanburg Herald,* June 11, 1879.

86. Judge Aldrich's charge to the Greenville County grand jury, cited in the *New York Times,* July 21, 1879.

87. *Charleston News and Courier,* June 18, 1879; *Greenville Enterprise and Mountaineer,* June 18, 1879.

88. See, for example, the *Charleston News and Courier,* June 18, 1879.

89. *Charleston News and Courier,* June 23, 1879.

90. *Anderson Intelligencer,* June 26, 1879, taken from the *Greenville News,* June 18, 1879.

91. Judge Aldrich's charge to the Greenville grand jury, quoted in *New York Times,* July 21, 1879.

92. *Greenville Enterprise and Mountaineer,* June 18, 1879.

93. *Carolina Spartan,* March 11, 1885. For indictment and trial, see Court of General Sessions, Spartanburg County, Indictments, March 1885, SCDAH.

94. *Charleston News and Courier,* September 16, 1885.

95. *Charleston News and Courier,* September 17, 1885.

96. Governor Hugh S. Thompson Papers, telegrams sent and received, box 1, folder 30, and letter book F, 287, SCDAH.

97. *Charleston News and Courier,* September 17, 1885. In an interesting coincidence, one of the people who figured in the Woodward/Moore case appeared in connection with the attempted lynching. Jeff O'Shields, who was the person to whom locals were directing Fannie Woodward, was reportedly "warned to leave the neighborhood as soon as he can close up his business." Some who had participated in the foiled lynching apparently believed that O'Shields had betrayed their plans to the sheriff. So angry were they that "if they had got hold of him they might have dispatched him in short order" (*Greenville News,* quoted in *Carolina Spartan,* October 7, 1885).

98. *Carolina Spartan* (from *Greenville News*), March 31, 1886.

99. Spartanburg County, Indictments, March term 1886, SCDAH General Sessions.

100. *Carolina Spartan,* March 3, 1886; *Charleston News and Courier,* March 2, 1886; Spartanburg County, Indictments, [filed] June 23, 1886, SCDAH General Sessions.

101. *Carolina Spartan,* March 31, 1886 (story from the *Greenville Daily News*).

102. Ibid.

103. *Charleston News and Courier,* March 3, 1886.

104. *Carolina Spartan,* March 17, 1886.

105. Joel Williamson, *The Crucible of Race,* cited in Brundage, *Under Sentence of Death,* 12.

106. *Carolina Spartan,* March 17, 1886.

107. *Charleston News and Courier,* cited in *Carolina Spartan,* March 10, 1886.

108. *Greenville News,* cited in *Carolina Spartan,* March 10, 1886.

109. *Carolina Spartan,* September 16, 1885. The *Spartanburg Herald* issues from these years do not survive; given the *Herald*'s reaction to the Moore case, however, it is likely that it would have agreed with the *Spartan.*

110. *Carolina Spartan,* March 10, 1886.

111. *Charleston News and Courier,* September 17, 1885.

112. Moore, *Carnival of Blood,* 53; Stephen A. West, *From Yeoman to Redneck in the South Carolina Upcountry, 1850–1910* (Charlottesville: University of Virginia Press, 2008), 13, 103–21.

113. *Charleston News and Courier,* September 16, 1885.

114. *Carolina Spartan,* November 4, 1885.

115. *Carolina Spartan,* March 24, 1886.

"May the Lord keep down hard feelings"

The Woodrow Evolution Controversy and the 1884 Presbyterian Synod of South Carolina

Robert B. McCormick

On the evening of October 22, 1884, Washington Street Presbyterian Church in Greenville, South Carolina, glistened in the lamplight. The newly constructed neo-Gothic structure, a major addition to the city, was a suitable setting for a discussion of the old and the new. In a region of the state where Scots-Irish Presbyterians had planted a firm flag, an august gathering of the finest Presbyterian leaders in South Carolina was readying to discuss an issue of tremendous gravity that held the potential to damage seriously the future of Presbyterianism. Greenville was hosting no ordinary annual meeting of the South Carolina Presbyterian Synod. Few in the audience had come to hear about missions or the labors of local presbyteries. Instead they had gathered to hear about evolution and how Rev. James Woodrow, the Perkins Professor of Natural Science in Connexion with Revelation at Columbia Theological Seminary, had thrust evolution and its relationship to Christianity and the seminary to the forefront of denominational debate.

Historians have examined the Woodrow evolution controversy, but brief attention has been focused on the synod meeting in Greenville where the first significant public debates took place. The most complete study of the controversy is in Ernest Trice Thompson's *Presbyterians in the South*. Thompson, like others, looked at the controversy in its totality, and although addressing the 1884 South Carolina Synod, he did not dwell on the debates or upstate South Carolina's reaction to the gathering.[1] The synod meeting, however, offered the first opportunity for Presbyterians across South Carolina to discuss evolution and the relationship between science and religion. It was closely monitored by southern Presbyterians, and its debates were deemed to be of such importance that synods and presbyteries throughout the region passed resolutions condemning the teaching of evolution at Columbia Theological Seminary. The debates demonstrated that conservative antievolution forces were not as strong among South

Carolina Presbyterians as one would assume. More than a few important voices supported Woodrow's views on evolution and expressed the belief that it was significant for seminarians to learn about evolution. Likewise the synod provided a glimpse into the intellectual positions held by Presbyterian leaders of the upstate, buttressing arguments that the South was far from a scientific desert.[2] Instead the erudite arguments presented at the synod only reinforce the position that vigorous scientific and religious debate was a part of South Carolina's landscape.

Evolution was far from a new concept, even in predominantly rural areas of the state. Various interpretations of evolutionary theory had been bantered about for years prior to Charles Darwin's famous works, and intellectuals within South Carolina had studied these theories. Beyond South Carolina, American Protestants had responded to the evolutionary challenge in many different ways. In 1875 Charles Hodge, Princeton Theological Seminary's great defender of biblical authority, published a careful study repudiating Darwin's views that became, to many, the final word against Darwin. *What Is Darwinism?*, published by Hodge in 1874, became the accepted Protestant defense of God's role in creation, denouncing the assertion that change through natural selection was the foundation of plant and animal life.[3] A leading Presbyterian, Hodge criticized Darwin for being unscientific and relying far too much on speculation. In particular he opposed Darwin's view that natural selection was taking place devoid of any direction or design.[4] Hodge's denunciations had great appeal for conservative southern Protestant intellects. Like almost all defenders of biblical authority of the period, Hodge used Harvard's famed naturalist Louis Agassiz as one of the keystones of his argument.[5] Agassiz was the most famous scientist in America and an outspoken opponent of Darwin's theories until his death in 1873.[6] Ironically, Agassiz and James Woodrow had been friends since 1853 when Woodrow spent a summer studying under Agassiz at Harvard.

Aware of controversies surrounding the theory of human evolution, citizens in the southern United States had been somewhat slow to react to the evolutionary debate triggered by Darwin's *The Origin of Species* and *The Descent of Man,* but it would be incorrect to suppose that southern intellectuals were removed from conversations about evolution. As early as 1878, Alexander Winchell of Vanderbilt University caused a scandal by questioning the historical record found in Genesis when he published a pamphlet titled *Adamites and Pre-Adamites.* Winchell, a geologist who believed in polygenesis, professed that humans had existed prior to the Adam of the Bible. This short book and other writings and lectures convinced Vanderbilt's board of trustees that Winchell's services were no longer needed, and he was summarily removed from the faculty.[7] In the upstate there had not been much vocal debate about evolution; however, Wofford College's Professor Daniel Allston DuPre was known to teach evolution to his young Methodist charges.[8] Evolution of a kind was also being taught at Davidson College, where Professor J. R. Blake was teaching nebular theory, the idea that the solar system was continually evolving.[9] Blake was the most prominent professor at Davidson, where many Presbyterian ministers from South Carolina had completed their undergraduate studies.

The majority of southern Protestants as well as their ministers remained suspicious of evolution theories and scientific investigation in general. This was no surprise, considering that among major Protestant denominations in the nineteenth century South, only "Episcopalians and Presbyterians required a seminary degree for clerical ordination."[10] Presbyterian ministers were marked by solid educations, especially in theology, and in general demonstrated a great interest in the world around them. Other Protestant denominations, such as Baptists and Methodists, deemed anyone holding formal education and seeking ordination a potential threat to the understood truths of the scriptures. Protestant leaders believed that formal education would make the clergy prone to questioning biblical authority and inerrancy. Although southern Presbyterians were more concerned with providing an educated clergy—they operated four seminaries—the popular religious culture worked against them. Southern Protestants placed scriptural authority on a level not seen among their northern brethren or overseas. As Kenneth Bailey wrote, "among both clergy and rank and file there was an awesome reverence for the Bible, literally construed, and hypersensitivity toward any subversion of hallowed beliefs."[11] Discussion of science that seemingly conflicted with the Bible was to be avoided at all costs and, if possible, ridiculed. Furthermore the conservative theology of leading figures in southern Presbyterianism, in part, was founded in a siege mentality that called some Presbyterian leaders to defend conservative theological positions against the winds of change in other parts of the country. Having split from their northern brethren in 1861 and having suffered defeat in the Civil War, those with southern Presbyterian identity were closely attached to the idea that it was the church's duty to preserve the purity of Calvinism and the Westminster Confession. Presbyterian leaders wished to defend order and stability against what they believed was anarchic change forced upon them by northern victory.[12]

Without intent James Woodrow fueled South Carolina's first significant evolution controversy when he delivered an address to the Columbia Theological Seminary's Alumni Association and its board of directors on May 7, 1884. Woodrow was an ordained Presbyterian minister with a sparkling reputation as a clergyman, scholar, businessman, and scientist. On the surface it appears that Woodrow was an unlikely instigator, but his heritage and training indicate that he was precisely the type of man to make a bold statement in favor of teaching about evolution to seminarians. A native of Carlisle, England, Woodrow was imbued with Presbyterian thought from his earliest days. His father was a

Presbyterian minister who moved the family from England to Canada and then to the United States. By 1853 Woodrow had graduated from Jefferson College, later Washington and Jefferson College, and moved south to teach at Oglethorpe University, a Presbyterian institution in Georgia. Later in the 1850s he traveled to the University of Heidelberg to continue his academic training, perhaps with the urging of his friend Louis Agassiz, the noted natural scientist. Woodrow performed brilliantly at Heidelberg, impressing the faculty and earning a Ph.D. in natural science. Declining offers to teach at Heidelberg and feeling the tug of his Presbyterian beliefs, he returned to Oglethorpe and was ordained a Presbyterian minister by Georgia's Hopewell Presbytery in 1859.

In 1861 he went to Columbia Theological Seminary in Columbia, South Carolina, as the first Perkins Professor of Natural Sciences, a new and unique post destined to raise eyebrows. Some wondered why a seminary needed a professor to teach about scientific matters. Judge John Perkins of Columbus, Mississippi, had provided a large endowment in order to fund this professorship, which was intended to reinforce biblical belief in the face of scientific challenges. Woodrow seemingly possessed the perfect qualities to hold this ambiguous but distinctive position, unlike any at other seminaries. During the Civil War, Woodrow served the Confederacy first as a chaplain and subsequently as chief chemist for the Confederate laboratory in Columbia. After the war he returned to work at the seminary and also assumed duties as editor and owner of the *Southern Presbyterian Review*. When South Carolina College reopened in 1880, Woodrow taught in several fields of science ranging from chemistry to geology to zoology. He was renowned for his classroom abilities, his devotion to Christianity, and the dignity with which he carried himself.[13]

The May 1884 address had its origins a year earlier when Columbia Seminary's board of trustees asked Woodrow to prepare remarks about evolution for publication in the highly respected *Southern Presbyterian Review,* the same journal he edited. Because the Alumni Association had selected Woodrow to give an address for them and the board was scheduled to meet at the same time, the board agreed for Woodrow to deliver an address on evolution at the Alumni Association meeting in May 1884. Ironically controversy and struggle were well known to the seminary, for it had suffered through the difficult war years and had been forced to close in 1880, reopening two years later. Furthermore considerable pressure from around the South had mounted for Woodrow to make a clear statement about evolution and theology, especially because he had turned down all invitations to do so.[14] Woodrow's hesitancy to speak about evolution was no doubt caused by a deeply held concern that his views would cause a firestorm among Presbyterians. He well understood that the address had to reflect his views accurately while allaying fears about the relationship between Christianity and science.[15]

Woodrow spoke to a large audience, many of whom were former students and friends. At the beginning of the lecture, the bespectacled Woodrow was careful to emphasize his belief in the truthfulness of the Bible, stating, "I have found nothing in my study of the Holy Bible and of natural science that shakes my firm belief in the divine inspiration of every word of that Bible and in the consequent absolute truth, the absolute inerrancy, of every expression which it contains from beginning to end."[16] As the address developed, he explained his opinion that the scriptures were not scientific texts, having nothing to do with science, and that the mode of creation was not mentioned or addressed in the Bible. He reasoned that fossil evidence demonstrated that animals and plants had changed over time and that such knowledge was in no way inconsistent with the nature of God or biblical accounts.[17] Regarding humans, Woodrow recognized that the scriptures were more precise, but they said nothing as to Adam arising of organic or inorganic matter and remained in a context that was not inconsistent with evolution. When forced to reconcile Eve's creation, however, Woodrow did not question the Bible's words that she was created from one of Adam's ribs. Because of this belief, Woodrow's views on evolution appear awkward and forced, but he was being consistent in biblical primacy, although he cannot be viewed as a strict evolutionist. Why would God have allowed for fossils to be buried if they did not speak to the truthfulness of God's creation, he asked. Underscoring his position was a lengthy argument defending evolutionary principles found from the tertiary world as well as in the solar system.[18] After demonstrating extensive study of the topic, Woodrow concluded that scientific evidence proved that evolution was probably true, emphasizing that evolution in no way contradicted God's message about creation found within the Bible. The Bible and science could not be expected to be in harmony on all matters because the intent of each was different. He stressed that the key was for the scriptures to not be in contradiction with science. In concluding his speech, Woodrow emphasized that evolution was not anti-Christian and that, "according to not unreasonable interpretations of the Bible, it does not contradict anything there taught so far as regards the earth, the lower animals, and probably man as to his body."[19]

The address, delivered at the First Presbyterian Church in Columbia, did not spur outrage or shock. Rev. Thomas H. Law, pastor at First Presbyterian in Spartanburg and a member of Columbia's board of director's, commented that the speech "created no special alarm or excitement in the Church."[20] Meeting in September, the seminary's board of directors voted eight to three approving Woodrow's teaching of evolution in the seminary, noting that he was consistent with the Bible's teachings. The board members were not, however, willing to go on record as agreeing with Woodrow's views, and in a rather inconvenient manner, they made that point clear in their statement supporting his work at the seminary but shying away from endorsing his opinions. The board most likely was reflective of other thoughtful Presbyterians who were unsure of evolution and its effect on the denomination.

Although there was limited immediate reaction about Woodrow's views, Presbyterian publications around the South began to attack Columbia's theologian. Woodrow's address in Columbia became front-page news for Presbyterian publications such as the *Southwestern Presbyterian,* the *Central Presbyterian,* the *St. Louis Presbyterian,* and the *Texas Presbyterian,* among others. Woodrow's *Southern Presbyterian Review* became the touchstone for debate, especially after printing Woodrow's speech in its July issues and spending most of the summer and fall of 1884 addressing editorials and articles critical of his speech.[21] Woodrow's masterful scientific knowledge combined with his theological knowledge made him difficult to assail. Unless one chose to damn him as a heretic, there was no easy way to attack his views since his most vocal critics possessed none of his scientific expertise.

With most of the evolution debate confined to Presbyterian circles, it took some time before the general upstate public was aroused. In its first report about the Woodrow controversy, the *Carolina Spartan* came to the professor's defense. On August 27, 1884, the editors pleaded for the public to read Woodrow's address, which had been produced as a pamphlet. "Let him not be condemned without a hearing," they urged.[22] Foreshadowing the debate at the South Carolina Synod, the editor explained that "crystalized opinions have boldly withstood the advance of science in all ages of the church and to-day prejudice has more force than independent thought. Science has never retarded the true work of the church nor has the church with all its efforts crippled science much. They both have their special work to do and there is no real contradiction among them."[23] Such comments from the most popular paper in Spartanburg demonstrated more than a little sympathy with Woodrow's support for evolution.

A month later the *Carolina Spartan* placed evolution in the middle of its front page, choosing to reprint a series of interviews conducted by the *Philadelphia Times* at a meeting of the American Association for the Advancement of Science. The interviews in the article, which featured some of the foremost names in American science, demonstrated that evolution was widely accepted in scientific circles and that there was, evolution notwithstanding, a generally accepted compatibility between science and religion.[24] The story was printed, no doubt, to counteract the growing opposition to Woodrow, evolution theory, and science in general. The choice to print this story in such a prominent position tells us that the newspaper's editor was not opposed to supporting generally unpopular positions and perhaps understood that there was a market for more progressive opinions.

The cool fall weather that descended on the upstate did nothing to chill the fervor with which Presbyterians as well as religious leaders of other denominations anticipated the synod opening in Greenville, South Carolina. A whirlwind of excitement could be felt throughout the city. At a few minutes past 8:00 P.M. on October 22, 1884, the synod began with the singing of "Oh, for a Thousand Tongues to Sing," an appropriate hymn for a gathering destined to feature much discussion. Next, Rev. Dr. J. B. Mack, the synod moderator at its convening, provided biblical direction for the synod by reading the first chapter of Genesis. Greenville's *Enterprise and Mountaineer* noted that it was "most impressively read."[25] Giving a clear indication that devoted Christians would be challenged by infidel scientific authorities, Dr. Mack, secretary of Columbia's board and a well-known opponent of Woodrow's views, chose the sixteenth chapter of John as the New Testament reading.[26] This passage focuses on the inevitable conflict that Christians would face from the unbelieving world. A small number of participants did not want the Woodrow controversy to be discussed at the synod, fearing the great damage that might be inflicted on the Presbyterian Church. Attempts to thwart discussion were overridden prior to the convening of the synod. The *Charleston News and Courier* reported that there was heavy support for the controversy to be fully discussed and a decision reached on Woodrow's beliefs as well as the wisdom of teaching evolution at Columbia Theological Seminary. The paper's special correspondent captured the weight of the synod, writing that "citizens of Greenville in common with the rest of the State, are awaiting with an unusual degree of interest the action of the Synod in the premises. The church will be thronged daily during the continuance of the debate. The ablest talent and the profoundest thinkers of the church are here ready to enter the lists on either side, and when the debate opens a field day may be expected."[27] At 10:30 P.M. the opening remarks were concluded and the crowd was dismissed in anticipation of the impending debate.

On the second day, with preliminaries finished, the evolution controversy reached center stage when members of Columbia Seminary's board of directors officially issued their report on James Woodrow's teaching, approving his views on evolution by explaining that they were convinced that they were in no way contradictory to scripture. The synod responded by charging the Theological Seminary Committee, composed of five members, with examining "at once such matters as pertain to the Perkins Professorship and report as speedily as possible."[28] The committee worked at remarkable speed and provided two reports to the synod in its evening session. Charleston's *Sunday News* reported that the building was packed to its utmost capacity and that the gathered crowd had the "keenest interest" in the affair about to transpire.[29] One report was favored by the majority of three and the other by the minority of two. The majority report sought to define evolution as a "purely scientific and extra-Scriptural hypothesis," thus alleviating the church from making any statement of support or rejection.[30] Recognizing that the evolution controversy had stimulated tremendous interest, the committee wanted to keep the synod from any pronouncement about evolution, explaining that the church's duty was to defend the faith and that it "can never, without transcending her proper sphere, incorporate into her confessions of Faith any of the hypotheses, theories or systems of human science."[31] Speaking in defense of James Woodrow, the report noted that while evolution was a topic germane to Woodrow's duties, "nevertheless, neither this nor any other scientific hypothesis is or can be taught in our Theological Seminary as an article of Church faith."[32] The report ended with resounding support for the seminary's board of directors, who in the majority had not found any incompatibility with Woodrow's teachings and articles of Presbyterian faith.

As with any issue of this nature, members of the committee were not unanimous in their judgments. A minority of two, one of whom was F. L. Anderson, an elder at Antioch Presbyterian Church in the upstate, filed a competing report critical of the board's majority position on James Woodrow. Anderson along with Rev. Robert A. Webb, a Columbia Seminary graduate as well as a close friend of Joseph B. Mack, contended that the synod was not to examine whether the "views of Dr. Woodrow contradict the Bible in its highest and absolute sense, but upon the question whether they contradict the interpretations of the Bible by the Presbyterian Church in the United States."[33] After resolving that the seminary board had "virtually" approved the teaching of evolution, they pronounced "the inculcation and defence of the said hypothesis even as a probable one, in the Theological Seminary, as being contrary to the interpretation of the Scriptures by our church."[34]

After motions to adopt the minority and majority reports could not win approval, vigorous debate ensued. An Oglethorpe and Columbia Seminary graduate, Rev. James S. Cozby of Harmony Presbytery offered an impassioned and convincing defense for Professor Woodrow, arguing that the church should steer clear from making pronouncements on science and should confine itself to the scriptures. Furthermore he stressed that Woodrow's position as the Perkins Professor mandated that he address evolution but that Woodrow "holds that where any hypothesis of science comes in conflict with the World of God, that that hypothesis must fall before the Word."[35]

Rev. John B. Adger, a fellow professor at Columbia Seminary, strengthened Cozby's position by remarking that natural science was not the enemy of the church and that no condemnation of Woodrow's teachings should be made. Adger was cut of a different cloth than many of his peers at the synod, because he had served as a missionary in Armenia and ministered to African Americans in Charleston for five years.[36] His experiences appear to have influenced his views in a more liberal fashion. He condemned the "wide-spread opinion that natural science is the enemy of the Gospel. Many excellent ministers have made themselves the laughing stock of infidelity because they have advanced such fearful absurdities in their endeavor to advocate the truth of the Scriptures, and that was the originating cause of this very Perkin's [*sic*] Professorship."[37] Adger echoed the argument for a separation of science and scriptures and endorsed Woodrow's continued discussion of evolution at the seminary. In a stinging assault on the opposition, he remarked that "if this Synod and the other Synods shall condemn this teaching and cast their censure, I shall hang my head, whatever the rest of you may do. I pray to God that no such dishonor as this is to be done to God's truth and to his Word; that no such dishonor will be done as to say that the Church has fear of the teachings of science."[38] Understanding that many in the South and beyond would be closely watching the synod, Adger drew an apt analogy between Galileo and Woodrow, urging the church not to do what Catholic leaders had done in 1633. After a discussion of evolutionary theory, he defended Woodrow's position on the scriptures, saying that the theologian had said nothing contradictory to the Bible and had only made statements in full support of and belief in its inerrancy.[39] Adger's passionate address ended emphasizing that unproved hypotheses such as evolution were discussed at the seminary on a daily basis among students and professors. Conversations of that nature were critical to furthering the education of seminarians.[40]

Since the hour was too late for J. B. Mack to develop a lengthy defense of the minority report, the synod adjourned until the next day. On October 24 at 9:30 the synod reconvened and discussed some of the more mundane matters, such as home missions. Anticipation was high, and after a short time the synod returned to the Woodrow controversy. A minister in the Charleston Presbytery, Mack again took the floor in favor of the minority report and emphasized that there was no effort or intent to brand Woodrow as an infidel or heretic. This was a difficult argument to make, considering that Mack and other opponents believed that evolutionary theory was a heretical position; therefore Woodrow would have to be a heretic for favoring it and espousing it. Nevertheless opponents of Woodrow repeatedly emphasized that they were not charging Woodrow with heresy, fearing that they would lose favor from some Presbyterians if they too strongly condemned Woodrow, the man. Instead Mack stated that "this discussion . . . was to decide whether the Southern Presbyterian Church is or is not the degenerate daughter of a noble mother."[41] He contended in typical fashion, for a leader in a church that believed itself under assault, that "the character of the Southern Church is on trial before the world."[42] Mack steered the discussion toward the synod's authority over the seminary curriculum and what was proper for its curriculum, emphasizing that the seminary must focus only on religious teaching and "should not admit the discussion of things imperfect and untrue."[43] As usual, Louis Agassiz was mentioned to support the allegations that the theory of evolution had no basis for belief and was inimical to the scriptures.

Mack's opinions were supported by a fellow member of the Charleston Presbytery, Rev. Dr. W. F. Junkin. Although ill, Junkin threw more fuel on the fire, arguing that the minority report was not as thorough or as resounding as it should have been. In no uncertain terms, he said that the synod should reject any teaching of evolution in the seminary. Addressing the Woodrow/Galileo analogy, he asserted that "the position of the Church of Rome in that connection is the one that the Church in all ages will be called upon to occupy. The Church, and very properly, said to Galileo, 'so long as you bear our credentials you shall not utter things which we believe to be untrue.'"[44] Denoting a fear of scientific thought, Junkin remarked that students who were introduced to evolutionary theory may become strident adherents to the concept. Ultimately the teaching of evolution would destroy the sanctity and holiness of God's word while diminishing religion to the role of having to respond to scientific ideas, whether they be proved or unproved.[45] The soul would become a meaningless concept broken on the altar of evolution. Junkin's remarks were the most direct attacks on Woodrow and doubtless found many receptive listeners.

One of the most convincing of Woodrow's defenders was Rev. C. R. Hemphill, the new professor of biblical literature at Columbia Theological Seminary. Hemphill, a former student of Woodrow's and a Columbia alumnus as well as a scholar fluent in Hebrew and Greek, reasoned that it was illogical for Woodrow's opponents to say that they were not accusing him of heresy when they went to great lengths to argue that his views on evolution were heretical to the Presbyterian Church. Defending Woodrow's right to teach about evolution and its relationship to Christianity, he explained that Woodrow did not "inculcate" evolution to seminarians but explained how science and Christianity were associated with one another.[46] Poking fun at synods that had already condemned Woodrow's teachings, the Chester, South Carolina, native remarked that it was obvious that the Kentucky Synod knew "what is, but also what will be. They look into the future and know what they will not believe."[47] Hemphill favored a Presbyterian Church that continued to explore God's world and did not limit itself to antiquated ideas that contradicted observations of any rational and logical person.[48]

The attacks continued with Rev. Henry B. Pratt of Bethel Presbytery quoting Genesis and explaining that Woodrow's teaching was "intra and contrascriptural, and that it infringed on the pith and core of the Word of God, and that therefore we are bound to express a condemnatory judgment."[49] Pratt, more than any other speaker, focused his attention on biblical inerrancy, using scriptural passages, especially from Genesis, to argue against Woodrow. He had little regard for examining the complex relationship between the seminary and its board ownership or the board's and the synod's role in curricula. He indicated that he opposed not only Woodrow's teaching about evolution but also the theory itself. In many ways Pratt's words were those in the minds of many Presbyterians, fearful of what evolution would do to their dearly held Christian beliefs.

After an exhausting round of debate, the synod adjourned until 7:30 P.M. After the synod reconvened, Professor Henry E. Shepherd, president of Charleston College, came to Woodrow's defense. The new president altered the synod's tone, bringing an academic approach to the question and stressing the need for science to be taught to seminarians. He abhorred the idea that ministers would be taught only what was proved, explaining that science was changing at all times and that it was necessary for ministers to understand the basic ideas of science. Shepherd was not an atheist or a follower of Darwin; instead he hoped to create a blend of faith, religion, and education.[50]

The synod membership was anxiously awaiting the speeches from the two titans who defined the controversy. All who had spoken to this point provided only a preface for the real debate. Along with Woodrow, John L. Girardeau was one of the most highly respected Presbyterian voices in South Carolina and among southern Presbyterians in general. A professor at Columbia Theological Seminary, he had worked closely with Woodrow for eight years. Girardeau was a native of James Island, South Carolina, and a graduate of the College of Charleston and Columbia Theological Seminary. He had spent much of his early career ministering to slaves in Charleston, having inherited this work from John Adger, one of Woodrow's defenders. Girardeau was extremely popular among the slaves and even after the war continued to serve free African Americans at what became Zion Presbyterian Church. In 1876 he accepted the post as professor of didactic and polemic theology at Columbia Theological Seminary. Girardeau and Woodrow had very different personalities and almost appeared destined to conflict. Although both were prolific scholars of great intellectual ability, Girardeau was famous for passionate sermons and speeches that captivated audiences, while Woodrow was a tamer, more sober voice. Girardeau's "strong Calvinism and strict ideas of church discipline" contrasted with the theories of Woodrow, who over the years had become "more and more engaged in secular affairs, in editing the church papers, and at the University."[51] Both were of extraordinary intellectual ability, but Girardeau had the more popular personality, and that counted for a great deal.

Girardeau's address to the synod, lasting three hours, was a masterful and eloquent defense of the conservative position. Because synod members had charged heresy in hushed and loud tones, Girardeau emphasized that Woodrow was in no way a heretic and that any charges of that nature would result in his coming to Woodrow's defense.[52] The issue before the synod was the board of directors' endorsement of Woodrow's teaching or "inculcating" an unproven hypothesis in a seminary.[53] As Girardeau explained, "the conflict in this case is between the Church's Bible and a scientific hypothesis; it is between theology and the science of the scientific man."[54] The board had erred by not agreeing with Woodrow's position on evolution while maintaining that his teaching about it at the seminary was satisfactory. Girardeau directly attacked Woodrow's position about science—in this case evolution—as being noncontradictory to the Bible, saying that Woodrow failed to understand that Presbyterians should be focused on "the harmony of non-contradiction," as contradiction by definition meant the acceptance of one position and the rejection of the other. He charged that Woodrow's belief in the evolution of Adam was contradictory to accepted church positions, stressing that Adam was formed from inorganic dust, not organic as held by evolutionists. The church's position was that Adam was created by God and not through a process of evolution from lower orders. The church argued that Adam had no parents, where evolutionists believed that he had animal parents. Supporters of evolution contended that Adam was an infant and child who matured to a man, but the church held that Adam was created a man. Like others, Girardeau emphasized that evolution was an unproven hypothesis that was contradictory to the Presbyterian Church's accepted interpretation of the Bible, the inerrant word of God. Therefore evolution "ought not to be inculcated and maintained in our Theological Seminaries," which were charged with "the church's interpretation of the word of God."[55] Moving beyond these arguments, Girardeau stressed that the synods that founded the seminaries and under whom they functioned held the authority to decide the curriculum, and the synods were under the authority of God, who was understood through the Bible.[56]

Toward the end of the lecture, which had been interrupted by an intermission, Girardeau's tone became more aggressive, emphatically emphasizing how Woodrow's position differed from those held by the southern Presbyterian Church. Girardeau summarized his views in four points:

> The Church is bound to cleave to her interpretation in her Standards of god's word, and to her traditional views, until they have been proved to be untrue and therefore untenable.
>
> No unverified hypothesis can afford such proof.
>
> No Professor in a Theological Seminary, as Professor, is at liberty in the class-room or in the chapel to inculcate views contrary to the Standards of the church or to oppose any element of those Standards. If he conscientiously holds views which are inconsistent with them, he ought to refrain from inculcating those views, or else retire from the institution.
>
> I add, that should he persist in claiming and exercising such liberty, it is the duty of the church through her constituted organs of control to arrest him.[57]

Girardeau attempted to demonstrate that Woodrow's views were well out of line with mainstream southern Presbyterians. "None of Dr. Woodrow's fellow

Professors agree with him; six of the seven leading church papers oppose him; not one of the Board of Directors of the Seminary will endorse his views," he charged.[58] Girardeau had attempted to move the argument toward a direct assault on evolutionary theory and away from the issue of whether Woodrow was teaching it to his students as fact. It was an easier case to make.

Rev. J. L. Martin was the next speaker to ascend the pulpit. He had the nearly impossible task of defending Woodrow's teachings while the powerful tones of Girardeau's words echoed in the synod members' ears. Martin, however, gave a clever response by wading into the disagreement over the definition of "dust," maintaining that "as the Bible has left the question an open one, the child of God can go through that open door into the domain of science to seek light."[59] Such words were not likely to convert those who had a negative view of scientific study. Martin added that the board members' approval of Woodrow's teachings and their denial of evolutionary theory were not "inconsistent" since Woodrow was conducting his duties as charged to him when he accepted the post of Perkins Professor.[60] Woodrow was not forcing his views on seminarians, but he was exploring the relationships between science and religion, consistently teaching the inerrant truths of the Bible and offering nothing beyond that which was expected of the professorship.

With exhaustion overtaking the speakers and the audience, the session was adjourned until Monday, October 27. Because the synod's other business occupied most of that day, anxiety and excitement grew in anticipation of the evening session. The synod had heard many compelling arguments to this point, but because of time constraints and the need for many in attendance to return home, the synod passed a resolution limiting speakers to fifteen minutes each, except for seminary board members, the current speaker, Rev. J. L. Martin, and James Woodrow. Later in the afternoon Dr. Junkin proposed that Woodrow be invited to speak before the synod and that the honor be given to him to make the final remarks before a vote was taken on the minority and majority reports. The synod approved and scheduled Dr. Woodrow to appear at 7:30 in the evening.

Washington Street Presbyterian was full of Presbyterian leaders anxious to hear Woodrow speak in his defense.[61] It is safe to say that the majority of prominent Presbyterians around the South wished for Woodrow to fail adequately to defend evolution and his teaching about it in the seminary. Woodrow's speech, which was not scripted and lasted for over seven hours, discussed timeless themes involving religion, science, and education. He addressed issues ranging from ownership of the seminary to evolutionary theory. He emphasized the problems of establishing religious truths as well as scientific truths, going as far as to question the church's oversight over its seminaries and colleges.

The Heidelberg graduate began his lecture with a welcoming tone by mentioning how many of the ministers gathered in attendance he had taught as seminarians or had served with in various capacities. After maintaining that he had never uttered a word contradictory to the scriptures and was devoted to their inerrant authority, statements designed to quell those who called him a heretic, Woodrow defended himself by stressing that he had never forced students to believe anything that he said other than the belief in the power of the one, almighty God. Placing his adherence to the scriptures on center stage, he remarked, "Science for its own sake I have never even remotely referred to in the hearing of any human being within the walls of that Theological Seminary."[62] Nevertheless the Perkins Professorship was charged by the board of trustees with teaching about science, and Woodrow explained that the board knew that he would teach various scientific theories such as instructing his students that the earth's age was a function of geological history and not shackled to the six days mentioned in the Bible. In this scientific theory and others, he saw no contradiction with the scriptures or the Westminster Confession, quoting from it to prove that they were synchronized. This was a wise move, because the 1647 Westminster Confession, save for the Bible, was the dearest document to Presbyterian theology. It was a central underpinning for reformed theology.

Woodrow addressed a charge in some of the earlier speeches that the board of trustees had the right to determine what he taught in the classroom. This foundational issue of academic freedom was dear to Woodrow, but it was by no means the central theme of the remarks he delivered at the synod. His argument was that there was no difference between the seminary and religious colleges such as Davidson. He asked whether the synod should year by year evaluate what is taught within its schools and asked if it was right for the synod to say, "'You shall not teach the other, because we, sitting as a court of the Lord Jesus Christ, pronounce it to be an unverified hypothesis.' Your responsibility terminates when you have selected those in whom you confide as to their general knowledge, as to their ability, and as to their fidelity, and, above all, as to this: that they shall teach nothing that contradicts the word of God. There and there alone, is the limit of your responsibility."[63] No doubt those words stung and angered many of his opponents. Regardless, Woodrow was making a bold statement for academic freedom, even in the context of religious instruction. Woodrow carefully demonstrated the flaws within his opponents' positions, noting that it was impossible to limit instruction to only that which is limited to the Bible. Did not seminarians need to understand the world in which they lived?

Woodrow directly attacked the contention that he was teaching an "unverified truth" when he spoke about evolution during his classes in Columbia. Laying down the gauntlet, he turned to his scientific training, saying, "I have followed the various lines of evidence connected with the matter during these past years so far that I can say that it [evolution] is probably true. And I do say it; I don't conceal it; I have no concealed opinions, notwithstanding all that

has been said about my trying to teach without letting the Church know."[64]
He pointed out that even when dealing with the scriptures, there was no unanimity on many points and other denominations and even Presbyterians themselves disagreed on interpretations. Did this mean that scriptures held unverified
truth? This led Woodrow into a lengthy and impressive list of scientists who believed in the basic ideas of evolution that far outdistanced that of his opponents
who placed so much emphasis on Louis Agassiz, having no other prominent
allies to cite. Woodrow even explained that Agassiz's son, Alexander, believed
that evolution was valid. At Davidson, Professor Blake taught that evolution
was probably true, and the same went for Wofford, the University of Georgia,
Central University in Kentucky, and many other institutions. Woodrow had
even consulted those who attended the 1884 meeting of the American Association for the Advancement of Science and discovered that almost all believed
in evolution. Belief in the concept was almost universal abroad and at home.
He produced a letter from the renowned botanist William H. Brewer, chair of
agriculture at Yale University's Sheffield Scientific School, stating that the belief
in evolution, even among mainstream Protestants, was dominant, if not almost
unanimous.[65]

Woodrow knew that he had to confront evolution directly in more detail,
and he did so with flair. As he had done earlier in the year, he took a moder-
ate approach to evolution using the phrase "descent with modification" to define evolution while emphasizing that change in species takes place over time.[66]
Woodrow took the position that Darwin and his followers did not discuss the
power that produced evolutionary change; therefore evolution could be conducted by God through the orderly laws of the world that he created. Adam
could have descended from more primitive life, because it was part of God's
plan that all plants and animals did this. The scriptures, in Woodrow's view,
were silent about the actual process that created Adam, so it stood to reason
that God led us toward this truth by directing man to study carefully the rest
of his creation. This in no way subordinated scripture to science, as Woodrow
was accused of doing. In Woodrow's opinion, the opposite was true with science, a discipline inspired by God's orderly creation of the world, in association
with the Bible, albeit the supreme authority, helping man understand the world
that God created and therefore providing a method for humans to move closer
to God.

Woodrow's address to the synod was adjourned because it was nearing 12:30
A.M. To give him the fullest opportunity to defend himself, he was allowed time
to complete his remarks the following day. In some ways similar to Martin Luther at Worms, Woodrow returned to the synod the next day, Tuesday, October
28, and offered a brief but devastating assessment of the church's relationship
to science. With the synod conducting other business, Woodrow did not regain

the floor until after 4 P.M. Critical of past church leaders and perhaps influenced by John Adger's words earlier in the synod, he charged, "I think I am right when I assert that every time the Church has undertaken to express an opinion on scientific matters, it has expressed an opinion that was wrong."[67] Obviously frustrated by those who condemned his teaching, Woodrow gave a spirited defense. "As you look backward over the dreary past, you will see that it has been taught in the Church's name that if you believe that human beings live beyond the torrid zone, you must reject the Scriptures as false; if you believe that the earth is a sphere, you must reject the Scriptures as false; if you believe that the sun doesn't revolve around the earth but that the earth revolves around the sun, you must reject the Scriptures as false; if you believe that the universe was created more than six thousand years ago, you must reject the Scriptures as false. Will you add to this dismal list of appalling examples your teaching, that if you believe that evolution is true, you must reject the Scriptures as false?"[68] These were damning and direct words, especially considering that they came from one of the most respected theologians in the southern Presbyterian Church.

With Woodrow's defense finished, the synod decided to vote on the majority and minority reports. The majority report was defeated with forty-four in favor but fifty-two against. Ministers from Enoree Presbytery, the presbytery that best represented upstate South Carolina, recorded a divided vote with four in favor of the majority report and five against.[69] Upstate Presbyterian leaders were split on their views toward evolution in the seminary as well as the theory itself. When the minority report was voted on, only three members of Enoree Presbytery voted for it, with six opposed. This vote appears to indicate that the opponents of evolution being taught in the seminary were in the clear minority. It is difficult, however, to determine whether the vote showed that upstate Presbyterian ministers were expressing confidence in Woodrow or making a statement on the merits of teaching evolution at the seminary. Since Woodrow's reputation was strong and so many Presbyterian ministers had been influenced by him, the former was more likely.

Since both reports were defeated, some compromise statement was necessary. The compromise resolved "that in the judgment of this Synod the teaching of Evolution in the Theological Seminary at Columbia, except in a purely expository manner, without intention of inculcating its truth, is hereby disapproved."[70] This resolution made few happy as well because the vote was very close with fifty favoring it and forty-five opposed. The Enoree delegation had six votes in favor of the resolution and three opposed.[71] Immediately after the vote, the synod passed unanimously a resolution introduced by Reverend Junkin, one of Woodrow's harshest critics, praising Woodrow as a devoted Christian of the highest character. It read "that the Synod of South Carolina hereby expresses its sincere affection for Dr. Woodrow's person, its appreciation of the purity of his Christian character, its admiration of his distinguished talents and scholarly attainments both in Theology and Science, and its high estimate of his past services."[72] It was a nice gesture designed to bring cohesion to what was a divided southern Presbyterian Church, but the division was too great to have much effect.

With the synod being adjourned, the *Southern Presbyterian Review* declared victory and a level of vindication for Woodrow. In the October 30 issue, the editors wrote that "the result is a complete victory for Dr. Woodrow and the Board of Directors, inasmuch as the Synod disapproves what he never had the remotest idea of doing, and authorizes his teaching in 'a purely expository manner'—the only way in which he has taught science in the Seminary, viz, expounding it and showing connexion with revelation."[73] Woodrow had survived, but his victory was tainted by the gathering forces fearful of his opinions and the damage they might do to Presbyterianism. As John Girardeau had rightly said, "if Dr. Woodrow is endorsed, the Seminary will be known as the Evolution Seminary."[74] By association the southern Presbyterian Church would be known as the faith that saw Jesus as a descendant of a heathen "brute."

The votes cast by Presbyterian leaders in the upstate demonstrated conflicting views about the evolution controversy as well as Woodrow. The debates had only deepened disagreement because voters were torn between their support for Woodrow and their personal views on evolution. Of the four from Enoree Presbytery who favored the majority report, James Fair, the pastor at Laurens Presbyterian Church, had been one of Woodrow's students while T. H. Law and D. A. Todd were known to be friends. Todd and Law, both 1862 graduates of Columbia Seminary, were among the keenest of Woodrow's supporters, and both opposed the final agreement. They were joined by Z. L. Holmes in rejecting the compromise. While most were willing to agree to the final compromise, the votes show that conservative theological positions were far from unanimous within the upstate Presbyterian leadership.

The debates in Greenville were of such magnitude and eloquence that according to R. A. Webb, "a member of Congress who heard it, told me at its close that, for ability, dignity, and force, he had never heard its equal in the Senate of the United States."[75] The words and actions at the South Carolina Synod triggered Presbyterians around the South to zealously join in the debate. Because Columbia Seminary operated under the auspices of the synods of South Carolina, Georgia, Florida, and Alabama, all had to discuss and give their judgment on Woodrow's teachings. Unanimously, all four state synods condemned the teaching of evolution at the seminary.

Greenville newspapers had followed the evolution debate far more closely than their Spartanburg brethren had. The *Enterprise and Mountaineer* was tired of the issue, reporting, "we have taken no part in the debate and made no comments because we have become rather weary of objecting to a theory which is 'not proven,' and because we have expressed ourselves distinctly and in full upon the matter heretofore."[76] Nevertheless they lambasted Woodrow's belief that Adam was a product of evolution and that his soul was breathed into him by God, while Eve was derived solely from Adam's rib. In particular they noted the problem with Eve's descent, saying that it "is very complimentary to the mother of all living, and is decidedly unique. It certainly would not have occurred to him, had it not been necessary to somehow save the Mosaic record."[77] The *Enterprise and Mountaineer* provided a thorough explanation of the paper's objections to evolution theory by questioning the lack of evidence that demonstrated the evolution of humans, contending that there was no evidence of one species converting into another species, and explaining that evolution had not been observed among humans or any other form above the smallest protoplasm.[78]

The *Carolina Spartan* followed events in Greenville far less than it did the presidential contest between Grover Cleveland and James Blaine. Presidential campaign news dominated the paper's pages throughout the period of the evolution debate at the synod. Nevertheless the paper, at the end of the synod, reported that evolution had silenced, at least for a few days, presidential talk. The paper predicted that the debate would only strengthen the Presbyterian Church.[79] It reported in late November, "you hear little of Evolution since the beginning of the election excitement."[80] Even with the enthusiasm over Cleveland's victory, however, the *Spartan* reported on December 3 that Baptist ministers meeting in Spartanburg had a grand time ridiculing and laughing at the concept of evolution. The ringleader was Rev. T. DeWitt Talmage, a New York Presbyterian pastor and one of the most prominent ministers in the country. In grand fashion he poked fun at evolution in an environment of clear unanimity, unlike that found among his Presbyterian brethren in South Carolina.[81]

Even after the last lamp had been extinguished in Greenville, the legacy of the bitter disagreements aired on the floor of Washington Street Presbyterian Church lingered. The Woodrow controversy did not end. The synods of Georgia, Alabama, and Florida had their say on Woodrow's teachings at Columbia and passed resolutions stating that evolution should not be instructed. What followed was an eight-to-four vote of Columbia's board of directors asking Woodrow to resign his post. When he refused, the board fired him, only to learn later that of the four controlling synods, South Carolina and Florida refused to agree that the board's dismissal had been the proper course of action. Being that there was no unanimity regarding his removal, the board reinstated Woodrow in late 1885 only to ask again for his resignation. Woodrow's doggedness and intransigence—he believed that he had taught and said nothing but what was consistent with the Bible and the Confessions—were on display again when he was charged with heresy by the Augusta Presbytery. His nemesis Girardeau led the attack. Although he was acquitted by the presbytery, the Georgia Synod, where the acquittal was appealed, convicted Woodrow. South Carolina again stepped into the fray when Girardeau at the 1886 meeting of the South Carolina Presbyterian Synod in Cheraw gained the approval of a resolution demanding Woodrow resign from Columbia. Woodrow still would not comply and was removed by the board in late 1886. Woodrow was not done. He sought and received a hearing at the Presbyterian General Assembly held in Baltimore in 1888, aware that the majority in attendance were in opposition to his views. Woodrow was defeated, and the southern Presbyterian Church issued a strong statement condemning evolution as a theory contrary to the Bible.

The long and complex debates about evolution and the Columbia Seminary were brought to the forefront of Presbyterian consciousness with the synod meeting in Greenville. More than simply a discussion of Darwin's theory, the synod's debates ranged widely from scriptural interpretation to academic freedom to the relationship between the church and its educational institutions. Far from being a backwater of intellectual thought, the 1884 synod demonstrated that scholarly debate on a vigorous intellectual level was not uncommon in upstate South Carolina and the entire state. Instead of offering simple arguments for or against the teaching of evolution, these Presbyterian leaders were, for the most part, deeply engaged in the complexities of scientific and theological debates well within the current of mainstream America. Woodrow's endorsement of evolution and his practice of teaching about it to seminarians forced the synod to come to terms with biblical inerrancy and the denomination's conservative traditions. Woodrow and his supporters believed that nothing in evolution contradicted the Bible, holding that one could believe in human evolution and biblical authority without being contradictory, while emphasizing that final authority rested with the Bible. Woodrow repeatedly stated that the Bible did not speak about science and therefore the synod had no business making pronouncements about science. His opponents, stymied at the synod meeting, in part because of Woodrow's prominent position in the state as well as his debating skills, eventually would win the day by professing as Girardeau did that evolution directly contradicted the Bible and that the church maintained the right to stamp out heretical positions.

The synod's work was necessary, but the pain caused by the debate harmed the church. William Jacobs, the founder of Presbyterian College and a former student under Woodrow, perhaps best captured the ill will caused by the evolution debate. In October 1884, prior to the Greenville meeting, Jacobs expressed pain and hope: "I am grieving over the fact that this 'evolution' question is to disturb the harmony of the church in the Synod. May the Lord keep down hard feelings and disturbance."[82] Two years later the controversy continued to bother him, as it did many other Presbyterians. Speaking of the 1886 synod, he wrote that "it was large, but evolution and Woodrow were the only themes. . . . But Girardeau and Mack had lifted the black flag. It is a sad pity to have such men in the church of Jesus with the spirit of hate that they manifest."[83]

Notes

This chapter could not have been completed without the assistance of many people. In particular, I wish to thank Nancy Griffith and Sarah Leckie of the Archives and Special Collections Department at Presbyterian College's Thomason Library for all their help and advice. Warmest thanks are extended to Rev. David Sutton, who provided invaluable assistance regarding the history of Presbyterians in the South and who graciously agreed to read an earlier version of this chapter. The support and good cheer provided by my colleagues in the history department at the University of South Carolina Upstate always served as an inspiration. Last, I would like to thank my girls, Cindy, Mary, and Anna, for helping make this possible.

1. Ernest Trice Thompson, *Presbyterians in the South,* 3 vols. (Richmond, Va.: John Knox Press, 1973), 2:442–90. Thompson's three-volume history is not simply the standard but a masterful work on Presbyterian history.

2. In Robert V. Bruce, *The Launching of Modern American Science, 1846–1876* (New York: Knopf, 1987), the author argues that the South was essentially bereft of scientific contributions and by association scientific debate. In Lester D. Stephens, *Science, Race, and Religion in the American South: John Bachman and the Charleston Circle of Naturalists, 1815–1895* (Chapel Hill: University of North Carolina Press, 2000), the author challenges Bruce, arguing that scientific investigation, at least in Charleston, made significant contributions to American intellectual life. For more information on scientific work in South Carolina, see Albert E. Sanders and William D. Anderson Jr., *Natural History Investigations in South Carolina from Colonial Times to the Present* (Columbia: University of South Carolina Press, 1999).

3. Frederick Gregory, "The Impact of Darwinian Evolution on Protestant Theology in the Nineteenth Century," in *God & Nature: Historical Essays on the Encounter between Christianity and Science,* ed. David C. Lindberg and Ronald L. Numbers (Berkeley: University of California Press, 1986), 375–77.

4. Charles Hodge, *What Is Darwinism?* (New York: Scribner, Armstrong, 1874), 48.

5. Edward Lurie, *Louis Agassiz: A Life in Science* (Chicago: University of Chicago Press, 1960), 252–303.

6. For a detailed discussion of Agassiz's views on evolution, see Edward Lurie, "Louis Agassiz and the Idea of Evolution," *Victorian Studies* 3 (September 1959): 87–108; and Edward Lurie, *Louis Agassiz: A Life in Science* (Baltimore: Johns Hopkins University Press, 1988).

7. George E. Webb, *The Evolution Controversy in America* (Lexington: University Press of Kentucky, 1994), 33. Also see Mary Engel, "A Chapter in the History of Academic Freedom—The Case of Alexander Winchell," *History of Education Journal* 10 (1959): 73–80; Edwin Mims, *History of Vanderbilt University* (Nashville: Vanderbilt University Press, 1946), 100–104. After being removed from Vanderbilt's faculty,

Winchell enjoyed a long career in Michigan as state geologist and as a professor at the University of Michigan.

8. James Woodrow, "Speech before the Synod of South Carolina," in *Dr. James Woodrow as Seen by His Friends,* ed. Marion W. Woodrow (Columbia, S.C.: R. L. Bryan, 1909), 752.

9. Ibid.

10. Kenneth K. Bailey, "Southern White Protestantism at the Turn of the Century," *American Historical Review* 68 (April 1963): 622.

11. Ibid., 628.

12. For more information, see John L. Girardeau, *Confederate Memorial Day at Charleston, S.C.: Re-internment of the Carolina Dead from Gettysburg* (Charleston, S.C.: William G. Mazyck, 1871); Erskine Clarke, *Our Southern Zion: A History of Calvinism in the South Carolina Low Country, 1690–1990* (Tuscaloosa: University of Alabama Press), 220–24; Robert T. Handy, ed., *The Social Gospel in America, 1870–1920: Gladden, Ely, Rauschenbusch* (Oxford: Oxford University Press), 8–13.

13. There are several sources for basic biographical information about James Woodrow. See Robert Gustafson, *James Woodrow: Scientist, Theologian, Intellectual Leader* (Lewiston, N.Y.: Mellon Press, 1995); Philip Graham, "James Woodrow, Calvinist and Evolutionist," *Sewanee Review* 40 (July–September 1932): 301–15; Clement Eaton, "James Woodrow and the Freedom of Teaching in the South," *Journal of Southern History* 28 (February 1962): 3–17. Marion Woodrow, James's widow, compiled a number of very favorable evaluations of her husband in her *Dr. James Woodrow as Seen by His Friends.* The volume is rich in biographical information.

14. Thompson, *Presbyterians in the South,* 459–61.

15. Eugene Daniel, "Some Reminiscences," in *Dr. James Woodrow as Seen by His Friends,* ed. Marion Woodrow, 99.

16. James Woodrow, "Evolution Address before Columbia Theological Seminary," in *Dr. James Woodrow as Seen by His Friends,* ed. Marion Woodrow, 622. The address was also reproduced and discussed in the July 1884 issues of the *Southern Presbyterian Review.*

17. Ibid., 632–31.

18. Ibid., 635–41.

19. Ibid., 644.

20. Thomas H. Law, "Personal Reminiscences," in *Dr. James Woodrow as Seen by His Friends,* ed. Marion Woodrow, 65. A native of Hartsville, South Carolina, and a Columbia Theological Seminary graduate, Law lived in Spartanburg for much of his professional life.

21. Most of the issues during the summer of 1884 were consumed by the evolution debate, to the point that the editors grew wearisome of having to defend evolution and annoyed by having to debate evolution with many having limited scientific knowledge.

22. *Carolina Spartan,* August 27, 1884, 2.

23. Ibid.

24. "Science vs. Religion," *Carolina Spartan,* September 24, 1884, 1.

25. *Greenville Enterprise and Mountaineer,* October 29, 1884, 3. Unfortunately editions of the *Greenville News* for 1884 have been lost. John Adger and the editors of the *Southern Presbyterian Review* used the *Greenville News's* reports about the synod to assist them in forming a record of the speeches delivered.

26. M. F. T., "Synod of South Carolina," *Charleston News and Courier,* October 25, 1884, 1.

27. Ibid.

28. *Minutes of the Synod of South Carolina* (Spartanburg, S.C.: T. J. Trimmier, 1884), 7.

29. M. F. T., "Science and Religion," *Charleston Sunday News,* October 26, 1884, 2. The Charleston newspaper, by a large margin, provided the most comprehensive coverage of the synod.

30. Ibid., 11.

31. Ibid.

32. Ibid.

33. Ibid.

34. Ibid., 12.

35. Ibid., 2.

36. John B. Adger, *My Life and Times, 1810–1899* (Richmond, Va.: Presbyterian Committee of Publication, 1899), 90–129, 164–200. Adger's education set him apart from other contemporaries as well. He was a native of Charleston, South Carolina, but had graduated from Union College in Schenectady, New York, and Princeton Theological Seminary.

37. M. F. T., "Science and Religion," *Charleston News and Courier,* October 26, 1884, 2.

38. Ibid.

39. Ibid.

40. Adger, *My Life and Times,* 462–63.

41. M. F. T., "Dr. Woodrow as Galileo," *Charleston News and Courier,* October 27, 1884, 2. In 1865 southern Presbyterians changed the name of the church from Presbyterian Church in the Confederate States of America to Presbyterian Church in the United States. In more casual speech it was common to refer to the church as the Southern Presbyterian Church. It is ironic that the intent in 1865 had been to avoid a regional name, as it was deemed confining.

42. Adger, *My Life and Times,* 463.

43. M. F. T., "Dr. Woodrow as Galileo," 2.

44. Ibid.

45. Ibid.

46. Adger, *My Life and Times,* 470. Adger was quoting from the *Louisville Courier Journal.* Nine years after the evolution controversy, Hemphill was one of the founders of Louisville Theological Seminary.

47. Adger, *My Life and Times,* 470.

48. Hemphill specifically mentioned the rabid debate about the geological age of the earth, emphasizing that it was now fully accepted by the Presbyterian Church that the earth was extremely old and that God had not created it in a mere six days.

49. M. F. T., "Dr. Woodrow as Galileo," 2. Pratt had served as a missionary to Mexico and had translated the Bible into Spanish.

50. M. F. T., "Dr. Woodrow as Galileo," 2.

51. Louis C. LaMotte, *Colored Light: The Story of the Influence of Columbia Theological Seminary, 1828–1936* (Richmond, Va.: Presbyterian Committee of Publication, 1937), 206–7.

52. John L. Girardeau, *The Substance of Two Speeches on the Teaching of Evolution in Columbia Theological Seminary, Delivered in the Synod of South Carolina at Greenville, SC Oct. 1884* (Columbia, S.C.: William Sloane, 1885), 4–6.

53. Ibid., 6.

54. *Southern Presbyterian Review,* October 30, 1884, 2.

55. Girardeau, *The Substance of Two Speeches,* 15–16.

56. Ibid., 18.

57. Ibid., 23.

58. *Southern Presbyterian Review,* October 30, 1884, 2.

59. Ibid.

60. Ibid.

61. The name of Washington Street Presbyterian Church was officially changed in 1912 to First Presbyterian Church of Greenville, South Carolina.

62. Woodrow, "Speech before the Synod of South Carolina," 729. Abbreviated and abridged versions of Woodrow's address were printed in newspapers in South Carolina and around the South.

63. Woodrow, "Speech before the Synod of South Carolina," 737.

64. Ibid., 749.

65. Ibid., 752–57. Woodrow's opponents had used Sir William Thomson's words as evidence of a prominent scientist in opposition to evolution. Thomson was a famed mathematician and a specialist in electricity and thermodynamics, and he remained a keen Christian, seeing laws of nature as reflective in the word of God. Woodrow, trying to make light of one of evolution's opponents, ironically said that Thomson had presented a paper in Britain that argued that meteorites had brought life to earth.

66. Woodrow, "Speech before the Synod of South Carolina," 761.

67. Ibid., 782.

68. Ibid., 783.

69. *Minutes of the Synod of South Carolina,* 20. The Enoree Presbytery was the newest of South Carolina's five presbyteries, having been formed in October 1878. It was comprised of churches in Spartanburg, Greenville, Union, and Laurens Counties.

70. *Minutes of the Synod of South Carolina,* 21.

71. Ibid.

72. Ibid., 22.

73. *Southern Presbyterian Review,* October 30, 1884, 3.

74. Ibid., 2.

75. R. A. Webb, "The Evolution Controversy," in *The Life Work of John L. Girardeau,* ed. George A. Blackburn (Columbia, S.C.: State Company, 1916), 234.

76. "Evolution Again," *Greenville Enterprise and Mountaineer,* October 29, 1884, 1.

77. Ibid.

78. Ibid.

79. *Carolina Spartan,* October 29, 1884, 2.

80. *Carolina Spartan,* November 26, 1884, 2.

81. "Knocking Evolution Out," *Carolina Spartan,* December 3, 1884, 1. Talmage was a celebrated religious figure in Brooklyn and throughout the United States. He was well known for delivering passionate sermons to huge congregations.

82. Jacobs, ed., *Diary of William Plumer Jacobs,* 246.

83. Ibid., 264.

Suggested Readings

Abbott, Martin. *The Freedmen's Bureau in South Carolina, 1865–1872.* Chapel Hill: University of North Carolina Press, 1967.

Anderson, James P. *The Education of Blacks in the South, 1860–1935.* Chapel Hill: University of North Carolina Press, 1988.

Ayers, Edward. *Vengeance and Justice: Crime and Punishment in the Nineteenth Century American South.* Oxford: Oxford University Press, 1985.

Baker, Bruce E. *This Mob Will Surely Take My Life: Lynchings in the Carolinas, 1871–1947.* London: Continuum, 2008.

Barnes, Albert. *The Church and Slavery.* New York: Negro Universities Press, 1969.

Brewster, Lawrence Fay. *Summer Migrations and Resorts of South Carolina Planters.* Durham, N.C.: Duke University Press, 1947.

Brundage, W. Fitzhugh, ed. *Under Sentence of Death: Lynching in the South.* Chapel Hill: University of North Carolina Press, 1997.

Burton, Orville Vernon. *In My Father's House Are Many Mansions: Family and Community in Edgefield, South Carolina.* Chapel Hill: University of North Carolina Press, 1985.

Butchart, Ronald E. *Schooling the Freed People: Teaching, Learning, and the Struggle for Black Freedom, 1861–1876.* Chapel Hill: University of North Carolina Press, 2010.

Carlton, David L. *Mill and Town in South Carolina, 1880–1920.* Baton Rouge: Louisiana State University Press, 1982.

Chambers, Thomas A. *Drinking the Waters: Creating an American Leisure Class at Nineteenth Century Mineral Springs.* Washington, D.C.: Smithsonian Institution Press, 2002.

Craig, Tom Moore, ed. *Upcountry South Carolina Goes to War: Letters of the Anderson, Brockman and Moore Families 1853–1865.* Columbia: University of South Carolina Press, 2009.

Edgar, Walter. *South Carolina: A History.* Columbia: University of South Carolina Press, 1998.

Eelman, Bruce. *Entrepreneurs in the Southern Upcountry: Commercial Culture in Spartanburg, 1845–1880.* Athens: University of Georgia Press, 2008.

Ford, Lacey. *The Origins of Southern Radicalism: The South Carolina Upcountry, 1800–1860.* New York: Oxford University Press, 1988.

Fountain, Daniel L. *Slavery, Civil War and Salvation: African American Slaves and Christianity, 1830–1870.* Baton Rouge: Louisiana State University Press, 2010.

Hindus, Michael. *Prison and Plantation: Crime, Justice, and Authority in Massachusetts and South Carolina, 1767–1878.* Chapel Hill: University of North Carolina Press, 1980.

Huff, Archie Vernon, Jr. *Greenville: The History of the City and County in the South Carolina Piedmont.* Columbia: University of South Carolina Press, 1995.

Jones, F. D., and W. H. Mills, eds. *History of the Presbyterian Church in South Carolina since 1850.* Columbia: Published for the Synod of South Carolina by the R. L. Bryan Company, 1926.

Martinez, Michael J. *Carpetbaggers, Cavalry, and the Ku Klux Klan: Exposing the Invisible Empire during Reconstruction.* Lanham, Md.: Rowman and Littlefield, 2007.

Matthews, Donald G. *Religion in the Old South.* Chicago: University of Chicago Press, 1977.

Moore, John Hammond. *Carnival of Blood: Dueling, Lynching, and Murder in South Carolina, 1880–1920.* Columbia: University of South Carolina Press, 2006.

Racine, Philip. *Piedmont Farmer: The Journals of David Golightly Harris, 1855–1870.* Knoxville: University of Tennessee Press, 1990.

Ryan, John. *Ten Years with Custer: A 7th Cavalryman's Memoirs.* Terre Haute, Ind.: AST Press, 2001.

Sanders, Albert E., and William D. Anderson Jr. *Natural History Investigations in South Carolina from Colonial Times to the Present.* Columbia: University of South Carolina Press, 1999.

Sefton, James E. *The United States Army and Reconstruction, 1865–1877.* Baton Rouge: Louisiana State University Press, 1967.

Starnes, Richard D., ed. *Southern Journeys: Tourism, Heritage and Culture in the Modern South.* Tuscaloosa: University of Alabama Press, 2003.

Teter, Betsy, ed. *Textile Town: Spartanburg County, South Carolina.* Spartanburg, S.C.: Hub City Writers Project, 2002.

Thompson, Ernest Trice. *Presbyterians in the South.* Richmond, Va.: John Knox Press, 1973.

Tindall, George. *South Carolina Negroes, 1877–1900.* Columbia: University of South Carolina Press, 1952.

Tolnay, Stewart, and E. M. Beck. *A Festival of Violence: An Analysis of Southern Lynchings, 1882–1930.* Urbana and Chicago: University of Illinois Press, 1995.

Tullos, Allen. *Habits of Industry: White Culture and the Transformation of the Carolina Piedmont.* Chapel Hill: University of North Carolina Press, 1989.

Waldrep, Christopher. *The Many Faces of Judge Lynch: Extralegal Violence and Punishment in America.* New York: Palgrave Macmillan, 2002.

West, Jerry L. *The Ku Klux Klan in York County, South Carolina, 1865–1877.* Jefferson, N.C.: McFarland & Company, 2002.

Williams, Heather Andrea. *Self-Taught: African American Education in Slavery and Freedom.* Chapel Hill: University of North Carolina Press, 2003.

Williamson, Joel R. *After Slavery: The Negro in South Carolina during Reconstruction, 1861–1877.* Chapel Hill: University of North Carolina Press, 1965.

Zuczek, Richard. *State of Rebellion: Reconstruction in South Carolina.* Columbia: University of South Carolina Press, 1996.

About the Contributors

Katherine D. Cann is professor of history and chair of the Social Science Division at Spartanburg Methodist College. She holds a Ph.D. in history from the University of South Carolina. Her publications include *Common Ties: A History of Textile Industrial Institute, Spartanburg Junior College and Spartanburg Methodist College* and "Improving Textile Town, 1910 to 1929," in *Textile Town: Spartanburg County, South Carolina.*

Timothy P. Grady is associate professor of history at the University of South Carolina Upstate. He holds a Ph.D. in history from the College of William & Mary. His publications include *Anglo-Spanish Rivalry in Colonial Southeast America, 1650–1725* and various articles on early North America and the Atlantic world.

Nancy Snell Griffith recently retired as archives and special collections librarian at Presbyterian College. She is a graduate of Dickinson College in Carlisle, Pennsylvania, and the School of Information Studies at Syracuse University. She is the author of several reference books as well as numerous books and articles on local history, covering both South Carolina and her former home in Arkansas.

Carol Loar is associate professor of history at the University of South Carolina Upstate. She holds a Ph.D. in history from Northwestern University. Her publications include "Under Felt Hats and Worsted Stockings: The Uses of Conscience in Early Modern English Coroners' Inquests," published in the *Sixteenth Century Journal,* and "Popular Medical Knowledge and the Early Modern English Coroner's Inquest," published in the *Social History of Medicine.*

Robert B. McCormick is associate professor of history at the University of South Carolina Upstate. He holds a Ph.D. in history from the University of South Carolina. He has published on topics ranging from reform in early twentieth-century Macedonia to war criminality in the twentieth century. He is the author of *Croatia under Ante Pavelić: America, the Ustaše, and Croatian Genocide.*

Andrew H. Myers is professor of American studies at the University of South Carolina Upstate and a lieutenant colonel of infantry in the U.S. Army Retired

Reserve. He holds a Ph.D. in history from the University of Virginia. His publications include the book *Black, White & Olive Drab* and the chapter "An American Professor with the Iraqi Army" in *Military Culture & Education*. He developed his interest in the federal occupation of the upcountry after performing similar duty with troopers of the Fourth and Ninth U.S. Cavalry Regiments. He received his gold spurs through the former.

Diane C. Vecchio is professor of history at Furman University. She holds a Ph.D. in history from Syracuse University. She is the author of *Merchants, Midwives, and Laboring Women: Immigrants in Urban America.* Recent published articles include "Making Their Way in the New South: Jewish Peddlers and Merchants in the South Carolina Upcountry" and "Connecting Spheres: Women's Work and Women's Lives in Milwaukee's Italian Third Ward," in *American Women Italian Style: Italian Americana's Best Writings on Women.*

Melissa Walker is the George Dean Johnson Jr. Professor of History at Converse College. She holds a Ph.D. in history from Clark University in Massachusetts. She is the author or editor of seven books, two of which are *Country Women Cope with Hard Times: A Collection of Oral Histories* and *All We Knew Was to Farm: Rural Women in the Upcountry South, 1919–1941.*

Index

Abbeville County: about, 1, 103n1; American Missionary Association efforts, 99–100; establishing schools for all children, 94–95; establishing schools for blacks, 91–94; Freedmen's Bureau in, 90–91; missionary activities in, 139; ownership of slaves, 87–88; ratio of blacks to whites, 89, 92, 94; school facilities and teachers, 95–97; school financing, 93, 95, 97–99, 100–101; school integration, 101–2; support of education, 88–90, 104n21; violence toward blacks, 88; white settlement, 87
Abbeville Press and Banner, 89, 90–91, 94
abolition, 15, 95, 99, 135, 137–40, 143–45
Adamites and Pre-Adamites (Winchell), 191
Adger, John B., Rev., 197–98, 205
African American Presbyterian Church, 154. *See also* Clinton Presbyterian Church; Sloan's Chapel
African Americans: Aiken County massacre, 77; churches in the black community, 124–25; clergy education and ordination, 145–46, 148–49, 150, 153; creation of own schools, 91–92; desire for education, 91–94, 102, 125–30; employment in textile industry, 111; employment in upcountry resorts, 18–19; free public education, 45; "grass widows," 70; land ownership, 118; laundresses for the army, 69–70; as local militia forces, 77, 113, 115, 149; military service, 55, 59, 81n35; political

power from Constitution of 1868, 56, 59; presence of upcountry slavery, 24n41; racial stereotypes, 180; Reconstruction era violence, 88; segregation and discrimination, 75, 101–2, 106n53, 123–24, 129–30. *See also* emancipation; race relations; slavery
African Methodist Episcopal Church (AME), 92
After Slavery (Williamson), 89
Agassiz, Alexander, 202
Agassiz, Louis, 191, 202
Age of Homespun (Ulrich), ix
Agnes Scott College (Georgia), 44
agriculture: black land ownership, 118; cotton, 29, 40, 42, 87, 108, 111, 117; Farmer's Summer Encampment, 17; plantations and slave ownership, 108–9; sharecropper/tenant arrangements, 100, 107, 110–13, 117–18
Aiken County, 77
Alabama, viii, 60, 150, 206, 207
Albany Law Journal, 171
alcohol, 21, 59, 71–73, 101, 175–76. *See also* drunkenness
Aldrich, Judge, 170–71, 172, 186n55
Alexander, R. M., 127
Allen, C. L., 91
Allen University (Columbia), 92, 129
Alston (town), 55
Alston, Joseph, 8
Altamont Hotel (resort hotel), 20–21
American Association for the Advancement of Science, 195, 204